Salafism Goes Global

RELIGION AND GLOBAL POLITICS

Series Editor

John L. Esposito
University Professor and Director
Prince Alwaleed Bin Talal Center for Muslim-Christian Understanding
Georgetown University

Piety and Politics
Islamism in Contemporary Malaysia
Joseph Chinyong Liow

Terror in The Land of the Holy Spirit
Guatemala under General Efrain Rios
Montt, 1982–1983
Virginia Garrard-Burnett

In the House of War
Dutch Islam Observed
Sam Cherribi

Being Young and Muslim
New Cultural Politics in the Global
South and North
Asef Bayat and Linda Herrera

*Church, State, and Democracy In
Expanding Europe*
Lavinia Stan and Lucian Turcescu

The Headscarf Controversy
Secularism and Freedom of Religion
Hilal Elver

The House of Service
The Gülen Movement and Islam's
Third Way
David Tittensor

Answering the Call
Popular Islamic Activism in
Sadat's Egypt
Abdullah Al-Arian

*Mapping the Legal Boundaries of
Belonging*
Religion and Multiculturalism from
Israel to Canada
Edited by René Provost

Religious Secularity
A Theological Challenge to the
Islamic State
Naser Ghobadzadeh

*The Middle Path of Moderation
In Islam*
The Qurʾānic Principle of Wasaṭiyyah
Mohammad Hashim Kamali

One Islam, Many Muslim Worlds
Spirituality, Identity, and Resistance
Across Islamic Lands
Raymond William Baker

Containing Balkan Nationalism
Imperial Russia and Ottoman
Christians (1856–1914)
Denis Vovchenko

Inside the Muslim Brotherhood
Religion, Identity, and Politics
Khalil al-Anani

Politicizing Islam
The Islamic Revival in France and India
Z. Fareen Parvez

Soviet and Muslim
The Institutionalization of Islam in
Central Asia
Eren Tasar

Islam In Malaysia
An Entwined History
Khairudin Aljunied

Salafism Goes Global

From the Gulf to the French Banlieues

MOHAMED-ALI ADRAOUI

Oxford University Press is a department of the University of Oxford. It furthers
the University's objective of excellence in research, scholarship, and education
by publishing worldwide. Oxford is a registered trade mark of Oxford University
Press in the UK and certain other countries.

Published in the United States of America by Oxford University Press
198 Madison Avenue, New York, NY 10016, United States of America.

© Oxford University Press 2020

All rights reserved. No part of this publication may be reproduced, stored in
a retrieval system, or transmitted, in any form or by any means, without the
prior permission in writing of Oxford University Press, or as expressly permitted
by law, by license, or under terms agreed with the appropriate reproduction
rights organization. Inquiries concerning reproduction outside the scope of the
above should be sent to the Rights Department, Oxford University Press, at the
address above.

You must not circulate this work in any other form
and you must impose this same condition on any acquirer.

Library of Congress Cataloging-in-Publication Data
Names: Adraoui, Mohamed-Ali, author.
Title: Salafism goes global : from the Gulf to the French banlieues / Mohamed-Ali Adraoui.
Other titles: Du Golfe aux banlieues, le salafisme mondialisé. English
Description: New York : Oxford University Press, 2020. |
Series: Religion and global politics | Includes bibliographical references and index. |
Translated from French.
Identifiers: LCCN 2019042375 (print) | LCCN 2019042376 (ebook) |
ISBN 9780190062460 (hardback) | ISBN 9780190062484 (epub) |
ISBN 9780190062491 (online)
Subjects: LCSH: Salafīyah—France. | Islam—France. |
Muslims—France—Attitudes.
Classification: LCC BP195.S18 A3513 2020 (print) | LCC BP195.S18 (ebook) |
DDC 297.8/1—dc23
LC record available at https://lccn.loc.gov/2019042375
LC ebook record available at https://lccn.loc.gov/2019042376

Contents

Preface	ix
Gilles Kepel	
Acknowledgments	xi
Introduction	xiii
Preamble	xiii
Salafism as Fundamentalism	xvii
A Movement That Draws from Common Sources but Reflects Contrasting Experiences	xx
Socialization as Political Language	xxvi
Methodology	xxxiii

I. THE REFERENCE GROUP

1. Genealogical Socialization	3
The Sociology of French Quietist Salafism	4
Typology	4
The Minhaj Salafi: An Antisystem Actor on the French Islamic Scene	22
The ʿAlim: The Maker of Salafist Meaning	27
The Daʾwa Salafiyya as Exclusive Islamic Paradigm	28
The Sociology of the Salafist Sphere: Rupture as an Effect of Historical Preaching on a Global and Local Level	33
The Salafi Habitus: Convert the Epistemic Rupture in the Social Arena	46
Call to Order: The Salafi as Guardian of Dogma	46
Orthopraxy	47
The Noah Syndrome	47
Resistance and Persistence	49
A Stranger among His Contemporaries	49
2. Pyramidal Socialization	50
Salafi Militant Apoliticism and the Control of French Islam's Political Agenda	50
The Quest for Status through Economic Independence	63
Social Rupture: Between Elitist Religious Practices and Cultural Desocialization	68
A Counterculture in Retreat and in Collision with the Dominant Culture: The Full-Body Veil	68

Elitist Proselytizing: A Conversion in a Mosque Attended by Salafis   73
Muslim Worship, Restorationist Practices with Elitist Effect:
   The Example of Prayer   75

3. Immunological Socialization   79
   Internal *Hijra*: Between Psychological Withdrawal and the First
      Fruits of Departure   81
      Rupture in Time and Space: The Logic of Religious Rationalization and
         Attendance at Mosques   81
      Protection against an Islamophobic Society: Media Discourse
         about Islam   84
   The *Hijra* to the Land of Islam: Leaving, Rebirth . . . and Fulfillment   88
      Egypt, or the Erasmus *Hijra*: Go East, Learn . . . and Return   88
      Algeria, or the *Hijra* of Origin: Go East . . . and Stay?   91

II. THE MEMBERSHIP GROUP

4. Filtered Socialization   101
   The Suburbs as a Symbolic Space for Differentiation and the
      Emergence of Counterworlds   101
      The Suburb: A Space for Forming an Antagonistic Habitus   101
      Militant Apoliticism: Between an Anti-imperialist Ethic, Disdain for
         Engagement, and Unfulfilled Politicization, a Relationship
         to Endogenous Politics?   105
      The Maghrebians: Inertia More than a Return to the Religious   118
      The Turks, or the All-Included Religious Socialization: A Turnkey Islam   124
      The Converts, or the Melting-Pot Socialization   127
   The Life Cycle of Quietist Salafism: The Generational Effect   129

5. Imaginary Socialization   133
   A New Age of Orientalism?   133
      The Orientalism of the French Salafis: To Begin with, a Western View
         of the Orient   135
      An Orientalism of the Interior, or How to Reify the Orient When
         You Are from It   140
      Reverse Orientalism: An Orient Better than the West   141
      Constructing a West as a Negative Mirror of the Orient, or Salafi
         Occidentalism   147
   The Invention of Tradition: Reifying Saudi Politico-religious Power   148
      The Salafist Sphere's Harmonious Character as Construction   148

6. Postmodern Socialization   157
   Salafi Socialization, or the Time of Religious Tribes: Atomization and
      Forming a New Organic Link of an Aesthetic Nature   157

Thriving on the Crisis of Islamism: The Minhaj Salafi as a Post-Islamist Mode 163
Islamism versus Minhaj Salafi: Militant Ethic of World Transformation against the Neofundamentalist Post-Islamism of Withdrawal 163
Conclusion 186

Index 197

Preface
Gilles Kepel

The study you are about to read fills a void by furnishing the fundamental reference points necessary for understanding a phenomenon that today has become a recurrent subject of debate and controversy in France.[1] More often than not, those who speak of Salafism know it only superficially, and they readily take offense at the "monstrous" appearance of this practice in contemporary Islam, buttressed by taking at face value the ritual and mimetic implementation of the Prophet's teachings. The phenomenon appears all the more bewildering in the French context, inasmuch as its practicants are products of the Republic's rationalist, secular schools. It reaches a fever pitch when it involves converts to Islam, often emerging from the suburban working class and socialized with a mostly Muslim youth. Here the Salafist commitment displays affinities with recruitment by sects laying claim to other beliefs but adopting similar paths: a break with the cultural background, resocialization, change of name, of dress and physical appearance, etc. Usually the distress of friends and relatives is extreme, as has been widely documented. Finally, although most Salafis stay away from politics and violent militancy and concentrate instead on proselytizing while vowing strict obedience to the great, mostly Saudi, Islamic scholars (or ulemas), and make of this interpretation of belief a church of sorts that is unknown in historical Sunni Islam, some individuals have gone beyond this engagement to cross over into jihad. The example of greatest concern in this regard is Mohammed Merah; since the drama that ensued after his crimes, he has cast a shadow over Islam's recent history in France.

Between its roots in the working-class "suburbs of Islam," where young people who have lost their bearings turn to an identity that corsets their faith and locks them in a citadel of certainties, and its signing onto the internet, where the fatwas of the Gulf ulemas circulate to circumscribe consciousness and feed dreams of emigrating from an impure France to leading a pure and

---

[1] Gilles Kepel is a university professor at Sciences Po and a member of the Institut Universitaire de France.

heroic Islamic life, Salafism constitutes an extreme case of de-integration. It registers in opposition to the French national narrative, whose credo is the integration of immigrants. Not only is integration detested here, but we also have the detachment of a certain number of young people alienated from their home country and their inherited culture.

Mr. Adraoui's rich study, conducted following numerous interviews in France, the Maghreb, Middle East, and Gulf, for the first time re-creates the complex journeys of France's Salafis. It pays a great deal of attention to their social, economic, political, and religious dimensions, and it exposes many of the everyday contradictions. This is indispensable reading for anyone who wishes to analyze developments of Islam in France today and those who, day by day, must deal with the social problems in the working-class suburbs where Islam's presence is crucial. This work makes a major contribution to the debate that promises to illuminate it decisively.

Acknowledgments

This work draws on a doctoral thesis that I had the honor of writing and defending in 2011, supervised by Gilles Kepel and Catherine Withol de Wenden at Sciences Po in Paris. It would certainly not have seen the light of day had it not been for the sage counsel and patience of these two individuals, who have never spared their efforts when it comes to their students. I also benefited greatly from a research allowance from Sciences Po's Mediterranean Middle East Studies Chair, where brilliant specialists in the Muslim world have been educated and contributed to the renaissance of studies in this field.

The advice by, exchange of views with, and friendship of many researchers were indispensable in my successfully pursuing this work. I therefore wish to thank Leyla Arslan, Sarah Zouheïr, Samir Amghar, Moussa Khedimallah, Adeline Braux, Fouad Nasri, Bernard Godard, Elyamine Settoul, Hamza Meddeb, Haoues Seniguer, El Yamine Soum, Nabil Mouline, Omar Saghi, Aurélie Daher, Vincent Geisser, Dominique Thomas, and Amel Boubekeur. Professors Jean-François Mayer, Jean-Pierre Filiu, Khadija Mohsen-Finan, Farhad Khosrokhavar, Hosham Dawod, Michel Wieviorka, Jérôme Ferret, Pierre Grosser, Tristan Mattelart, Samy Cohen, Nonna Mayer, and Marie-Hélène Bayle allowed me to test my hypotheses in lectures and seminars. I further want to thank Joas Wagemakers, Martin Van Bruinessen Martijn de Koning, and Roel Meijer of the Netherlands, Madawi Al-Rasheed, Sadek Hamid, Fawaz Gerges and Toby Dodge of the United Kingdom, Zoltan Pall, Ali Kadiri, and Victor Kattan of Singapore, John Esposito (who has made this English version possible), Jonathan Brown, Lorenzo Vidino, and Marc Sageman of the United States, and Jordi Moreras of Spain.

I also wish to express my deepest gratitude to Olivier Roy, Franck Frégosi, and Bernard Haykel, who were members of my thesis jury and who, by their counsel, attentive reading, and proximity contributed decisively to my work. Olivier Roy'help, especially, has been amazingly precious for so many years.

I personally benefited from the reception given me by Marie Masdupudy, the French consul, during my sojourn in Egypt in July 2009. A very special thank you goes to Josiane Valladeau, Giancarlo Ripoli, Bocar Alpha Ba,

Erwan et Priscille Hebré, Vincent Terrier, Mourad and Maamar El Maktafi, M'Hamed El Mansouri, Yassine Amanzou, Anouar Bouadjela, Randianne Peccoud, Hatim Achikhan, Mohammed Ghazi, Kader Smail, Hassan Chahdi, Karim Chaibi, and Delphine Patétif.

At Oxford University Press, I am thankful to Cynthia Read, Hannah Campeanu, and Prabhu Chinnasamy for their kindness, patience, and constant availability. As an independent translator, Henry Randolph has done a stunning job in translating my words and ideas making this English version possible, that is why I am so grateful to him.

My love goes to my parents, Ahmed and Khadija, and my brothers, Charafdine, Hisham, and Issam, my nephews Adam, Samy and Issa, to whom this book is dedicated. These efforts of mine find their meaning and raison d'être in them.

Finally, I am indebted to the individuals who answered my questions and welcomed me in their mosques and other places where this religious ethic is deployed and has not ceased raising questions for the rest of society.

Introduction

> It is, it seems, a highly prevalent failing to prefer the schematic authority of a text to direct human contacts that risk being disconcerting. But is this an ever-present flaw or are there indeed circumstances that, more than others, make textual attitudes prevail?
> —Edward Saïd, *L'Orientalisme: L'Orient crée parl'Occident*, 2005

> The radicals question existing arrangements, demand reforms or the abolition of what they view as unjustifiable on the level of principle. It is more a matter of an attitude than an organized current of political thought. Its practical content varies as a function of the circumstances that the radicals find themselves confronted with.
> —Alexis de Tocqueville, *De la démocratie en Amerique*

Preamble

From the most progressive of tendencies to fundamentalist movements, the Muslim religion is characterized by a multitude of currents. The intellectuals laboring to "make Islam enter modernity"[2] and the practitioners of a "return to the sources" demarcate the vast spectrum of Islamic belief, the object of many interrogatories stimulated by recent events staged by actors with manifest ambitions to revive the Islam that was in the beginning. Thus the public debate, particularly since September 11, 2001, has seen numerous questions surface concerning the religious ethic justifying such actions. The conception of Islam that is invoked to legitimize this type of engagement is based on Salafism, understood ever since that date as a radical movement advocating the destruction of the "enemies of Islam," by armed combat if necessary. It

---

[2] Malika Zeghal, "Intellectuels de l'islam contemporain: Nouvelles générations, nouveaux débats" (Intellectuals of contemporary Islam: New generations, new debates), *Revue des mondes musulmans et de la Méditerranée*, no. 123 (2008): 32–201. Unless otherwise specified, all translations are mine.

Salafism Goes Global. Mohamed-Ali Adraoui, Oxford University Press (2020). © Oxford University Press.
DOI: 10.1093/oso/9780190062460.001.0001

turns out that this current, in the plural, crystallizes multiple interpretations. In existence since the first centuries of Islam, it postulates alignment with the ethic of those early times as the best way to live this religion, while eschewing any other form of allegiance. This justifies its foundational dynamic of a constant quest for purifying the faith by an unswerving return to basics. If this paradigm is systematically distinguished by an attempt to revive the original Islam of Salaf Salih,[3] its implementation nevertheless can take contrasting approaches. Certain approaches legitimize the resort to violence, in the process adopting a violent reading of jihad.[4] Several integrate lawful politics to push their religious agenda. Others, finally, seek to purify their practice while abjuring any interest in political activism; in France today, the majority identify with this quietist approach. Hence Salafism means different things. Its clerics,[5] the principal vectors for interpretations of scriptural sources, debate, make speeches, or struggle to assert their reading of the sacred references. Therefore Salafism may under no circumstances be reduced to specific organizations like Al-Qaeda, even if it is one of its most mediatized heralds.[6]

Of the multiple discussions variously focused on the violence of some Salafist groups, for several years the path of Mohammed Merah (although very far removed from the majority profiles in France), or the place of the one-piece veil worn by some women followers of this dogma or the proselytizing by integrating imams, all have put their stamp on the public debate in France and attracted attention to this particular form of faith, to the point where the term "Salafi" has often taken on the meaning of a radical, extremist, or sectarian way of thinking.

The novice will no doubt be surprised by the use of a term imported from the Islamic referential coming from the mouth of a secular republic's minister with portfolios that are removed a priori from the problems of worship and church-state relations. An article in *Figaro* dated March 17, 2005, headlined

---

[3] "Pious forebears," "virtuous precursors," or "ancient sages." This expression designates the first generation of the faithful, whose faith and practice are perceived as the most exact expressions of piety because these persons were formed in the wake of the Prophet and some are held to be contemporaries of his apostolate. Salafiyya, which expresses the return to the example of the "pious forbears," is generally translated in English as "Salafism."

[4] It is a question of the attention paid by the believer to his faith and his practice to become a better Muslim; this may occur through a spiritual, social, or political combat in order to get rid of forces that work to destroy the spirit and the reality of Islam.

[5] Islamic clerics are the '*oulama* (ulemas) who are responsible for defining the religious norm based on mastery of the sacred logos ('*ilm*, from the root '-l-m, "the one for science" in Arabic, from which comes '*alim*, meaning "scholar" in the Muslim tradition, including the one who specializes in the study of religious disciplines).

[6] Jean-Perre Filiu, *Les neuf vies d'Al-Quaïda* (The nine lives of Al-Qaeda) (Paris: Fayard, 2009).

"UMP Digs through Its Tool Box," quotes the minister of employment, labor, and integration of youth, Gérard Larcher, as criticizing the alleged rigidity of legislation for saying "We have a Salafist reading of the labor code, as if it were untouchable, permanently not subject to interpretation, except by the Ulemas on the Highest Court of Appeal." Aside from the remark's caustic nature, lifting such words from Salafism's semantic field to characterize a debate bearing on the most profane public business illustrates the radicalistic sense of a current that raises questions and unease as its visibility grows. And yet the Salafi dynamic[7] in France is essentially quietist and structured around a desire to wall itself off against society so that it can lead a life free of the minutest element that might contaminate the process of purification sought after by its adherents. This current has fed a host of fears centered on a rampant communitarianism, the corollary to an Islamization of the suburbs that would make relations problematic between some Muslims and the rest of society. Counting several thousand faithful today, the Salafist current is also the object of numerous questions concerning the "sectarian" way of life that it encourages or about the "entryism" that it promotes with the goal of "testing the values of the Republic."[8]

Its followers often have a long beard; like the first believers of Islam, they dress in a *qamis* (a man's plain long garment on a simple pattern) that never reaches below the calf, and sometimes they wear a skull cap to cover a shaved head. Their speech is systematically punctuated by pious formulations as signs of devotion, such as *Inch'Allah* (By the grace of God), *Ma Cha Allah* (It is God's will), or *Soubhan Allah* (Glory to God). Their faith aims for rigor and presents itself as reproducing the Islam practiced at the time when Muhammad, Islam's Prophet, and his Companions as well as their immediate successors promoted the purest form of this religion. You notice the Salafist presence primarily on the outskirts of large French cities, where some people raise the specter of districts surrendered to Muslim fundamentalists. They frequent mosques, shopping centers, or stairwells with equal facility. It is common to hear them preach the need for reforming the morals of the

---

[7] Historically fundamentalism's raison d'être does not lie in scriptural sources but in "a literal reading, ahistoric and nonhermeneutic, of papal encyclicals." John Coleman, "Catholic Integralism as a Fundamentalism," in Lawrence Kaplan (ed.), *Fundamentalism in Comparative Perspective* (Amherst: University of Massachusetts Press, 1992), 76.

[8] See Jean-François Copé, "La burqa, ce sont des intégristes qui veulent tester la République" (The burqa, fundamentalists who want to test the Republic), *Huffington Post*, October 17, 2009, http://www.lepost.fr/article/2009/10/17/1746909_jean-francois-cope-laburqa-ce-sont-des-integristes-qui-veulent-tester-la-republique.html.

strayed faithful, whose manner of living out their faith no longer has much to do with that of the pious forebears. They can also be seen in the airports, taking off for or returning from Middle Eastern countries they love traveling to if not settling there permanently. Their religiosity is more and more visible in the Paris region and elsewhere in the country. They quote the great Sunni names and subject to public scorn any Muslims who do not profess the same need for reconnecting with the orthodoxy as they do and to which their return to the sources is supposed to lead. The majority do not vote, since that would be tantamount to legitimating an impious order, and they favor a partisan spirit over the unification of the umma (community of believers) around the divine Uniqueness (*tawhid*). Their ambition is to devote themselves to God in exclusive worship, without regard for such things as politics that supposedly keep them from fulfilling this agenda. They reckon that their environment is unhealthy, and they are emphatic in their desire to break the ties that attach them to it so that they can establish themselves in a Muslim society more welcoming than a France that is hostile, as they see it, to their practice of "true" Islam. They dream of reviving the original faith, inspired by the *'oulama*. In addition, the adepts seldom preface their speech when evoking religious subjects without the consecrated formulation *qala Cheikh* (the sheikh[9] has said), suggesting in this way that they take their rules for living from the maxims and opinions of authorized clerics.[10] Salafi wives in some cases wear the burqa, which was a hot media and political topic in 2009, before the law was passed in 2010 to prohibit leaving the house with the face concealed.[11] While they are not hostile to many aspects of modernity, such as technological progress and economic success, they are nonetheless Salafis;[12] in other words, they take as their model the most virtuous Muslims who lived in the time of Revelation, the Salaf Salih, and the first generations of Islam. They are exclusively inspired by the latter's morality in the quest for salvation. They seek separation and accept it. The new life they seek to

---

[9] In Sunni Islam, the title conferred on clerics mastering the Islamic logos and its interpretation.

[10] These opinions are offered in the form of the fatwa (from the root *f-t*, which designates the promulgated opinion). This is a legal opinion concerning problems that confront the faithful. It is the principal vector for achieving conformity with orthodoxy.

[11] Law No. 2010-1192, dated October 11, 2010, prohibiting concealment of the face in public spaces.

[12] In 2005 a general information report put forward a figure of 5,000 Muslims of this persuasion in French society. After September 11 the general perception was that of a growing religious group whose visibility caused concern (see Xavier Ternisien, "L'essor des salafistes en banlieue inquiète policiers et musulmans" (The rapid expansion of Salafists in the suburbs worries the police and Muslims), *Le Monde*, January 24, 2002; Piotr Smolar, "Mouvance éclatée, le salafisme s'est étendu aux villes moyennes" (Spreading out, Salafism has reached the midsized cities), *Le Monde*, April 4, 2007).

embrace is meant to remake them into human beings who are faithful to the appeal of the original Islam. Their reason for living is to revive a sacred norm forgotten by the rest of humanity, without heeding the social cost of such an approach.[13] They care little what others think of their way of life. This is a revivalist project, and no consideration can get in the way of this desire to resuscitate the original Islam in all its presumed forms. In the quest for absolute religiosity, this path must allow them to break all ties that shackle them to a detested society, the avatar of a lost age.

Salafism as Fundamentalism

Despite the multiplicity of discourses and postures that characterize the identification with Islam's earliest times, the presupposition for all the mobilizations of the Salaf referent remains identical: Islam, from the perspective of dogma, practice, and temporal civilization, was authentic only when the believers were close to Muhammad's apostolate. The faithful who kept company with the Prophet and then, shaped and inspired by his example, propagated his Message (*rissala*) instituted what is perceived now as a veritable Golden Age. Cultivating a pure rapport with the faith and the social practices stemming from it, Muslims were able to live according to a moral paradigm, one of whose principal effects was to permit advances in civilizational terms. Such is the basic premise of numerous movements today for which a return to Islam is bound to let them project themselves propitiously into the future. The history is a paradoxical challenge, running the risk of altering the Truth, and full of nonexistent data, the believer having to reproduce the original model without taking into account different evolutions; this is why Salafism must be understood as an assumed fundamentalism. Muslims can truly be themselves only through full and total identification with the first generations of the faithful, for the most correct standard is not the most recent one but the oldest one. The premise of the Golden Age explains why any religious, social, or political enterprise apart from the way

---

[13] Regarding this actor profile, Leyla Arslan speaks of "kamikazes," meaning those who put [their] considered differences forward in a very negative manner, to be righteous in their own eyes despite the social and economic disadvantages that it brings. Leyla Arslan, *Enfants d'Islam et de Marianne: Des banlieues à l'Université* (Children of Islam and Marianne: From the suburbs to the university) (Paris: PUF, "Proche Orient," 2010), 16).

that is supposed to lead to Salaf will be struck ipso facto with the seal of illegitimacy.

To understand the essence of Salafism it is therefore suitable to think in terms of a "mental topography." The contemporary situation that Muslims find themselves in is the consequence of centuries of erring ways and of forgetting the authentic norm that would have guided believers toward a different, necessarily more favorable plane, since it would have ensued from respecting a morality with the unaltered principles of Islam as its starting point. Thus, in order to connect again with the Truth, righteousness, and happiness, it behooves believers who are aware of this break caused by the straying of their coreligionists to retrace their steps in a way that rewinds the course of history and recovers the sole form of practice authorized in theory. The foundation of the Salafist ethos resides in this "topographical" thinking,[14] which makes the believer responsible and holds him accountable for Islam's crisis. This vision presupposes two possible courses. The first means a turn to the past, since it is necessary to return to Islam's early times to recover the lost purity. The second leads to the future, because the newly aware faithful must reform the corrupted morals of their coreligionists within a purified framework. This dual movement is fundamental to Salafist socialization.

The faith of Muslims is deemed sick as long as they do not clearly identify with this religious movement that is perceived as curative. It will not know how to regenerate itself other than through puritan reform proceeding from a return to the past to reconnect with the foundations laid by Muhammad and put into practice by his first followers. Salafis therefore argue that types of worship different from theirs cannot be considered Islamic since they have been infiltrated by scoria, distorting the primal authenticity. They alone have remained faithful, alone did not deviate from the way. Reviving this system of values and norms is feasible, provided the footsteps of the first believers are followed; more specifically, by following their contemporary heirs, namely the clerics, they have been anointed by their respect for orthodoxy.[15]

---

[14] We understand that the practicants most often present their religiosity as a "way" (*minhaj*) to better distinguish it from the other "roads" supposedly leading nowhere. We were also able to observe that Salafism, in the clerical literature and daily vernacular of the practicants, took the name Minhaj al-Haqq (the true way) or Minhaj Sahih (the real way). Insisting on the predicative characters of their conception of Islam, this religiosity is also called Da'wa Salafiyya (Salafi preaching). The reference of the Sunna, the example of the Prophet, also is the object of an exclusive appropriation ("scholars of the Sunna," "return to the Sunna," etc.). As for the practicants, they also think of themselves as *oussouliyun* (partisans of the return to the root), the word *oussoul* also referring to foundations.

[15] Salafis see themselves as orthodox, that is, persons whose doctrine (*doxa*) is right (*orthos*). This is also the reason they frequently present themselves as "the steadfast ones" or "the people of

Salafism thus explicitly echoes religious fundamentalism since, in the very definition of this reform movement, reference is made to the generation that was present when the principles were established. Promoting a Salafist morality means identifying with the first believers of the Muslim religion, the Salaf Salih, who are, in essence, seen as the most ardent defenders of the credo and of the orthopraxy. The first term, Salaf, points to anteriority. It designates the people "who were there before," those "who preceded." Differing from the Khalaf, later generations who, for example, live in contemporaneous centuries, the Salaf are blessed with historical and, especially, moral precedence. They are the guarantors of the most authentic Islamic norm because it flows directly from their closeness with Muhammad, through whom Revelation, mediated by the Archangel Gabriel, was delivered to the human being (the word of God creating itself in the Koran). The example provided by the Prophet, be it in religious affairs (vertical)[16] or social relations (horizontal),[17] is the other source of morality and Islamic law. The Salaf witnessed the deployment of these two holy sources that form the matrix of Sunnism, in contrast to the Shiite Muslims, for whom the Truth reposed in the Prophet's lineage after his death, access to which is difficult for someone who does not admit the primacy of *ahl al-bayt* (men of the House of the Prophet).[18] The second term, Salih, means "value" and "virtue" in Arabic. The root *s-l-h* stands for "intrinsic value." Thus the first generations of believers rank on top of the historical scale of spiritual greatness and moral merit.

What is involved here is a dynamic of a return to a period endowed with moral qualities that are lacking in contemporary times. In this way, all fundamentalism is foremost a discourse about the present. It is not a pathology of modernity, since any advent of a norm contains in its very essence a ruing of what came before and, as a result, nourishes a nostalgia for origins and lost authenticity. Put another way, the fundamentalist ethic is organically integrated in the broad spectrum of modes of worship and appropriation of the sacred. The recourse to the past in order to surmount the present and

---

righteousness." See Franck Frégosi, *Penser l'Islam dans la laïcité* (Islamic thought in secularism) (Paris: Fayard, 2008), 123–127.

[16] The Arab term for these is *al-ʾibadat*, from the root ʿ-b-d, "adoration."
[17] The Arab word here is *al-mouʾamalat*, from the root ʿ-m-l, which stands for the relational dimension in human life.
[18] Shiism's organizing idea is that, following the death of Muhammad, his Truth passed down the line of his descendants, which explains the reverence, if not adoration in certain cases, starting with his cousin and son-in-law, Ali Ibn Abou Talib, who, some Muslims have it, was chosen to succeed the Prophet and guide the umma.

influence the future is that much more understandable when the religious is interrogated by the faithful who think of themselves as being in crisis, as is the case today.

Numerous movements, sometimes conflicting ones in the history of Islam, have fed the ambition of bringing back the origin. They all share this project of reactivating the first norm in order to recapture fidelity to the Message. Some are organized around political action and want to influence history; others advocate a more detached vision and focus on a purification dynamic without aiming to transform the social framework by an activist ethic. Salafism is pluralistic and must be differentiated according to whether accepting it leads, for example, to an assumed politicization or not. The latter is the more important should it restore, in reality, a rapport with history to society and even the notion of religious reform. Fundamentalist enterprises,[19] if they are joined to the imperative of returning to religious bedrock,[20] may nevertheless be divided into two groups, as underlined by Jean-François Mayer: "The distinction between groups that withdraw and groups that choose the political offensive in the name of religious values constitutes an important line of demarcation: there are 'fundamentalist' attitudes that are essentially religious and others that are by nature politico-religious."[21]

A Movement That Draws from Common Sources but Reflects Contrasting Experiences

Salafism starts from the belief that Islam exists in objective terms and that the faithful can legitimately control history, conceived as a path to follow in order to arrive at the "illuminated destination" that is the original religion. No other consideration may interfere with religion, as it alone will let Muslims find happiness. To identify yourself with the Salaf as you progress in your religious apprenticeship results from an implacable logic because the more faithful you claim to be, the greater is the theoretical alignment with the

---

[19] Geoffrey F. Nuttall, *The Puritan Spirit* (London: Epworth Press, 1967), 11.
[20] The term "fundamentalism" came into use sometime in the early twentieth century in the Anglo-Saxon Protestant sphere to designate the willingness of believers who "notably affirmed the inspiration and infallibility of Scripture in the face of Biblical criticism, harking back to fundamental truths such as the divinity and virgin birth of Christ, pushed evangelization and energetically criticized Roman Catholicism." Jean-François Mayer, *Les fondamentalismes* (Fundamentalisms) (Geneva: Georg, 2002), 12. See also George M. Mardsen, *Understanding Fundamentalism and Evangelicalism* (Grand Rapids, MI: William B. Eerdmans, 1991), chapter 1.
[21] Mayer, *Les fondamentalismes*, 74.

norm inherited from the virtuous predecessors. For the Muslim, it suffices to reconnect with what is inscribed in his subconscious since Revelation to rediscover the morality that will assure his prosperity and salvation:

> Islamic society struggles between slogans and conscience, futile slogans and blessed conscience; slogans crying out words without substance and conscience calling to the right way; to the solid guide rope of Allah and the illuminated path, back to Allah's Book and the tradition of His Noble Messenger according to the understanding of the pious Ancients; slogans affiliated with noble names for deceiving the public but whose affiliation is denied by their positions, proving the falseness of their pretensions, a conscience that devotes itself to the way of the pious Ancients, that it lays claim to, identifies with, whose foundations and its truths it follows all the while searching for the "illuminated destination"[22] [*al-Mahajjat al-Baydā*] where the night is as bright as the day and which only the damned shrink from.
>
> The identification with the Ancients [al-Salaf] and with *Salafism*[23] is an ancient thing and well known by the imams, the ulemas, and the Ancients and the Moderns. More than one man of learning is identified by using these names, numerous are those among them that have affiliated themselves with this way, because it is a noble, majestic, and respectable membership.
>
> However, there are in today's society numerous persons who falsely and dishonestly associate themselves with this noble identity; their line of conduct takes the path opposite that of the pious Ancients, both generally and specifically. It even contradicts it in specifics and especially in its foundations. On the one hand, it is the nobility of this identity that has impelled them to assimilate themselves to it; but let us also assert, on the other hand, that in fact they lead people away from the correct belief or again, from a last point of view, through ignorance of the nature of the way of the Ancients.[24]

This excerpt comes from an introductory text for Salafist preaching edited by one of the movement's emblematic figures, Sheikh Al-Albani, who here

---

[22] In red lettering in the original text.
[23] Also in red.
[24] Cheikh Muhammad Nāsir al-Dīn al-Albāni, *Le salafisme: Du mythe à la réalité. Fondements, équivoques, positions, vérité. Texte présenté et annoté par 'Amr 'Abd al-Mun'im Salîm* (Salafism: From myth to reality. Origins, ambiguities, truth. Text presented by 'Amr 'Abd al-Mun'im Sālim) (Brussels: Al-Hadīth Editions, 2008).

sets down the basics of his religious approach and touches on one of the principal characteristics of the debates that it arouses. The symbolic superiority of the call of the Salaf and the legitimacy that it imparts lead many Muslims to claim they follow it but without actually adopting the exact substance of this religiosity. The cleric even so calls for distrust and for deepening the concept of Salafism. Sheikh Al-Albani specifies here that this reference can hide many religious postures that violate, sometimes gravely, the prescriptions that he views as having been issued by the first generations. Many Muslims may seek the "illuminated destination," but every version of being Salafi defends its own perspective. The currents debate; they try to have the others fall into line; they contradict each other; sometimes they get entangled. But the contemporary fragmentation of the Salafi scene really calls attention to the plurality of this symbolic reference in which every re-Islamization actor claims to have the interpretive monopoly.

In order to return to the spiritual, legal, and moral roots of Islam, Salafism opposes any spirit of codification as well as any enterprise that would bar the interpretation of the religious norms laid down by the Prophet. Therefore it cannot be understood apart from a Sunni interpretation, which holds that the Islamic credo and worship define themselves, starting from the uncreated word of God that is the Koran (*al-Quran al-karim* [the perfect recitation]), as well as the ideal practice and morality represented by Muhammad and contained in the Sunna. This explains why the followers love to present their religiosity as the sole incarnation of orthodox Sunnism: not everyone is fit to serve as model, and if the Messenger is essentially the incarnation of Islamic virtue become man, then the believers must imitate the example of the first human beings through whom his example shone. In this resides the founding dynamic. The principal fallout from this thesis is the dis-intermediated reappropriation of the treasure that is the original Islam. Although a great number of clerics over the centuries have taken the part of the Sunna against heterodoxy, this does not mean that the interpretation has been sealed. Thus one of the key effects of this approach bears on the bypassing of the Sunni legal schools such as they were conceived over the course of Islam's first centuries.[25] Any cleric can claim orthodoxy whenever he relies exclusively on

---

[25] These are the Hanafi, Maleki, Chafi'i, and Hanbali *madahib* (plural of *madhab*, which designates the source of guidance and hence, by extension, the school), each founded by one of Sunnism's great names. If each of them is presented as a leading light, its teaching is suspect unless it is based on the Koran and the Sunna, the Sunnis being hostile to the idea of servile imitation by any cleric (*taqlid*), instead leaving him the freedom of interpretation permitted within the framework of orthodoxy. It is not surprising that historically the reform movements in Islam in the name of Salafism often took the

the canonical sources, which are the Koran, the Sunna, and the trail (*athar*) of the pious forebears who organize the Community and the Consensus that no Muslim may distance himself from on pain of forfeiting his salvation.[26] If there is any debate, it must be settled within the confines of this "epistemic framework"[27] bounded by the Salafite religious paradigm. It is based in particular on the duty of possessing as much religious knowledge (*'ilm*) as possible in order to be able to live in faith as the world evolves. This helps us to better understand why one of the most telling manifestations of this religious ethic today is tracking down signs of deviance or impiety, of having "associated" (*chirk*)[28] someone or something with God, leading to a nonexclusive adoration, thus breaking up the worship of Him alone (*tawhid*).

Three types of definitions make it easier to grasp the Salafite dynamic. It first of all thinks of itself as paradigmatic. The practitioners structure their religiosity around their vocation of serving as a scientific model based on correct mastery of the Islamic logos. If Islam has never again been as pure as it was in the beginning, then no interpretation of this system of meaning may be made except by reference to the first generation of believers. Next, it is a matter of a methodology according to which a norm cannot be legitimate if it does not get the "shadow of the Salaf," be it that of the Companions, their successors, or the *'oulama* like Sheikh Ibn Hanbal, Sheikh Ibn Taymiyya, or Sheikh Ibn Abdelwahab,[29] who, for their entire lives, affirmed the primacy of this epistemology above any other. The final element in the dynamic is an orthopraxy that the Muslims may determine out of respect for this religious

---

form of a rediscovery of the *ahadith* scholasticism (plural of "hadith," which designates the words left by Muhammad and on whose authenticity the clerics have been holding forth for centuries). This was the case with the medieval age of Islam, when several generations of *ahl al-hadith* (men of hadith) appeared whose teaching focused on the sayings of the Messenger.

[26] Muslim unity (*chaq saf al-oumma*) must rigorously start with rallying around the Koran and the way of Muhammad. Those who abide by it are the *ahl Sunna wal-jam 'a* (men of the Sunna and the Community/of the Consensus/of the Assembly), as opposed to the sectarians, the deviants who, in straying from the *jam 'a*, spawn *ahzab* (plural of *hizb*, "party" or "partisan group," defenders of an ideology and no longer Islam as revealed Truth).
[27] Samir Amghar, "Les salafistes français: Une nouvelle aristocratie religieuse" (The French Salafists: A new religious aristocracy), *Maghreb-Machrek*, Spring 2005, 13–31.
[28] According to the *'oulama* (religious scholars), if the *chirk* is "minor," it makes the Muslim a "deviant" (*moubtadi'*), and if it is "major," it makes him a "heretic" who has fallen into "atheism" (*kufr*).
[29] See first part, chapter 1. Other figures have appeared in the Muslim world around the Salafi agenda, such as Sheikh Muhammad Al-Chawkani (1759–1834) in Yémen in the late eighteenth and early nineteenth centuries and Shah Wali Allah (1703–1762) in India in the eighteenth century. See Bernard Haykel, *Revival and Reform in Islam: The Legacy of Muhammad al-Shawkani* (Cambridge, UK: Cambridge University Press, 2003), and "On the Nature of Salafi Thought and Action," in Roel Meijer (ed.), *Global Salafism: Islam's New Religious Movement* (London: Hust, 2009), 33–57.

proceeding. Islam is a palpable experience, and no sincere faith can be declared if it is not translated into recognized practices blessed by the clerics. Salvation requires right belief and faithful practice.

Nonetheless, putting these principles into practice has been impeded historically by numerous contradictory readings. The Salafiyya of the second half of the nineteenth century around Jamal-Dine Al-Afghani and Muhammad Abdou[30] and the Muslim Brotherhood movement beginning in Egypt in 1928 laid claim to a return to the Ancients, but today this paradigm has different meanings. Between the violent enterprise of destabilizing the apostate Muslim regimes and their Western allies initiated by Osama bin Laden and the quietism of thousands of puritan believers in France, or the participation in Salafist parties in Kuwait[31] and in Egypt since the fall of Hosni Mubarak, the map is the same (Koran, Sunna, and *athar*), but the destination differs.[32]

These postures most often are antagonistic, but at times they are complementary or mutually supporting, as in the case of the Kingdom of Saudi Arabia, the country that is key to understanding the Salafism of our time. While the quarrels over dogma and interpretation are quite real and do not fall within the main framework of this book, we can keep the link to politics as a discriminating criterion for analyzing the references to Salafiyya today.

The version of this approach that has gotten the most media coverage, in particular with regard to the attacks of September 11, 2001, is jihadism. It refers to groups that seek the advent of an Islamic society by means of armed combat against iniquitous entities. It targets both Western states—in whose front rank figures the United States, allegedly hostile toward Muslims—as well as regimes that are nominally Islamic but that are in religious disrepute

---

[30] See second part, chapter 6. The reference here is to the "Salafism of lights" (Salafiyya tanwiriyya) based on the compatibility of reason and revelation, immanent order and transcendental order. See Haykel, "On the Nature of Salafi Thought and Action," 47.

[31] Carine Lahoud-Tatar, *Islam et politique au Koweït* (Islam and politics in Kuwait) (Paris: PUF, "Proche Orient," 2011).

[32] This view of Salafism that distinguishes between the jihadist, the quietist, and the participationist derives from the typology of Quintan Wiktorowicz, "Anatomy of the Salafi Movement," *Studies in Conflict & Terrorism* 29, no. 3 (April–May 2006): 207–239. Wiktorowicz differentiates among "jihadist," "purist," and "political" Salafists. The first are adept at violent organized action; the second, on which our work centers, are theoretically quietist; and the third are participationists, in that they integrate politics in defending their conception of society and participate in elections and public debates. The jihadists can be compared to those Samir Amghar calls "revolutionary Salafis," a reference to their project of overthrowing states whose leaders have "apostatized" Islam in having refused its laws and by being in solidarity with Western powers that are "enemies of Islam." See Samir Amghar, "Le salafisme en Europe: La mouvance polymorphe d'une radicalization" (Salafism in Europe: The polymorphous movement of a radicalization), *Politique étrangère* (Foreign policy), no. 1 (Spring 2006): 65–78.

because they do not apply the letter of the laws of Allah. Among those, Saudi Arabia certainly occupies first place.[33]

This propensity of the revolutionaries to declare those who hold political authority (*wilayat al-amr*) anathema represents an abomination in the eyes of quietist Salafis, one of whose dogmatic principles is a prohibition on defying the political power from the moment that it proclaims allegiance to Islam. If criticisms are to be formulated against it, they may emanate only from clerics, the people not being a legitimate political actor unless called to the rescue. In putting the preservation of orthopraxy in the center of political thinking as well as the physical and moral safety of believers for fear of fomenting sedition (fitna), the Salafis are, in a certain sense, Hobbesian: prepared to abdicate their sovereignty in exchange for having their religion protected and safety assured. The jihadists can be viewed more as Lockeans, since they hold the view that obeisance to power is legitimate only from the moment that it abides by the canonical prescriptions. Outside this framework, it is permitted (*yazouj*) to defy power in the name of divine precepts. The quietist practitioners, in fact, legitimize the different political orders under which they live. If it is a non-Muslim society, they are obligated to separate themselves from it physically, in the manner of the Prophet and his Companions, who had to abandon Mecca for Medina in order to safeguard their lives and faith. This practice of *hijra*[34] is essential for grasping the content of Salafist socialization under way in France. It constitutes one of the analytical points on which we are most reliant in studying this religious movement, and it must be viewed as an isolation undertaken for safety purposes, a physical migration preceded by a moral separation from a flawed environment. French order is not legitimate; it is a place of perdition for anyone wanting to continue living there. Although the quietists declare their disinterest in engaging in an assumed political activism (*harakiyya*), you can detect in them an attraction to Saudi Arabia, the key hub for spreading this norm in the contemporary era,[35] because here the implementation of the orthodox social

---

[33] The principal jihadist organization is Al-Qaeda (the Base), whose current leader, Ayman Al-Zawahiri (since the death of Osama bin Laden in May 2011), after years of fruitless combat against the apostate Islamic regimes, has theorized the need to turn again against their most powerful supporters, starting with the United States. This change of priority target, from the "close enemy" to the "remote enemy," constitutes the frame that led to September 11, 2001. See Gilles Kepel, *Fitna: Guerre au coeur de l'islam* (Fitna: The war in Islam's heart) (Paris: Gallimard, 2004).

[34] From the root *h-j-r*, which reflects departure, movement, migration. *Hijra* represents uncontestably the most original characteristics of quietist Salafism at work in France.

[35] The globalization of Salafi norms is largely due to the kingdom's proselytizing activity, whether it is through a university policy welcoming students eager to be educated in orthodoxy or an institutional cluster charged with propagating these conceptions on a global scale. This is the case, for

contract aiming to unite learned men and politicians for expanding an authentic Islam is perceived as being the most accomplished. The preaching has as its purpose reforming the hearts and morals of Muslims, which makes teaching just as important as activism as far as Salafi militants are concerned. The quietists say they practice a scholastic or scientific Salafism (Salafiyya 'ilmiyya). Engaging in politics makes sense only for Muslims possessing souls that are not cleansed.

The latter conception of contemporary Salafism is both militant and participationist, because it means operating within the legal political game. This form of preaching can be found in Kuwait, most prominently in the circle of Abderahman Abdelkhaliq,[36] and in Saudi Arabia, where it is incarnated by the Sahwa (Awakening) movement, organized around clerics like Safar Al-Hawali, Salman Al-'Awda, and 'Aīd Al-Qarni and which was born after the first Gulf War out of a growing religious challenge to Saudi policy.[37] Influenced by the radicalism of the Muslim Brotherhood, this current is reformist on a religious level but engaged on the political level, distinct from the quietists, and it is the object of strident warnings, just like the revolutionary version.

Socialization as Political Language

We now turn to examining the concept of socialization and, more specifically, the effects of identifying with a religion that advocates a permanent split from society. What does it mean to integrate with a puritan community and foster rapport with a world defined by this new reference? These queries derive their legitimacy from questioning a way of life that breaks

---

example, of the Muslim World League, founded in 1962 in Mecca. While these are important factors, they do not exclusively explain the growing visibility of Salafi codes. We will see that this religious norm enjoys its own legitimacy in the history of Islam beyond any proselytizing action by any particular actor, as Haykel underlines, pointing out the facility of identifying with it because of the feeling of basing one's practice on a "tangible" proof (*dalil*). See Haykel, "On the Nature of Salafi Thought and Action," 36–37; Samir Amghar, "La Ligue islamique mondiale en Europe: Un instrument de défense des intérêts stratégiques saoudiens" (The Muslim World League in Europe: An instrument for defending Saudi strategic interests), *Critique internationale* 2, no. 51 (2011): 113–127, and "Acteurs internationaux et islam de France" (International actors and French Islam), *Politique étrangère*, no. 1 (Spring 2005): 12–22.

[36] Lahoud-Tatar, *Islam et politique au Koweït*.
[37] Stéphane Lacroix, *Les islamistes saoudiens: Une insurrection manquée* (The Saudi Islamists: A failed insurrection) (Paris: PUF, "Proche Orient," 2010).

with everything that does not fit into the authentic Islamic framework. Many things have been said about Salafism in France, particularly in the media and the security realm, but little light has been shed on the nature of the socialization it induces. If this religiosity is primarily a form of preaching, it is also a way of living life in relation to God and man. The attempt to strictly and finally cut itself off from a society told ceaselessly it is ungodly takes a presumption, that is, a knowledge that appears to be objective but in fact reflects a superficial understanding of the studied reality.[38] This is linked to a shared sense based on experienced feeling and not on the criterion of scientific truth drawn from an in-depth analysis and conforming to certain quite precise empirical rules. If Da'wa Salafiyya (Salafi Preaching) is an undertaking to restore Islam to a fundamentalist and puritan mode, the socialization engendered by it favors separation as the social horizon. The practicant must strive to emancipate himself from the impious society so he can be reborn improved in the light of a veracious message that from now on will organize his entire existence. In other words, the situation he aspires to proceeds from a dual movement: desocializing himself from a society destined for perdition, then resocializing himself in a peer group that aims to deploy a new social identity opposed to the theoretically dominant value of society. The quest for desocialization also explains why the term "Salafist" often has extremist, violence-prone, obscurantist, or dogmatic connotations attached to it. In a sense, this addresses only one aspect of the approach, both empirically and compared with other contemporary social groups. The idea driving this book is this: separation does not reflect any sociological reality because everything is subject to socialization. Adopting a new way of life induces a different form of identification that will add itself, contradict, complete, nuance, value, or nullify dispositions previously assimilated in the course of other social "lives"[39] that organized as many identity factors able to explain the appropriation at a given moment of a system with precise meaning.[40]

We thus develop the hypothesis of the relational dimension of socialization, which allows us to situate any approach to acquiring specific values in a dynamic of social construction of reality and of identity factors by which

---

[38] Émile Durkheim, *Les règles de la méthode sociologique* (1894) (The rules of sociological method) (Paris: Payot, "Petite Bibliothèque Payot," 2009), foreword.

[39] Bernard Lahire, "Prédispositions naturelles ou dispositions sociales?" (Natural predispositions or social dispositions?), in *L'Esprit sociologique* (The sociological mind) (Paris: La Découverte, 2005), 305–307.

[40] Nancy Venel, *Musulmans et Citoyens* (Muslims and citizens) (Paris: PUF, "Partage du savoir" [Shared knowledge], 2004), 3.

one cognitive framework is preferred over another. Socialization is simultaneously process and language, assimilation and prescription, discovery and refuge, renewal and perpetuation, as well as questioning and confirmation. It is foremost the integration of values and norms that the individual has not recognized until then as part of his personal ethic:

> Socialization therefore is . . . the ensemble of processes by which the individual is constructed—it can also be said "formed," "fashioned," "made," "conditioned"—by the global and local society in which he lives, a process during which the individual acquires—"learns," "interiorizes," "incorporates," "integrates"—ways of doing, thinking, and being that are socially situated. . . . [It is the] manner in which society forms and transforms individuals. . . . Indeed, socialization does not denote a "domain" of acts, unlike school or the family, for example, but instead a notion, a manner of envisaging reality and constructing a way of looking.[41]

This first definition, a functional one, echoes one from the field of social psychology that also stresses the incorporation of norms and values:

> Socialization denotes the process by which individuals acquire the values, roles, and norms that govern the functioning of groups, institutions, and society at large. From the individual's point of view, its function is to integrate the subject in his society and lead him to acquire in apprenticeship the ways of thinking, acting, and feeling that are characteristic of the culture. Seen from the collective plane, its function is to permit social regulation and ensure a certain level of social cohesion.[42]

In a manner of speaking, socialization is above all determined by construction of the identity and the reality that puts the individual in touch with his context. As Georg Simmel underlines, it echoes the interaction which specifies, first and foremost, the process that he defines as the "structuring of the solitary juxtaposition of individuals with the forces of communal and interdependent existence."[43] Behind the desocialization[44] that the Salafi call

---

[41] Muriel Darmon, *La socialisation* (Socialization) (Paris: Armand Colin, "128," 2006), 6.
[42] Youcef Aïssani, *La psychologie sociale* (Social psychology) (Paris: Armand Colin, 2003), 56.
[43] Georg Simmel, *Sociologie et épistémologie* (Sociology and epistemology) (Paris: PUF, 1981).
[44] While we agree with Alain Touraine when he writes that "[the] desocialization is due to new social actors and the appearance of new cultural movements that give and produce meaning [and who] take it upon themselves to answer this crucial question: 'Where is the meaning?,'" we do not agree

for we can detect material for more pointed questioning. We postulate that it must inform us about the biographies of the principal parties and what they look for in this religiosity. While it is necessary to study the manner in which an aspired to[45] identity is acquired, our main thesis hinges on the second dimension of socialization. We mean to interest ourselves in the resocialization that Salafist separation leads to, in order to study if the values and behaviors henceforth to be formulated under the seal of the sacred in fact grow out of an intractable antagonism toward modernity. Should the Salafist affiliation be analyzed more as an object of interaction or as the translation of a purely fundamentalist essence? No socializing dynamic is neutral, and if, as in the case of this current, it insists on a system of counternorms in open conflict with the surrounding society, it must nevertheless be studied as both a desocialization and a resocialization whose logic may escape the motivations put forward by the actors themselves. They readily see themselves as being away from the path that society wants them to take. That is why the objective of reestablishing an identity that they came close to losing forever, had they not awakened in time to orthodox Islam's injunctions, must be understood with the tools provided by the sociology of deviance. The practicants imagine themselves as escaping from a *mainstream* morality, which, on a microsociological level, sets up an antagonistic trajectory; however, a more global approach allows us also to compare the effects of a socialization of separation to what can be observed in society at large.

This general problematic must be dealt with by confronting the spread of this religiosity in the French sphere and the world with several pertinent hypotheses. Because we are interested not just in the manner in which Salafist norms are assimilated in practice but what role they play in the path taken by certain individuals in a more global social, political, and religious context, we perceive in this journey a form of secondary socialization. It takes place when an actor with an evolving vision interacts with a world that has some objective manifestations[46] but is first and foremost understood subjectively.

with him when he states that "desocialization [is] the decline of the social . . . [and rejects] all 'social' norms and values." Alain Touraine, *Un nouveau paradigme: Pour comprendre le monde d'aujourd'hui* (A new paradigm: Toward understanding today's world) (Paris: Fayard, 2005), 28.

[45] The practicants are in a "state of certainty." Luc Boltanski, *Les cadres: La formation d'un groupe social* (The cadres: Formation of a social group) (Paris: Minuit, "Le sens commun" [Common sense], 1982), 33.

[46] It is also a question of institutions, space, media, and family or other social groups, which are just as much objective realities, interpreted by an individual who turns them into social worlds that he treats subjectively: "We can define 'reality' as a quality belonging to phenomena that we recognize as having an existence independent of our own will (we cannot 'wish them'), and we can define

Enrollment in this special system of meaning echoes the evolution of personality and relationship with the world that a person undergoes after having his infancy defined by primary socialization.[47]

We will therefore ask if the Salafist socialization inserts itself into a clear dialectic, and if certain factors more than others can explain today's emergence of such a religious field in France's fragmented Islam and, more broadly, in a society more than ever stamped by individualism, by secularization as well as by modernism. Regarding a secondary socialization, it amounts to asking about the historic dimension of the identification with the Salafi norm. Because we approach this question in a relational manner, we need to see if it is due to certain profiles evolving in a given context during a defined period. Blending the subjective and objective, micro- and macrosociological approaches, we postulate, "Socialization always takes place in the context of a specific social structure. Socio-structural conditions account for its content and also the measure of 'success.' In other words, micro-sociological or socio- psychological analysis of the phenomena of interiorization must always take place against a background of macro-sociological comprehension of their structural aspects."[48]

Socialization thus is a cardinal object of analysis that will allow us not only to understand how assimilation of a meaning different from others occurs and its effects, but especially to come to grips with the evolution of a society and the nature of the interactions that it maintains with a specific group of individuals. In addition, studying a given form of socialization informs us about the structure and the transformation of relations as well as the representations that link the actor to his environment:

> Socialization is constantly taking place and unwinding, and it renews itself among humans in an eternal flux and ferment that connect individuals, even in cases where it does not result in characteristic forms of organization. People watch each other, they envy each other, they write letters and dine together, they feel sympathy and antipathy over and above any tangible interest.... To the extent that it happens progressively, society always

---

'knowledge' as the certainty that the phenomena are real and that they possess specific traits." Peter Berger and Thomas Luckmann, *La construction sociale de la réalité* (The social construction of reality) (Paris: Méridiens Klincksieck, "Sociétés," 1986), 7–8.

[47] "In the course of the primary socialization . . . the individual's first world is constructed." Ibid., 186.
[48] Ibid., 222.

means that individuals are linked by influences and determinations that are felt reciprocally.... "Society" in this case is only the name applied to an ensemble of individuals, linked to each other by reciprocal actions.[49]

The same goes for identity, which must also be analyzed in constructivist and interactionist terms since it results, to the extent that socialization goes on, from the constantly mutating linkage between an individual formed by a given context and an environment that he helps to fashion as well:

> Identity is, of course, a key element in subjective reality and, like any subjective reality, it finds itself in a dialectical situation with society. Identity is formed by social processes. Once crystallized, it is preserved, modified, or even reshaped by social relationships. The social processes involved both in maintaining and forming identity are determined by the social structure. Conversely, the identities produced by the interaction of the organism, of the individual consciousness, and the social structure in turn influence the given social structure, maintaining it, transforming it, or giving it a new form. Societies have a history during which specific identities emerge; this history, however, is produced by human beings possessing a specific identity.[50]

The Salafi identity does not escape this rule because the actor is marked, even if not consciously aware of its happening, by the phenomenon of this system of meaning being a personal construction. He finds in it particularly that which he thinks is compatible with certain characteristics of his prior socialization, one that took place, for example, within an immigrant Muslim family or in the suburbs, as is the case with many practicants. In other words, there always exists a projected part of a self that escapes the discourse the individual has developed about himself by virtue of a socialization that he may think is exclusive of any other allegiance. It falls to us, therefore, to search for what sociological regularities characterize this deeper self.

Our hypotheses address three types of interrogatories. Above and beyond the antagonistic posture taken by Salafism, to assess the substance of the

---

[49] Simmel, *Sociologie et épistémologie*, 90. He also notes that the study of socialization allows us to "see how individuals and groups act reciprocally, how the individual approaches or distances himself from the group, how the dominant values, the accumulations and prerogatives progress or regress under certain social conditions—all of this perhaps comprising the real coming to be of an era" (95).
[50] Berger and Luckmann, *La construction sociale de la réalité*, 235–236.

resocialization which emerges in this mode of relating to the world, we need to ask three questions.

First, are there profiles that are more likely than others to embrace the ethos of Da'wa Salafiyya? If we take at face value the practicant's Salafist universalist thesis that this religiosity would touch social groups indiscriminately, it seems paradoxical to observe a significant predilection for this practice in certain ethnic, geographic, or generational circles. If so, what elements possibly explain the formation of a separation identity relative to an environment reified for reasons linked to the sacred? In other words, are there even specific primary[51] characteristics able to shed light on the adoption of such a way of life? By extension, if we adopt a comparative approach with other of Islam's offerings, could we succeed in evoking, if not a causality, at least a correlation between certain characteristics and the identification with a given religious norm? Is it therefore possible, given a certain political and media discourse that for many years has interrogated the belonging to Islam and the manner of living this religion in light of integration factors, to upend the reasoning and to question the influence of preexisting ties with society in the adoption of one religious conception over another? Beyond Islam in/of France, does interesting ourselves in the sociology of this religion in our society not lead ultimately to learning more about how it functions intrinsically rather than in what Islam says or does not say? Between the offer and the demand of Islamic meaning, which comes first? Is the aspiration to radicalism that the preaching is assumed to contain due to the message that is being conveyed in theory, or is it the fruit of prior interactions that are looking for justification in the sacred?

Second, taking a larger view, we can ask what the emergence of Salafism in the Islamic field covers. September 11, 2001, marked a rupture in the representations linked to the militant—or potentially radical—character of this religion. In this regard, it crystallizes a paradox: one of the most mediatized and most feared manifestations was anxiety about communities that no longer felt obliged to convert their moral norms in the political domain, especially on non-Muslim territory. Echoing a posture that some judged to be sectarian and separationist, or at least apolitical, this identity offer enjoins the faithful to remain apart from a social order not based on Islam. The activist, engaged translation of the Muslim reference characterizes

---

[51] That is to say, linked to primary socialization that defines the relationship with the world until adolescence and that organizes the capacity to orient oneself to other forms of socialization.

a precise moment in the sociology of this religion. How to explain the upsurge of quietist Salafism in the midst of French society during the 1990s, even when the practicants posed the ahistorical and atemporal aspects of this religion? In this respect, the relationship to politics constitutes a pertinent indicator, to the extent that the craving for a religious practice that is a priori remote from this type of contingency perhaps finds its microsociological basis in previous and macrosociological socializations on the one hand and in a crisis of militancy in all contemporary societies on the other hand. To sum up, it makes sense to historicize the emergence of quietist Salafism.

Third, what does fundamentalism echo? What describes a relationship with the world that is imprinted with distrust of what, in the view of its practicants, does not qualify as the realm of the acceptable? Beyond the discourse, what is it that organizes such an approach to society in the wider sense? Analyzing Salafism provides a glimpse of a certain attraction to multiple aspects of modernity, starting with the most unabashed consumerism, material success, or, even more, the entrepreneurial spirit. If the relationship to these values is formulated in sacred terms and results from a translation of Islamic revivalism, there again the comparative approach allows putting this posture into a context where these very same values are widely shared. This then prompts questions about certain religious justifications, indeed the fundamentalist project itself. This leads us to confront a type of discourse with the reality of its implementation and with other groups' ways of being, thus allowing us to judge what is modern in something that represents itself as exclusively focused on the past.

Methodology

To take the measure of a phenomenon like the French version of quietist Salafism, we need to confront a dual theoretical argument.

First, there is the subjective argument: The individual is the actor of his existence and relations with the social world. The relationships he weaves, the positions he takes, as well as the identity chords that he plays to produce the meaning by which he is going to try to understand society—all this results from a choice. We therefore adopt a subjectivist postulate that echoes the comprehensive (Weberian) tradition of sociology. Still, this angle of analysis does not suffice; an individual relationship with society must also be grasped in its interaction with an environment that is neither a tangible nor even an immutable given. Rather it inserts itself in a reality constructed as much by the actor, whose vision determines a representation of the world that in turn will affect the meaning that he imparts to his actions, as it is affected by others who position themselves around different issues and with whom he interacts in interpreting a situation.

The second argument has a rather more holistic understanding of the social space since, while the observation of Salafism in France and other societies is characterized by the emergence of a singular relationship to the world, it does not permit ending up with a total exclusion of what are at bottom sociological tendencies detectable in this religiosity underneath the superficial layer of sacred language. We will translate this intuition with an attitude that detaches itself from the actor's perspective by taking into account the weight of certain social structures and collective representations. In other words, beyond the real motivations advanced by the actors, what can explain the choice of such a process of identification? Here we formulate the hypothesis according to which the analysis of the latter must be rendered by more than a purely psychological study, to the extent that the phenomenon constitutes a social fact that must be decoded as such by paying particular attention to changes in the rest of society. As social material, Salafism must be explicated by the social[52] and not by an investigation of an exclusively religious nature that could only spark an essentialist reflection on the nature of this phenomenon.[53] In short, what are the factors framing the growing visibility of Salafism in French society?

In light of this, we will opt for a constructivist sociology and a symbolic interactional methodology that we will seek to enrich by a Durkheimian approach as being the more explicative. The combination of epistemological potentials of these differing analysis grids ought to allow us to inquire into the reach of socialization within the system of Salafi meaning. Our approach is constructivist in that neither the structures of a society nor the actors are independent. Indeed we start from a position that is both comprehensive and explicative, but no identity process can be derived with an approach that is entirely personal or that weights the social exclusively.[54] In fact if we simultaneously opt, for a second time, for a more holistic approach, we will not lose sight of the need to explain the emergence of Salafism and to not end up

---

[52] "The first origin of a social process of any importance must be sought in how the internal social milieu is constituted." Durkheim, *Les règles de la méthode sociologique*, 111.
[53] Olivier Roy, *L'islam mondialisé* (Globalized Islam) (Paris: Seuil, 2002), 12.
[54] Philippe Riutort, *Précis de sociologie* (Handbook of sociology) (Paris: PUF, "Major," 2004), 214.

with a definitive primacy of society over the individual. On a methodological level, the symbolic interactional reading will be mobilized in order to grasp the Salafi condition as a sociological career, to study the meaning given by the actors to their practices and evidence the strategic and distinct character of this identity. As for the explicative approach, it should permit us to determine the possible explanatory factors behind this choice of career. In other words, the first grid determines the group of the practicants' references, while the second specifies the membership group, since it insists on Salafism's place within the field of French and global Islam and on that which symbolizes this fundamentalist religiosity in contemporary times.

Utilizing an interactional symbolic grid offers three advantages: it allows us, first, to apprehend reality as an entity constructed and proceeding from an interaction between the actor and his environment; second, to apply a concept that permits grasping the Salafi identity process in its progressive and strategic dimension—that of the deviant path; and third, to adopt a fitting empirical approach, that of ethnomethodology.

Reality is interrelational and constructed. It results from differing individual interpretations of the world. Cognitive access to reality depends on the symbolic dimensions assigned to objects, to social practices, or to institutions. In other words, actors function in life by dint of how they interpret reality; the meaning they accord to their actions proceeds from the interactions that organize society (between one actor and another; between an actor and an institution, political party, or journalist; between a religious community and a society viewed as impious and bad; etc.). The situations in which Salafis find them themselves are as much chances for deploying a meaning that, if perceived as unequivocal and arising from their fundamentalist approach, in reality arises from the interaction of differing subjectivities. It is also going to be our task to see to what extent it is possible to explain sociologically the subjectivities of actors embracing the canons of their religiosity. Even if the practicants perceive their daily life as a natural, unconstructed given, this does not preclude an interest in what factors might shed light on their propensity to apprehend reality in sacred and exclusive terms.[55] Next, we will try to consider the reasons why a certain framing of reality is privileged among certain profiles.[56]

---

[55] Berger and Luckmann, *La construction sociale de la réalité*, 34–35.
[56] Ibid., 29–30.

The second advantage of the interactional symbolic approach is linked to the concept that is key to our way of looking at the Salafist journey: the deviant path. The notion of deviance must be handled with caution inasmuch as the practicants use it in a pejorative sense. (Their preachings insist on tracking the augmentations that have corroded Islam since its origins.) So we will use it in the sense that Howard Becker does. In studying the relationship of marijuana smokers and jazz singers to the rest of society during the 1950s in the United States,[57] Becker developed the concept of the deviant path, which means the path and the progressive apprenticeship of persons considered deviants because of their transgressions against social norms, a concept that can be understood only in a subjective fashion. Sociological deviance is not a state but a relationship. The transgression does not conform to any preestablished definition and therefore cannot be considered unequivocal. The deviance that the way of life of the people Becker met echoed results from a system of interrelational and interpersonal perceptions. The author thus distinguishes deviance as a transgressive process that relates different subjectivities, but he does not dwell on the reasons that lead an individual to stake out such posture—what is for some a gap with the norm may be perfectly ordinary for others.[58] If we take this basic distinction back to symbolic interactionism, our work will comprise an extra explanatory breadth for the phenomenon. As for the Salafis, they consider their way of life and their relationship with the world completely normal, since they proceed, no less and no more, from identification with the only religion blessed by God and, within it, the required authentic form of adoration. At the same time, this orthodox pretension is accompanied by a supplemental characteristic: they willingly will consider themselves deviants compared to what French society expects of them. It even represents a source of pride that a devalued

---

[57] Howard S. Becker, *Outsiders: Études de sociologie de la deviance* (Outsiders: Studies in the sociology of deviance) (1963; Paris: Métailié, 1985).

[58] All deviance is born in the transgression of a norm, in other words, the breaking through this imprescriptible limit beyond which an act, an attitude, or an event suddenly ceases to be acceptable, comprehensible, or recognizable. This general definition raises at least two questions: When, how, and why does one determine a transgression? and What is a norm? The sociology of deviance is essentially fixated on responding to the first of these and on imposing the idea according to which the social reaction is the crucial element in the characterization of an infraction. As for the problem of the nature of the norm, it has received a purely empirical answer: most of the time, the research has contented itself with deducing the existence of a norm from a deviance that has become the object of an identification and treatment that are already institutionalized. "La déviance est un jugement exprimant une relation pas un état de fait" (Deviance is a judgment expressing a relationship, not an established fact). Albert Ogien, *Sociologie de la deviance* (The sociology of deviance) (Paris: Armand Colin, 1999), 201.

and morally delegitimized society decrees them to be asocial, sectarian, or extremist. To put it another way, the Salafis accept the idea that their orthodoxy will be considered deviant in the impious context that characterizes the society in which they are evolving or in relation to the religious deviance that defines Islam's other branches. Their thinking takes on a dual dimension: they see themselves right on a moral plane and view themselves as distinct on a sociological plane. In this, the career describes both the empirical path of the actor as part of this socialization and a precise dynamic on a moral plane.

Every breaking away, every realization goes back to the idea that holds that Salafism realizes itself by achieving certain points of passage, the most emblematic being that of the salutary migration to the land of Islam. The interactional current puts a concept in the heart of the analysis that can better grasp the meaning given to representations, social practices, and the otherness of identity while inserting the actor in a constant construction of the real. We understand career above all as moral trajectory:

> The advantage of the career concept resides in its ambiguity. On the one hand, it applies to intimate significations, self-image and feelings of one's own identity, which everyone entertains securely and secretly; on the other hand, it refers to the individual's formal situation, his relations to the law, his living environment, and it thus enters into the social relations framework. The concept of career in this way authorizes a to-and-fro movement from the private to the public, from the I to its social environment, which avoids mistakenly falling back on the individual's statements about himself or the idea formed of his own person ... to the moral aspects of his career, that is, to the cycle of changes that intervene in the personality because of this career and the changes in the system of representation by which the individual is aware of himself and understands others.[59]

The concept of the deviant career as defined by Becker thus permits taking into account both what the Salafis think of their coreligionists, and a fortiori non-Muslims, i.e., that they are damned dogmatic "deviants," and also that they can live without difficulty with being perceived sociologically as

---

[59] Erving Goffman, *Asiles* (1963; Sanctuaries) (Paris: Minuit, "Le sens commun" [Common sense], 1975), 179.

Table I.1

	Individual	... abides by the norm	... violates the norm
Society perceives as deviant		Accused wrongfully of being deviant	Clearly deviant
does not perceive as deviant		Conforming or normal	Secretly deviant

"deviants" who are dedicating their existence to realizing an assumed identity in the proper, antagonistic sense of the term:

> Becker intends to show how the two worlds, one of normality and the other of deviance, do not just coexist with each other, but penetrate and overlap each other at numerous points of contact. To visualize these differing, always two-way gateways, Becker uses the notion of "career" in the world of deviance. He thus intends to describe how an individual penetrates by stages or plateaus, always reversible, into the world of deviance.[60]

Becker points out that the actors' deviance can be understood in four large classes that stem from the confrontation between the individual and society. The first may or may not transgress the norm. In Islam's case, this is the identification with the system of republican values (secularism, liberty, modernity, etc.). As for society, it either perceives persons as deviants or not. Therefore we have Table I.1.

The Salafis are "clearly deviant" in that they are aware they are violating a norm that, unlike the rest of society,[61] they do not recognize as legitimate.[62]

---

[60] Martine Xiberras, *Les théories de l'exclusion: Pour une construction de l'imaginaire de la deviance* (The theories of exclusion: For an imaginary construct of deviance), 2nd edition (Paris: Armand Colin, "Sociology References," 1998), 101–102.

[61] In another scenario, some Islamic actors in France are perceived in some quarters as "secretly deviant" because, though they are not necessarily seen as rejecting normality, they are suspected of doing so in secret. A typical example is Tariq Ramadan, who is accused of double-talk. In the view of his defenders, he is wrongly accused of deviance since he favors a respectful dialogue with the system of republican values, while his detractors suspect him of the opposite. As for other figures, they are considered normal in that they respect the existing value system as a given and abide by its principles. This is the case with the rector of the Grand Mosque of Paris, Dalil Boubakeur.

[62] Here we find the meaning of the term "outsider" that we will adhere to: "[The] individual who is ... labeled a stranger can see things differently. It may be that he does not accept the norm according to which people judge him or that he denies to those who judge him the competence or

The break is therefore explicit and claimed to be a natural practice: the two parties (individual and society) no longer speak the same language, nor do they share the same values. To get to the heart of the matter, we then have to study the apprenticeship in deviance that characterizes the Salafi career, a process marked by numerous rites and the assimilation of certain principles that reinforce the anchoring in this system of meaning.[63]

Finally, the interactional symbolic interpretation grid provides us with the most pertinent method for highlighting the traits of the examined socialization. We have turned to good account the field approach advocated by the pioneers of this school, who share the principal perspective of paying attention to concrete actions of actors and to their daily life, the social tie that is forming as the system of interpersonal relations is deployed.[64]

This explains why we have adopted a pragmatic approach[65] without assigning a great deal of importance to the purely religious debates, the objective being to remain faithful to the empiricism that is indispensable for studying this socialization. Our approach has also been sensitive[66] to making connections with practicants and heads of mosques when proposing to discuss Islam in France and, in particular, Salafism as part of a university research project. The places of worship constituting the chief locations for these socializations, we thought it well to gain the confidence of the imams or preachers in a way that helped us gain acceptance by the regulars. This worked out well. We carried out the work between 2005 and 2011, and it allowed us to meet with more than a hundred Muslims of this order with whom we discussed a variety of subjects: the reasons for their religious engagement, their views on political events, the place of Islam in France and in the world, their conception of religious alterity, in some cases their relationship with their country of origin, as well as their relationship with their family. Compared to the order of magnitude generally reported of five thousand practicants in 2005, this sample represents 2% of France's estimated Salafi population. Of the hundred practicants we talked with,

---

legitimacy to do so. He derives a second meaning from the term (the first one being 'estranged from the group'): the transgressor can imagine that his judges are strangers to his universe." Becker, *Outsiders*, 25.

[63] Xiberras, *Les théories de l'exclusion*, 103–104.
[64] David Le Breton, *L'interactionnisme symbolique* (Symbolic interactionism) (Paris: PUF, "Quadrige Manuels" [Quadriga textbooks], 2004), 6–7.
[65] Ibid., 10.
[66] Ibid., 3.

about half gave us interviews long enough to be useful, i.e., lasting at least thirty minutes, if not forty-five. The longest went on for several hours, and some even spanned several days, since we often formed sufficiently reliable contacts with actors that let us make repeat visits over several years and so judge eventual continuities or breaks in their careers. In parallel, and on a more global theoretical plane, we chose from the start to set in motion a pluridisciplinary approach with the objective of posing questions from different angles about the Salafi movement operating today in France and the world.[67]

As a result, our ethnomethodological line was organized along three practical axes, although with reference to the central focus on studying the daily lives of the actors as productive of meaning for the external observer:

> Ethnomethodology is the study of the knowledge and practical activities in the ordinary lives of individuals as they interact and relate to society. It asks itself how reality is produced without letup in their continually renewed collaboration. Its objective is the process of elaboration of the thinking and rules applied during interactions; it relies on the actors' capacities for interpretation that assumes the tension between their competence and their performance. In no way is it the wish to understand the world itself but rather to relate the procedures of meaning, the profane methods of construction of the social life that it constitutes for the actors. As microsociology rooted in the study of a particular context, it does not postulate that knowing is informed by the individual's consciousness, but that reflexivity enters materially into his deeds and gestures.[68]

We conducted fifty-one interviews, the majority with men. They took place in mosques, in the homes of the key stakeholders, or in public venues, most often cafés or fast-food emporiums. These conversations gave us the opportunity to delve into the actors' biographies and, in particular, the meaning they attributed to their religious journey. The interviews were deliberately left unstructured to give the practicants a maximum of freedom as they were observed in telling their story of how their path was constructed.[69] Although we each time refocused the questions toward the reasons for the religious engagement, we reaped the benefits of the

---

[67] Boltanski, *Les cadres*, 7–8.
[68] Le Breton, *L'interactionnisme symbolique*, 143.
[69] Ibid., 180.

autonomy the actors had in explaining their journey. It is known that "a biographical story has nothing to do with an account of diverse facts; it is a social action through which an individual adds up his life (the biography) and the ongoing social interaction (the interview) by means of an interactive narrative";[70] for this reason, the interviews made up the principal biographical material we worked with.

In order to deepen the relationship with politics, we sought to have the practicants react when circumstances were "hot," using the term in the sense that Mounia Bennani-Chraïbi does in his study of Moroccan youth for comparing the reactions of the individuals he encountered when the political development involved "hot times" or "cold times."[71] We thus tried regularly to have the actors respond to polemics, crises, or wars involving the image of Islam or coreligionists, such as the "affair of the caricatures," the project of a law forbidding the wearing of the full veil, and the 2008–2009 Gaza War. The second methodological axis was participant observation in situ, which constitutes the "hallmark of the interactional approach."[72] It echoes an inductive approach coupled with empirical work:[73]

> [Participant observation] is the concrete demonstration of the pragmatic accent of the practice. The methodology utilizes the sociologist's self as a tool for exploring social processes. It makes the sociologist plunge himself into the scenes that he hopes to report and to become observer of and participant in them at the same time. His justification comes from the definition of knowledge as being linked to the movement of the actors' practical activity, from the argument that the sociologist cannot understand what is going on by introspection or supposition and from the injunction to respect the reality of appearances.[74]

We therefore favored the Paris region as the main territory for our research, after previously having scouted places of worship where figures

---

[70] Franco Ferrarotti, *Histoire et histoires de vie: La méthode biographique dans les sciences sociales* (History and life stories: The biographical method in the social sciences) (Paris: Méridiens Kincksieck, 1983), 53.
[71] Mounia Bennani-Chraïbi, *Soumis et rebelles: Les jeunes au Maroc* (Subjects and rebels: Youth in Morocco) (Paris: CNRS Éditions, 1998).
[72] Le Breton, *L'interactionnisme symbolique*, 173.
[73] Ibid., 172.
[74] Ibid., 178. Also see P. Rock, *The Making of Symbolic Interactionism* (London: Macmillan, 1979).

from Salafi preaching in France regularly discoursed. This is why we went over a span of several years into the towns of the inner and outer Paris suburbs: Mantes-la-Jolie, Les Mureaux, Stains, Argenteuil, Saint-Denis, Nanterre, Villeneuve-la-Garenne, Montreuil, Levallois-Perret, Athis-Mons, Corbeil-Essonnes, Sartrouville, La Courneuve, Clichy-sous-Bois, Montfermeil, Asnières, Gennevilliers, Colombes, La Garenne-Colombes, Maisons-Alfort, Courbevoie, Vitry-sur-Seine, Draveil, Juvisy-sur-Orge, and Épinay-sur-Seine, not counting Paris *intra muros*. To this must be added the mosques of certain provincial towns. Finally, we made a research stay in the North of France in 2008, in Lille, to be exact. After it was all over, we had visited more than fifty Muslim places of worship as much for interviews as for many hours of neutral or participant observation. We also observed the practicants in their daily life: at home, in their neighborhood relationships, and as they moved about, etc. In addition, we followed them whenever feasible in their migration to a Muslim country. This took us to the beacon countries of the *hijra* for French Salafis: to Egypt (Cairo) in July 2009, to Algeria in August 2009, and to Morocco on several occasions during the years of empirical work, interrupted only by a stay in the United Arab Emirates in April 2005. In this way, we were able to observe as closely as possible the implementation of one of the cardinal principles of this socialization: the abandonment of the impious society.

A third methodological avenue allowed us to empirically examine the quietist Salafism at work in France and in the world. This is not directly related to symbolic interactionism, but it is no less essential for grasping the spread of this religious ethic. It consists of the study of the movement's website, which constitutes the favored interface between clerics and practicants. It is indeed on the web that the norms for life and principles meant to guide their new socialization are researched. We spent many hours studying the productions accessible via the internet, as they represented a first-rate source of information, even if the web could not be as rich as the interviews. In addition, over the course of several years, and with the popularization of video-sharing sites, we noticed a growing tendency to utilize this *medium* for broadcasting the Salafist position; this is why we refer to it in numerous places of our demonstration. Finally, with orthodox Islam finding a great deal of its raison d'être in systematically confronting Islam's other offerings, our work also consisted of shuttling back and forth between the practicants' discourse and manner of being, between the Salafi norms and those of competing offers. Thus, in the analysis of their socialization we made a point of referencing other systems of Islamic meaning on any given point (relationship with institutions, relations with non-Muslims, the role of cultural practices, politicization, etc.). Addressed here also are media figures as well as traditions imported from some home countries, missionary groups focused on conversions, and organized militant groups.

Studying the socialization of individuals in the Salafi system first tallies with an analysis of how they construct their meaning. In other words, it is a matter of taking an interest in their subjectivity as it develops in the course of their career and how it positions itself with respect to the rest of society in the Islamic field in France and globally. This first part can therefore be understood as examining their reference group:

> An individual's vision of the world, and particularly the one he has of himself, forms under the influence of different partners. These can be direct but also indirect. Especially once he has achieved his primary socialization, the individual refers to individuals or groups of which he has only indirect knowledge, to which he compares himself and on which he constructs stereotypes. The concept of reference group makes it possible to think about this ensemble of phenomena.[75]

Still, while it is essential to see how this puritan, fundamentalist meaning is turned into daily practice, or more specifically, when certain political crises occur, we have stated our wish of putting forward an explanatory grid for this identity process. How to explain that this socialization in the interior of these perceptions relates to certain profiles sharing certain sociological regularities? This is where we pick up again the relational dimension of assimilating values and norms through others. After a fashion, it is a question of objectivizing certain discourses by resituating them in a context that sometimes escapes the actors themselves. Studying the groups the actors belong to lets us detect more profound logics that frame the emergence of quietist Salafism in our era. It involves analyzing the environment that influences the socialization within this system of meaning. By putting in perspective the factors

---

[75] Jean Manuel De Queiroz and Marek Ziolkovski, *L'interactionnisme symbolique* (Symbolic interactionism) (Paris: Presses Universitaires de Rennes, 1994), 51. The reference group "continually restructures the individual's cognitive perspective" (52). The Salafi group, on top of which throne sit the clerics, is thus the "orientational other." See Manford Kuhn, "The Reference Group Reconsidered" (1972), in J. G. Manis and B. N. Meltzer (eds.), *Symbolic Interaction: A Reader in Social Psychology* (Boston, MA: Allyn & Bacon, 1978).

that explain the identification with this religion, we mean to leave aside the reasons put forward by the individuals in order to focus on patterns observed during our fieldwork that inform us on the deepest motives for such a religious engagement. The membership group is where the interactions that determine the growing visibility of this offer of Islam take place.

PART I
THE REFERENCE GROUP

In the first part of this book, will be highlighted the Salafi subjectivity of the people we have met. We will see how their socialization within a certain web of significance works. More specifically, three types of socialization will be addressed: genealogical, pyramidal and immunological. The first one sheds light upon the historical and religious construction through which Salafis come to identify with certain values and norms that they claim to be the purest form of Islam. The second one deals with the construction of a feeling of social superiority and genuineness thanks to which Salafis come to consider themselves to be at the top of the religious and social scale. The third one presents them as trying also to build a barrier with the rest of the society, which is seen as potentially dangerous for their morality and purity.

1
Genealogical Socialization

Genealogical socialization is the process by which the actor acquires an identity derived from appropriating a different heritage and which determines a concept of the world and of life that will provide an exclusive frame for thought and action. It is genealogical because the process inserts itself into a sacred temporality with which every believing Muslim identifies, being sincere and strong enough to live with whatever ruptures with his environment he needs to make while seeking to reproduce the habitus of Islam's first believers. It is linked to the establishment of a symbolic lineage between the time when this religion appeared and modern times, when a minute portion of believers show themselves to be faithful to the demands of the true faith. Muslims, while constituting the best "religious community" created by God,[1] have turned away from the dogmatic and cultural implications of the founding-era reference. It corresponds to the appropriation of the entire canonical array of the Minhaj Salafi (Salafi Pathway): primordial, consubstantial with all other forms of identification with the Salaf Salih, it strives to perpetuate their heritage and their memory, a source of paradigmatic imitation developed through contact with the Prophet Muhammad himself, who did not omit specifying in one of his authenticated pronouncements that "the best men are those of my generation, then those who come after them, then those that come after them."[2] It constitutes the initial stage of this puritanical career.

---

[1] "You are the best community that has been raised for mankind. You order what is fitting and you prohibit the blameworthy and believe in Allah." Koran, sura 3, Al-'Imran (The family of Imran), verse 110. This verse notably institutes the principle of *hisba*, "commanding the right and forbidding the wrong," which must guide all Muslims. Michael Cook, *Commanding Right and Forbidding Wrong in Islamic Thought* (Cambridge, UK: Cambridge University Press, 2001).

[2] Hadith 4603 of the authenticated compendium of the Imam Muslim. (It also appears in that of the Imam Bukhari.) This pronouncement is key for the practicants, who see in it the basis for their identification with Islam's beginnings. Muhammad also specified that after the blessed first three generations, the divine approval would go to any of the faithful who would have followed in the footsteps of the Companions (*sahaba*), those who succeeded them (*tabi'oun*), and those who came after (*tabi'tabi'in*).

Salafism Goes Global. Mohamed-Ali Adraoui, Oxford University Press (2020). © Oxford University Press.
DOI: 10.1093/oso/9780190062460.001.0001

The Sociology of French Quietist Salafism

Typology

Besides the ethnogeographic markers of Salafism, we retain as an analytical perspective a series of ideal types constructed from the intrinsic rationales of the undertaking. Based on our observations and conversations, more than half of Salafis (between 50% and 60%) come from a Maghrebian family. Individuals coming from a non-Muslim background form the second component, between 25% and 30%. The remainder includes Muslims originating from sub-Saharan Africa (Mali, Senegal, etc.). Salafis from Turkish families are extremely rare in French society.

Among Maghrebian practicants, the children of the Algerian immigration are overrepresented and make up the majority of Arab Salafists (more than half of believers we met and identified in the mosques). Among them are a not insignificant portion of individuals from families of Kabyle origin who remain faithful to the religious reference, in contrast to those who abandoned it to embrace instead the former French colonial power's cultural codes and live according to them outside the Islamic reference. The Moroccans outnumber the Tunisians in this case. We also met Salafis of Egyptian origin, who, in essence, are immigrant preaching cadres, distinct from the majority of Maghrebian Salafis who were born in France or arrived there at a very early age.

The converts fall into two categories: those who come from West Indian and African Christian families and those from European Christian families; the former comprise the more numerous category by far.

Albeit a very important[3] characteristic, the age of the faithful—youthful for the most part—is not enough for drawing pertinent lines of cleavage if we set as our goal developing a typology of Salafis in French society.

On the other hand, the study of subjectivities allows us to highlight four main types of Salafist profiles. If the practicants are to be believed, entry into their career is motivated by Salafism's proven authenticity; however, an analysis of the reasons for their religious commitment reveals common features

---

[3] The median age of individuals we met clusters around thirty years. Very few (fewer than 10%) were over forty. The age of conversion seems to go with youth: a near majority chose this religion before the age of thirty (a very large portion at around twenty). The sole notable exception relates to the postmilitant profile (discussed later), in which are grouped Salafists who joined after several years of socialization in Islamic political and militant groups.

that existed before conversion. One constant is thinking of piety as a reaction to deviationist changes in the Islamic environment. In presenting itself as the bearer of an ethic of righteousness and of constancy confronting a false Islam, quietest Salafism integrates alterity as a defining characteristic, with two intrinsically associated paradoxical dimensions: the perpetuation of a religious morality bounded by and understood in orthodox fashion (supposedly signifying that the Da'wa Salafiyya is sufficient unto itself) and the puritan reaction to attempts at diluting the dogma and original practices (which supposes that the Islamic alterity must preexist for an independent and antinomic Salafist field to be historically constituted).[4] Thus we get this from a well-known French-language Salafist website:

> The term "Salafist" applies to anyone who sincerely clings to the Salafs. *It is not an attachment to a particular person or a group of people*, rather it is the attachment to a path that never departs from the way of the Prophet (peace and Allah's blessing upon him) [*sic*], of his companions, and those who truly follow them. Moreover, the Salafia does not rely on the act of following a particular Sheikh or an imam; it means adhering to the Koran and the authentic Sunna as understood and practiced by all the pious predecessors (*as-Salaf us-Salih*). The true Salafi emphasizes the *TAWHID* [divine uniqueness] which means devoting of all one's acts of worship exclusively to Allah: in the invocation, in the plea for help, in appealing for refuge whether in ease or in difficulty, in sacrifice by fire, in sermons, in fear, in hope, in the total reliance on Him.[5]

The "Redirected Upward" Salafis (Mainly the Post-Tablighis)

The first ideal type of convert is someone "redirected upward." For this profile, the Salafist viaticum is a religiosity of fixation, which structures itself spiritually and dogmatically as a contemporary pious movement. The redirection toward an Islamic authenticity is a qualitative leap from the previous religious experience to entry into the Minhaj. Coming in their majority from the Tabligh mass preaching whose exclusive way of portraying Islam they retain, the Salafis who are "reoriented upward" explain their change of reference point as stemming from their realization that they have strayed onto a

---

[4] Henri Laoust, *Les schismes dans l'islam: Introduction à la religion Musulmane* (Islam's schisms: Introduction to the Muslim religion) (Paris: Payot, 1965), "Bibliothèque historique," 84.
[5] "What Is the Minhaj Salafi?," http//www.al.baida.online.fr/quest-cequeleminhajsalafi.htm.

deviant path. Gaining access to an eminently superior form of practice, the redirected adept in the majority of cases is a former Tabligh,[6] whose principal deviation is to have missed out on one of Islam's fundamental principles: having access to a first-rate scientific capital, the intent never erasing the inconsistency.

We have a good example of this type of progression in the person of Adnan, born Pierre in 1981 to a Bosnian Christian family living in Lille for several decades. Now married to a woman of Moroccan descent from Lille and the father of a young daughter, Adnan had taken a course in Islamic sciences at the University of Medina after several years of graduate studies in geography at the University of Lille. Since 2009 he has been the manager of an Islamic bookstore in the Wasem working-class neighborhood. His Christian parents and Muslim in-laws both reacted unfavorably to the marriage, the former becoming intensely angry on discovering their son's new faith, which is why the couple appeared to us to be that much closer and animated by the serenity brought on by the fact of feeling persecuted by an environment that is hostile toward "orthodoxy."

Of small build, blond and blue-eyed, and wearing the obligatory beard, Adnan welcomed us in his home, a small apartment in an old apartment block in Wasem. He made it a point of honor to share with us a typical Moroccan meal prepared by his wife, the meat for which came directly from the animal sacrificed by the couple during the ʿAïd al-Adha (feast of sacrifice), a gesture of respect for a visitor wanting to learn about the Daʾwa Salafiyya. Our interview had a humorous start, the Salafi announcing, with a frank smile tinged with irony, "I researched you! I googled you and saw what you do. You really are a researcher [*laughing*]. You see? This is the Salafi FBI [*laughing*]." The meal proceeded, and we were able to establish the importance in

---

[6] Founded in 1926 in the Indian province of Mewat, the Jamʾat at-Tabligh (Association for Propagating the Faith) may be defined as an Islamic movement of revivalist (re)conversion, like Salafism but centered on a minimalist religious vision. The key objective being to bring Muslims who happen to be de-Islamicized, perhaps because of colonialism, back to the path of God, it envisions no need for complex preachings and, more precisely, for making too much of debates related to tradition or, even more so, to differences linked to staked-out positions in the sociopolitical domain. Consequently, and particularly dating from the preachings of the movement's founder, Muhammad Ilyas al-Kandhlawi (1885–1944), which, although originally adhering to Sufi doctrine, were aimed at newly Islamicized Hindus, they dealt little with the religion's fundamentals, the movement's principal objective being reinforcing the necessity of focusing on Islamic mainstays such as ritual prayer. The movement has been present in France since the 1970s and the creation of the Faith and Practice association. See Gilles Kepel, *Les banlieues d'Islam: Naissance d'une religion en France* (The Islamic suburbs: *The Birth of a Religion in France*) (Paris: Seuil, 1991); Muhammad Khalid Masud, *Travelers in Faith: Studies of the Tablighi Jamāʾat as a Transnational Islamic Movement for Faith Renewal* (Brill, Social, 2000).

Salafist socialization of a process of cognitive reframing and moral repair, at which point the discussion turned to polygamy. Adnan's response was explicit: "Why should I deprive myself of benefits that God had authorized for me? It is allowed, right?" To keep the party amicable, our host proposed postponing our interview to the next day, when he would demonstrate that the false image associated with his religion stems from a misunderstanding.

After the meal we had a chance to check out the websites that he surfs on his computer. We ascertained that nearly all the links listed under his "favorites" pointed to Salafist websites, the only exceptions being those pointing to newspapers (in Arabic) or job searches. When we asked him to describe the reasons for his conversion to Tablighi Islam and the circumstances that led him to embrace the Salafist career, this is how he answered:

ADNAN: Why did I convert? [*Reflects for several seconds.*] Yes, it was in the winter of '96, I remember it well. I was in high school. But see, I prayed since September '98. Before that I was unenlightened. I didn't pray, so that's why I am telling you that I pray since '98. . . . I was living in the Gayant housing project in Douai. I had Arab friends and I had French friends, but I had more French friends. I tell you this because I know how researchers are, they will say it is because he has Arab friends. No, it was not that the little Frenchman followed his Arab friends, the way I understand it. [*We underline the fact that Adnan seems to be acquainted with sociological theories explaining how certain individuals born outside a Muslim milieu come to Islam through their circle of acquaintances who are of that religion.*] Besides, my Arab friends did not talk to me about Islam, we didn't discuss it . . . except of course the problem of ham, of Ramadan, et cetera. Yes, you could say they paid attention to that. Where I lived in the Gayant-Douai projects, there were Arabs, blacks, French. . . . Subsequently, in fact, it was a friend who afterwards became my best friend who was the one that prayed, but he never discussed it. He never talked about Islam. That's how I came to know someone who was a sincere practicant.

AUTHOR: And so that is where you in some fashion discovered the "true Islam"?

ADNAN: [*After a few seconds of reflection*] I meditated a lot. I've always meditated. I've always asked myself lots of questions, since I was little, like, for instance: death, God, what makes the mosquitoes fly, the colors of parrots, and beyond that, extraterrestrials. . . . In the second class, there was a course on Islam. That made a mark on me, not like in the fifth in college, where you quickly pass over things. In the former, the teacher told us everything, he was honest. One day, I recall, I asked a question. I wanted to know "What do the Muslims think about Jesus?" I'm telling you this because I liked Jesus. I really liked his story, his life. I didn't care for Christianity, how it portrays Jesus, the innovation, all that. At the time, I called it *bid'a* [faulty innovation]. [*Laughs.*] I found it to be far removed from what a religion should be.... Moreover I always conceived of the prophets as not being ordinary people. How to explain to you about the monotheistic religions? I sensed that there was a truth behind them. I always thought there was something.... So, during his course, I turned to my school friend Mehdi, I asked him what the Muslims thought of Jesus. He answered, "Bah, he's a prophet...." And that did something to me. I'd never have thought of such a thing. For me, that they called Jesus a prophet in the Muslim religion ... for me, Allah, at least what I knew of him, was, how shall I say? A statue that you worshipped, the great demon.... I went to see the teacher after the class, I wanted to find out. I asked him with regard to Jesus if the Muslims considered him a prophet. He said yes. Afterwards the conversation turned to the Koran, the Bible; the prof told me that there are actually several versions of the Bible and only one Koran. That was it for me as far as Jesus was concerned. It turned me off....

AUTHOR: And so then how did you come to the Tabligh?

ADNAN: And then, afterwards, I got into it in more depth. I read books, but especially I went back to my friend Nadir, the practicant. I started doing everything like him. After the class, I always went to his house, we were always together, I met his parents, I went to his home, I ate couscous there and all that, and I can say that's where I became a Muslim just like that.... He laid out everything he knew for me. Admittedly not everything was good, like it is in the Salafiyya. The Salafiyya was not around at that time. There was no book on Salafiyya, for instance. After, for the Tabligh? I attended mosques.

AUTHOR: Would you mind going into details?

ADNAN: I attended mosques and wound up meeting a *da'i* [preacher]. He impressed me from the start, because I didn't know anything. I listened and I thought that he was [darned good]. I thought he was competent, and also he talked a lot. He was egocentric, even a bit Sufi. He said some things some things, interpreting the Koran that, frankly [*a brief exclamation of disbelief*]. He did things, when I thought about them afterwards, when I knew the Salafiyya! For example, about the Salafis, he held his head in his hands and said, "It's the Salafis, they cast a spell over me. They're plotting against me." Me, I didn't understand, I did what he told me to do. I did the *khourouj*[7] and I preached with him, all based on the book *Riyad as-Salihin*.[8] We did the *khourouj* generally once a week. That went on for a year. I had a bad image of the Salafis. After I started to have a different view, I distanced myself a bit from the fellow in question. I started talking with some Salafis and that's when I understood. . . . They detested each other, him and the Salafis, and me, since I was hanging out with him. I could only follow him. I didn't know. For example, when I went out with him, I never said a thing, I kept quiet when he talked and when they turned to me, hah, all I did was agree.

AUTHOR: Can you tell me more about it? How did they convince you that the Minhaj-Salafi is the true Islam?

ADNAN: In encounters, as it were. Initially I didn't like the Salafis. I considered them to be . . . in fact . . . not good Muslims . . . how to say . . . in the West. . . . You might even say I couldn't stand them. That's because I was hanging out with people like the one I just mentioned. They had a negative view of the Salafis, the Wahabis they called them, those close to Saudi Arabia. . . . With the Tabligh guy I told you about, I therefore did the *khourouj*, but there came the moment when I distanced myself from him. I remember it was in 2000 that I dropped out. He did too many odd things, I told myself, so, okay, that's it. He wrote on the back of things, in Arabic, to protect himself, he said, that it was normal. If he just coughed, it was the Salafis, blah blah blah. I therefore dropped the Sufi [*a reference to the Tablighi ex-companion*], the one who was brainwashing me, the Salafis saying *bid'a, bid'a*. . . .

AUTHOR: So then how did you come from that to the Salafiyya?

ADNAN: I started going to a mosque in Douai near Flers. That's where I met some Salafis. They were literal, they had proofs when they shared their religion. You could say there is where I truly discovered what the Da'wa

---

[7] Khourouj fi Sabil al-llah (Exit from the path of God). The root *kh-r-j* denotes both a purely physical as well as a mental exit. For example, the revolutionary Salafists are called "new Khawarij" in reference to the Muslims who have left the path of orthodoxy by taking political positions counter to the last righteously guided caliph and son-in-law of Muhammad, Ali Ibn Abu Talib.

[8] *The Garden of the Virtuous*. This is an important work on the Muslim preaching scene. The author, Imam Muhi ad-Din an Nawawi (d. 1271), has compiled forty of the most celebrated prophetic sayings (*ahadith*).

Salafiyya was. It took me a long time to realize that I was lost and that what I believed was false. The things that I saw were clear, everything was explained with a proof. What the Salafi brothers did was clear. There was a big difference from the Tablighis. One more thing needs to be said, naturally [*tone of voice changes*]. The Tablighis are all on the dole. They won't give up the *khourouj* in order go to work [*irritated tone*]. Say false things, sure, but work and make money, no. . . . From when I was a student at the uni, I often talked with the Salafis at the mosque. . . . From the time I started going to this mosque, I talked with Salafis, and I started being interested in what they were saying. That's how it happened. I saw that what they were saying made sense. One day they gave me some pamphlets by al-Baïda.[9] At the time, at the uni, I was hanging out with some preachers in the place. I put some questions to them, and since I knew the Salafis, I started comparing. And that's where I started to see the differences and also the fact that with the Salafis, everything that was said was proven, there was a proof. It wasn't just idle words. When they gave an opinion, it was given by a scholar who had proofs from the Koran and the Sunna. With others, I won't say they are not sincere, that they weren't Muslims. It's something else. They didn't always argue with proofs necessarily. Things were said. After I compared them with what the Salafis said, it had its limits. To tell the truth, really, there was quite a difference.

AUTHOR: And when was it that you told yourself, "That's it, I'm a Salafi"?

ADNAN: I recall in the summer of 2001, some *chouyoukh* [plural of "sheikh"] came to the Aulnay-sous-Bois mosque. I remember, seventeen days of classes, frankly, teaching tradition, right. There, with me hanging out with the Salafis, I wanted to come and meet these scholars, and there is where it became clear. I really benefited from it. I was able to ask tons of questions and so on. . . . Most of all, there were two Saudi recruiters who told us about scholarships and the chance to go study in Saudi Arabia, and then, since I was drawn to the religion, I told myself, "I absolutely have to go there." . . . In 2001, 2002, I wanted more. I couldn't do anything else. I no longer wanted to attend the uni, I could have cared less, I was too strongly drawn to the books, I had my nose stuck in books all the time. I told my mother, "I want to go to Yemen." Over there, that's the country of Sheikh

---

[9] A well-known quietist Salafi website is www.al.baid.online.fr, celebrated for posting the teachings of one of the most influential clerics, Sheikh Rabi' Ibn al-Hadi al-Madkhali, a teacher at the University of Medina and one of the movement's influential voices.

Muqbil,[10] that's what I was after. However, Sheikh Muqbil died during the seminar. We were just taking some *dourouss* [plural of "classes," "lessons"] when someone came and told us Sheik Muqbil is dead. You can imagine the reaction in the mosque. Everyone called out, "Allah." ... My mother was in a panic, but she said to me, "It's your life, if you're sure that's what you want." Still, I took my time. I gave myself between September 2001 and January 2002 to find work and put aside some money, but Uncle bin Laden came along. The Yemen Embassy stopped handing out visas except to tourists. So then I started again at the uni in geography.... What a contrast: nothing but Salafis in geography, while in ecology there was nothing but Arabs and Africans.... And what happened one day? Surprise, I received a letter: I was invited to Medina. The application I put in with the recruiters from the Gulf at Aulnay had been approved. Me, I'd forgotten about it. I was concentrating on Yemen. In fact a response typically took a year; I'd stopped thinking about it, but there it was.

AUTHOR: And then?

ADNAN: I spent three and a half years there. Two years to learn Arabic. I got a diploma for that level.... Afterwards, for a year and a half, I was at the hadith uni. I had another two and a half years to go, but I wanted to get married and I didn't manage to get an *iqama* [residence permit], for the papers, for my wife, and all. I came back in March 2006. My father was sick, and my mother, ah, it weighed on her and so I came back.

The Emancipated Neotraditionalist Salafis

The second profile linked to developing a Salafist identity of rupture is that of the emancipated neotraditionalist. This category includes believers socialized primarily in an immigrant family in which Islam is the foremost moral referent but does not provide rules for speech and acts. The Salafis coming from this type of sociocultural structure accuse their parents and siblings of straying from authenticity. The family's Islam offers a strong communitarian connection but not a substantive moral or religious education. Therefore the

---

[10] Sheikh Muqbil Ibn Hadi al-Wadi'i al Yamani (d. 2001) was a Yemenite *'alim* among the most celebrated and influential of contemporary Da'wa Salafiyya. Considered to be a revitalizer of Islam (see later discussion) and a perpetuator of the orthodoxy, he is equally well-known for having directed a religious study center where many Muslims from throughout the world came to study, the Dar al-Hadith (House of the Hadith), in the village of Dammaj. See Stéphanie Lacroix, *Les islamistes saoudiens: Une insurrection manqué* (The Saudi Islamists: A failed uprising) (Paris: PUF, "Proche Orient," 2010), 111–114, 142–145.

emancipated neotraditionalist's principal criticism is that the Islam he grew up with is more container than content. While his parents follow an Islam of the masses, diluted by the horrors of local anti-Islamic, hence deviant, traditions he searches for an Islamic morality centered on a qualitative puritanical and demanding approach.

Observation of these emancipated Salafis suggests that, despite their refractory positioning with regard to parental customs, there is no profound break with the family except in extremely rare cases. This is because they never established a durable religiosity to break away from. Instead the emancipated Salafi has experimented with several Islamic traditions, in contrast to the post-Tablighi, who has known only a single version. Once the Salafist career has been embraced, other forms of socializing continue to be tied to parental opinion, starting with the choice of a spouse, in which father and mother have a say. And relationships with childhood and neighborhood friends remain intact. Whereas the post-Tablighi erases his former connections to a deviant Islamism, the emancipated maintains a great number of connections with his circle, but this is accompanied by proselytizing as well as a moralizing and normative discourse.

Born in 1980 in Algiers in the Bab-el-Oued quarter, Abdelwahid immigrated to France with his family at a very early age and was raised in Paris. Scarred by a parental divorce that he does not wish to dwell on, he goes so far as to admit that his father now lives in Italy, where he has started a new family. Abdelwahid followed a protracted course of study at a business school (École des Affaires), where he "met many Jews and bourge[oi]s." He has a good command of English and is drawn to the business world and succeeding economically. Finding in the example of the Prophet Muhammad his justification for rejecting paid employment (the Prophet being seen by him as a merchant and business-oriented person), this Salafi, a fervent fan of capitalism (as long as he can keep from behaving immorally), is the practicant most invested in business and entrepreneurism that we encountered. Cofounder of the Al-Mouslim (The Muslim) bookstore, a mecca for circulating Salafist literature on Jean-Pierre Timbaud Street, and the owner of a restaurant in the Bois des cars quarter of the Algerian capital, he presents the most dynamic intellectual and sociopolitical profile.

A first impressions on entering his (the bookstore-boutique is that the air is perfumed by the scent of musk, prized by the Prophet, according to tradition. Part of the fifteen square meters of floor space is set aside for selling clothes, especially for women. The managers of the *maktaba* (bookstore) set aside one a day a week for their female coreligionists so as to forestall any mixing and to allow the women to feel at ease patronizing a place frequented by men. Abdelwahid revels in describing the bookstore's opening day, when they rang up sales of more than seven hundred euros, with free mint tea and pastries helping to attract customers.

Although, for the time being, he follows the advice of the ʿoulama when it comes to voting, he confides that the prohibition on political participation in an impious land frustrates him because he wants to agitate against Islamophobia and for Palestine. He is convinced that Muslims must be active in defense of their religion and their people. His intention is to be a player in the socioreligious debate in France, thanks to his Islamic bookstore, which is frequented by a clientele seeking orthodoxy. Because of his wish to sensitize his coreligionists to causes affecting the Muslims of the world, starting with Palestine, Abdelwahid is identified by some as close to the Ikhwan ([Muslim] Brotherhood). Love for his native country, Algeria, is transmuted into a devaluation of the French condition. His wish to take part in electoral life thus must be understood as a way of defending Muslims and not as belonging to the body politic.

In contrast to the redirected post-Tablighi who aspires to a de-ethnicized, denationalized, and transcultural dimension of Islam, we find among the emancipated Salafists in traditionalist circles a continuity of affiliation with their country of origin. They seem to disconnect their national origin from the form of Islam practiced in the country of their parents.

The Post-Christian Salafis
The third profile is the path taken by Salafis born into non-Muslim families that identify as Christian (and more precisely Catholic) but whose religious reference has been diluted over successive generations. Before converting, they were nonpracticing believers, frustrated at not having been sufficiently grounded in the theoretical and practical aspects of Christianity. Accepting the heritage of Jesus, a positive personage whose ultimate message is represented by Muhammad's apostolate, these post-Christian Salafis are distinguished by a critical relationship with Catholicism and see in their entry into the Minhaj Salafi an awakening to a more "rational," "more scientific," and, in fine, "more logical" version of faith. Islam in its Salafist mode gives them a complete and immutable version of the religion, a normed and coherent system that provides a modus operandi for living life. Their conversion to Salafism is defined not so much by a discovery of the sacred as by

the delivery of a turnkey Islam whose practice contrasts with an uncertain, anomic Catholic faith.

The Salafist framework becomes a mirror held up to the shortcomings and approximations they believe is inherent in the Christian religion. We observe in this category of converts a pretension to a higher spirituality as well as a propensity to rhyme a puritan religious affiliation with the fight for the rights of Muslims and defense of Islam's image. The post-Christians stand out for their greater inclination to talk about the political and social issues with which Muslims in France and throughout the world must contend. Beyond that, we find among them some hints of racialism: they reproach the emancipated Salafis (mostly Arabs) for not drawing on the full complement of the faith's teachings, for their communitarian spirit, as well as for having a taste for the things of this world (a defect mostly attributed to the Maghrebi). Better versed in social debates and less well-represented than the first two profiles in business and entrepreneurial careers, post-Christians are distinguished by a more personal trajectory; once they have embraced the Salafist career, they do not deny their individuality to the same extent. They frequent the mosques, but solitude plays a large part in their devotion. The post-Christians criticize their coreligionists who came from (neo)traditionalist families for being more attracted to the prestige inherent in the Salafist condition than a true religious equilibrium, while the post-Christians claim to have a better grasp of what is to be expected from an authentic Islam.

Kamal-dine (formerly Ayrton) is a first-year student pursuing a master's degree in geography at the University of Paris I Panthéon-Sorbonne. He is writing his dissertation on the requalification of the Massy-Antony housing complex (low-rent housings where most of the families living there are migrants). An account of his progression illustrates the journey of Salafis who, erstwhile practicing Christians, discovered a faith they regard as more standardized and more concrete.

AUTHOR: Can you tell us a little bit about yourself? Where do you come from? Where do you live?

KAMAL-DINE: My name is Nelson Kamal-dine. I'm twenty-four years old and come from Cameroon. I belong to the Bassa tribe. I'm studying at Paris in the Geography Masters I program, concentration in maps and geography. I live in 91 at Massy-Palaiseau. That's where I live. My family is there.

AUTHOR: Can you tell me how you came to Islam? Or how Islam came to you? How did you become a Muslim, as it were?

KAMAL-DINE: Actually, I converted four years ago, in February 2005, *inch'allah*. I easily recall the date because it was St. Valentine's Day, February 14. I remember it well, it was the day I said the *chahada* [Islamic confession of faith]. That's when I went to a mosque and said the *chahada* in front of witnesses.[11] . . . Why did I convert to Islam? [*Thinks for a few seconds after drawing out the last syllable.*] Why did I choose Islam? I come from a Christian family, actually a practicing one. I was a Christian myself before. I regularly attended church. My family is Catholic, practicing Catholics. Okay, I had a Muslim circle of acquaintances, Muslim friends, even a lot of Muslim friends, but I was Christian. I knew my religion. I knew what my religion was all about, not like some people, who are Christian in name only. I can say about myself, that I had a good grasp of the Catholic religion. I went to church, I knew the catechism and all that, so that, for example, when I engaged in discussions with my Muslim buddies, we often debated, how shall I say, I could hold my own.

AUTHOR: Where was that? At Massy-Palaiseau?

KAMAL-DINE: No, it was at Verrière-le-Buisson, not far from Massy, in the 91370 postal code. But listen, I didn't grow up in a ZUP [Urban Development Zone]. It was Emmaus housing. There were many Muslims in my town, also converts, lots of them. There were roughly . . . sixteen thousand inhabitants, or something like that, but there were lots of Muslims.

AUTHOR: And so how did it happen that you embraced the Muslim religion, you, a practicing Christian?

KAMAL-DINE: I always kept company with Muslims. I had many Maghrebian friends, some of whom are Salafis today. Well, some of them did not really have a change of character, but that is in Allah's hands. In fact I always had a circle of Muslim acquaintances—in school, later at university. We talked about everything, we talked about religion, and we debated, with me telling them, "You Muslims, you have a right to this, you don't have a right to that." In the same way, they told me, "You Christians, blah blah blah." We kidded around a lot, but gradually I began to ask myself questions. Like I told you, I knew how to debate, I didn't keep quiet, I tried to defend Christianity. It turned out, frankly, I'll try to explain, the fact of

---

[11] The Tradition specifies that a person embracing Islam must make the profession of faith before at least two Muslims as witnesses. In practice, this explains why a number of new Muslims go to a mosque for the occasion.

having talked about Islam for a long time, the fact of having to a certain extent made comparisons—how do I say this? I began to feel a need to do research.... I felt I needed to understand Islam. I saw more and more people convert, to choose Islam. Moreover, everything that I heard about Islam, I didn't get it, so I began to want to understand it, to know it myself.

AUTHOR: And then?

KAMAL-DINE: There came a moment, like I said, when I started searching on my own. I had to see with my own eyes. It was diffuse in the beginning, I was simply looking. But gradually I became more certain.... It was especially on the internet, as a matter of fact, that's how I did most of my research. I researched Islam in general: history, beliefs.... And, sure enough, it's normal, all the time I was making comparisons with Christianity. I saw the difference. Islam, how to say it, it is a religion, and that's all, no, that's not fair. You believe, and that's it. For almost a year I meditated a lot. I asked myself many questions. And one day it clicked.

AUTHOR: Do I need to ask you to go on?

KAMAL-DINE: [*Laughs.*] Oops, careful, we're going to disturb everyone here that is cramming. [*We were in a library.*] The light came on when I read a hadith, one of the Prophet's hadiths. It was on an Islamic blog.... *Bismillah.*[12] [*Takes candy from his bag and, opens and eats it.*]

AUTHOR: Which one?

KAMAL-DINE: Really, I don't remember.... Wait.... I believe it was *Skyrock Islam Blog*, something like that. It was a blog for sixteen-to-twenty-year-olds, as its name implies.

AUTHOR: Then what?

KAMAL-DINE: I came across a hadith, how can I say this, that changed, transformed me. I read things about Islam, and I researched a lot of things about the Prophet Muhammad, *salatu salam*. [*Prayers and Peace Be Upon Him.*] And so there I read a hadith. It's the one where he says that a person that sneezes is saying "Alhamdoulillah" [Praise be to God]. And then, if he sneezes a second time, he again supposedly says "Alhamdoulillah." And if he sneezes a third time, it's the same: "Alhamdoulillah." But if he sneezes a fourth time, it means nothing, it mean s he's sick.

AUTHOR: And that's how the light came on?

KAMAL-DINE: Oh yeah. Because you know what? I told myself, with that kind of saying, this is no ordinary Prophet. When I read that, I had an

---

[12] "In God's name." With this formula, believers preface any kind of action.

"aha" moment, it was so precise. There was in it, let's say, a way of bringing the religion to life, not distanced from daily life. It was too much on target to be false. That a Prophet can teach something that's not purely spiritual, it's life as it's lived, I found that . . .

AUTHOR: And so, for example, in what respect did you think this differed a great deal from the Christian religion?

KAMAL-DINE: Bah, for a start, my father, he is Protestant, and my mother, she is Catholic. Me, I was Catholic like my mother. But for me, the two were the same, I saw no difference. The same thing applies to the dogma. The difference is in the hierarchy; in Catholicism you can't bypass the hierarchy: the priest, the pope. . . . In Protestantism anybody, provided they study, can be a pastor. . . . As for the said hadith, there's nothing like it in Christianity. In Christianity all the world is beautiful, the whole world is nice. In Islam there are rules. Humans need rules to respect.

AUTHOR: And why did you tell me about St. Valentine's just now, the day you became a Muslim?

KAMAL-DINE: Oh, yeah, that'll interest you. What happened, I started going to mosque regularly, but I never did the *chahada*. Well, on that day I did the *chahada*. I went to the Verriére mosque, to the foyer in Verriére, in fact, without ever having performed the *chahada*. One of the brothers one day told me, "Are you a convert?" I answered no. Then he told me they were going to do the *chahada*. So then I did it. I remember very well, it was on St. Valentine's.

AUTHOR: So it was a great occasion for you, then.

KAMAL-DINE: A great occasion, oh yeah, naturally. I became aware of the responsibility that comes with being a Muslim.

AUTHOR: Excuse me, I want to ask about your given name. How did you come to choose Kamal-dine? Didn't you call yourself Ayrton before?

KAMAL-DINE: I still do at times. My parents call me Ayrton. It doesn't bother me. As it happens, my parents chose Ayrton for two reasons. My father was a fan of the pilot Ayrton Senna. As for Kamal-dine, I always liked that first name. I had a childhood buddy, he came to our house, we did homework together, his name was Kamal-dine, and I adored that first name, I just found it exceedingly beautiful. Therefore, when I was looking for a Muslim first name, guess what?

AUTHOR: And why, then, the Da'wa Salafiyya?

KAMAL-DINE: Why the Da'wa Salafiyya? [*Thinks for a few seconds.*] In effect, ever since I joined Islam, I've always known one thing. When I entered

Islam, I knew full well that some people don't understand Islam the way it should be understood. Instinctively I knew, without anyone telling me, that the Islam that I saw in the street, on TV, in Muslim homes was not, how to put it, the true Islam. I was always convinced of that. I knew that there was something else. After that, how precisely did I come to the Salafiyya? Let's say I went to several schools of one kind or another. When you are a convert, you are new. Before I was a Salafi, I was ignorant. When a convert enters Islam, he knows nothing. He's like a baby emerging from his mother's womb. What happens when you don't know anything, you attach yourself to the person closest to you. Little does it matter if that person is Salafi, but I knew that I would not remain a Tablighi for long. Okay, I made a few sorties [*khourouj*], but I quickly went elsewhere to look. I did a *khourouj* at Auxerre, at Sainte Geneviève des Bois. This was during the first four months after my conversion, but, still, how to explain it? I knew perfectly well that some people did not have a good understanding of Islam.... To give you an example, I never dressed like the Tablighis, and I never found their way of doing things very logical, although I won't hide from you that it happened that I went to people to preach. They told me to go see such and such a person, and I went there, but down deep I didn't agree, now that I think of it. When you know nothing, you accept everything. When they told me to see such and such a person in the street, bah, I went there at the cost of making mistakes. I spoke without knowledge, I spoke about something I knew nothing about.

AUTHOR: And how did the discovery of the authentic Da'wa come about? of the science?

KAMAL-DINE: Like I told you, for four months after my conversion I spent time with some Tablighis. But I soon tired of them. From then on I started talking about courses by Abdeljalil (a young Salafi preacher that we find in this mosque and is the one who teaches and takes care of the prayers). They said to me, "Come to Montreuil, there are some super courses there." And there, believe me, that was truly science talking: What is it that Allah expects from us? What does he approve of? I felt at peace, serene, sure of myself.

AUTHOR: That's when you said, "That's it, the Salafiyya, it is good and that is for me"?

KAMAL-DINE: For a while longer, I continued taking courses by the Tabligh, it was at the Évry mosque, on Thursdays, while I was also going to courses by Abdeljalil. There [*stressing the word*] I saw the difference, that's when it clicked. A second click. After that, I gradually proclaimed myself a Salafi. I told myself, "I'm Muslim, but in contrast to the people of innovation, I am a Salafi."

The Postmilitant Salafis
Postmilitant Salafi practicants, in the past arrayed against the powers that be in Muslim countries or in the battles for influence in France, explain their rapprochement with Salafism as a rediscovery of one of Islam's first aims: comprehending and putting into practice a dogma that is beyond any partisan and political contingency. Having strayed by bringing Islam's values into all areas of life (political, intellectual, etc.) or by spreading the Muslim position to social evolutions, they see themselves as returned from a political mirage far removed from the original scope of the Revelation, the worship of God. Having risked pure transcendence for the immanence of an engagement as protester or citizen, these postmilitants are distinguished by moral fatigue as well as disillusion tied to the failure of the attempt at a sociopolitical Islamization.

Often born in Muslim countries, older than other peers, and previously in conflict with authority, they were forced to leave their country under a repression proportionate to the destruction they were ready to inflict on the state. Their adherence to quietist precepts is motivated by their sin of having wanted to reconstruct the Islamity of a state that had strayed from the divine precepts. Sheikh Mansour, a Tunisian living in France for several years, illustrates the path from Islamism to Minhaj Salafi. He is a well-known, respected figure among practicants in the Paris region, most of whom do not know that this cadre of the French Salafiyya started out in Ennahada,[13] a movement that branched off the Muslim Brotherhood, whose leader, Rashid al-Ghannouchi,[14] is a well-known herald of contemporary Islamism.

AUTHOR: May I ask you to introduce yourself? Where are you from?

---

[13] Having taken up the baton from MTI (Mouvement de la tendance islamique, Harakat al-Itijah al- Islami), created in Tunisia in 1981, the Ennahada movement, born under this name in 1989, positioned itself very clearly in the wake of the global, militant vision of Islam that was developed in Egypt starting in the 1920s by Hassan al-Banna and the Muslim Brotherhood Association that he founded in 1928. See François Burgat, *L'islamisme au Maghreb: La voix du Sud* (Islamism in the Maghreb: The voice of the South) (Paris: Payot, 1995).

[14] Born in 1941, this graduate in theology, professor of philosophy, and former admirer of Nasserism is one of the founders of MTI and then of Ennahada. Having moved to France, he was

SHEIKH MANSOUR: I'm forty-two years old. I was born in Tunisia. I have been a French citizen for the past seven years. I come from Tunis. I was born and grew up in the town of Ben' Rouss like Rashid al-Ghannouchi, who also comes from there. . . . I live in Saint-Denis, with my family. I have five children.

AUTHOR: Can you please describe your religious journey for me?

SHEIKH MANSOUR: I've been associated with Rashid al-Ghannouchi ever since Tunisia, Ennahada and all that, the Mouvement de la tendance islamique [MTI] before that. I was with them since high school. I received my baccalaureate in '86, F1 in engineering. Next I specialized by studying turbines that produce electricity. This is why afterwards I worked for an electric utility, Tunisia's equivalent of the EDF (Electricité de France, a French national company for electricity-supply). I was the assistant engineer, but I stayed in the movement. All the movements are represented in the high schools, just as in the university.

AUTHOR: And what was it like in the movement then?

SHEIKH MANSOUR: We had meetings in the movement, there were marriages, but, ultimately, we talked politics more than anything else. It was like in the Muslim Brotherhood.

AUTHOR: So you are saying that you belonged to the Muslim Brotherhood in your life?

SHEIKH MANSOUR: Yes, if you like, from 1982 to the early 1990s. Ben Ali (former Tunisian president who passed away in 2019 and was overthrown by the Tunisian revolution in 2011) made peace with the Muslim Brotherhood in 1987. It was very good. He freed the Muslim Brotherhood. It went very well for two years. In 1989 elections were held. That's when the problems started. With Ennahada, the Muslim Brotherhood was a heavyweight, and there was something like a state of war, you might say. After that, there came the arrests, et cetera. That's why most people came to Europe. . . . Before 1986 Ennahada was MTI, al-Itijah al Islami. The government held out the hope to the Muslim Brotherhood that it could become a political party.

---

a preacher of the Jama' at Tablighi for a time during the 1960s and developed a vision of Islam that increasingly opposed the secular politics of Habib Bourguiba, president of Tunisia. In 1981, after becoming embroiled in conflict with the Tunisian regime, he was arrested and sentenced to eleven years in prison, with three years effectively taken off the sentence. Until the Tunisian Revolution of 2011, he was a political refugee in London. Having returned to his country thanks to Ben Ali's fall, he won the free, democratic elections of the post–Ben Ali era in 2011. He wrote the first volume of his autobiography, titled *From the Village to Zeitouna*.

AUTHOR: And so, after that, you came to France?

SHEIKH MANSOUR: Yes, I came in '93. I arrived in Paris.

AUTHOR: And why France? Why did you choose France?

SHEIKH MANSOUR: Because of the language, it is a very familiar country in Tunisia, everything, the history.

AUTHOR: And so in France you continued to agitate with the movement people, or not?

SHEIKH MANSOUR: I continued to see Ghannouchi. Indeed I saw more of him than in Tunisia. In Tunisia, over there, I only saw him twice. Even the movement people. I saw them more often in France than in Tunisia.

AUTHOR: But explain to me how you came to break with Ghannouchi's Islam, the Muslim Brotherhood, and adopt the Da'wa Salafiyya.

SHEIKH MANSOUR: I will answer you very precisely. I will give you the exact reason.

AUTHOR: Please do. In general, I've been told it is because in the Minhaj Salafi there are proofs of what is said. The science, et cetera. The Salafis tell me that for them it is the authentic Islam.

SHEIKH MANSOUR: No, that's not . . . Yes, of course, it's true, there is that. The scholars, yes, all that. But I'm going to give you two precise reasons.

AUTHOR: Which are?

SHEIKH MANSOUR: Actually, I realized that the work done in Tunisia is not what is going to change things. Why, you ask me? Like I told you, in reality, there are two reasons. First of all, because people look after their own interests. When they came to France, many people who were in the movement abandoned the Da'wa and went into business. They ceased their religious work, they were more interested in business, all that. Therefore, when they talked about religion, in fact, you could say it was not by necessity. . . .

AUTHOR: And the second [reason]?

SHEIKH MANSOUR: The second was that people didn't have foundations. They were more interested in politics than anything else. With them, there were no imams, no foundations, no Da'wa. You go with them, you stay twenty years with them, but you won't know anything. That is very serious, especially for the young. If they have no foundations, no clear goals, anyone can come and manipulate them.

AUTHOR: And so it is more the fact that the old Brothers weren't all that interested in the Da'wa, this is what convinced you?

SHEIKH MANSOUR: Yes, you could say that. The fact that is that, yes, they were more interested—excuse me for what I'm about to say—in their delusions.

The Minhaj Salafi: An Antisystem Actor on the French Islamic Scene

The fracture line drawn by the Salafis in the Islamic camp is ideological and doctrinal. The dynamics characterizing the battles for influence in managing the salvation of the faithful derive from the traits of the Muslim population in France as well as the interweaving that unites certain believers with an Islamic offer outside French society. Thus among the structures of internal opposition exists a tension between the actors (individuals or groups) born or socialized in France and their elders striving to maintain ties to their native countries. Consular Islam is nourished by this feeling of a persisting allegiance. The national logics are important, because for certain of the faithful identification of the self with the Muslim norm depends on the feeling of belonging to a community of national origin without evoking the influence peddling of states. On the other hand, the French Islamic sphere also is characterized increasingly by a gender logic: it divides practicants of a patriarchal Islam from partisans of a feminist reading of Islamic references, conceived as a vector of intellectual emancipation and as a factor that facilitates access to the public space. There are other lines of fracture, such as the degree of organization and of proximity to the public authorities, which—with the creation of the French Council of the Muslim Faith in 2003[15]—benefit from a tool for anointment. The appearance in this instance may amount to a symbolic resource. However, Salafist socialization must be understood above all as a propensity to interpret feelings of similarity and alterity from an ideological angle. Religiosity must be the *primum movens* of every human being. The religious is the infrastructure of human societies' evolution, for it is the ultimate explanation of people's behavior.

The French Islamic sphere is in fact nothing more than a subsphere. Because the tensions and dynamics that touch on the Islamic faith in French society cannot be conceived of outside the epistemic frame imposed by the Salafis,

---

[15] "Le Conseil français due Culte musulman" (The French Council of the Muslim Faith), special issue of *French Politics, Culture and Society* vol. 23, no. 1 ().

the only feasible demarcation leads to a return to the foundations of authentic Islam. It does not makes sense to conceive of a competition in a national market because France is merely the field of expression of a universal historical and ontological rivalry between the Truth and the lie, even if the latter is dressed up in holy fripperies. France's Islamic field is understood in georeligious terms without any geographic specificity. The national social space can be nothing more than a receptacle for an antagonism inherited from Islam's first centuries between the practicants of the true and all others. Islamic *meaning* was the object of a fight born of the double division brought about by Muhammad's apostolate: believers and miscreants/associators[16] on the one hand, "orthodox" Muslims and Muslim deviants/deviationists on the other.

For the Salafis, this double antagonism structures the global and the French Islamic sphere. The quest for a monopoly of interpretation can be conceived of only if there is a preexisting "space of Islamic meaning"[17] whose structures are explained by a conjunction of geopolitical factors[18] that have made of the Kingdom of Saudi Arabia, starting in the 1960s, the principal pole of a puritan offer addressed to Muslims worldwide and thus influencing the French Islamic sphere. In this space the actors connect, confront each other, and mobilize specific resources in order to appear as the sole custodians of an authenticity that they deny in others. The Salafist resource vilifies other offers of Islam that sacrifice the demands for religious conformity to the French context when they ought to condemn it instead. The Salafist strategy consists of a subversion of norms accepted as legitimate for the Muslim community in France. It opposes the practicants against insufficiently solid believers in order to stand up to the contemporary idols: philosophical modernity, secularism, democracy. By positioning itself as an actor external to the institutional Islamic sphere, this religiosity thereby adopts a subversive posture, setting itself up as a "countersphere"[19] whose mission is to destroy the players who think of their religion as having a stake in the official landscape:

---

[16] The so-called associators (*mouchrikin*) recognize God but do not devote themselves to worshipping him exclusively, because they adore another element, for example money, an ideology, or a person, as much as him.

[17] Zaki Laidi (ed.), *Géopolitique du sens* (The geopolitics of meaning) (Paris: Desclée de Brouwer, 1998), 9–10.

[18] Gilles Kepel, "Genése et structure de l'espace de sens islamique contemporain" (Genesis and structure of the contemporary Islamic meaning space), in Laidi, *Géopolitique du sens*, 201, 203–204, 206–209.

[19] Franck Frégosi, "Champ religieux official et contre-champ islamique" (The official religious sphere and the Islamic countersphere), in François Lorcerie (ed.), *La politisation du voile en France, en Europe et dans le monde arabe* (The politicization of the veil in France, Europe and the world) (Paris: L'Harmattan, 2005), 53–63.

It is in this sense that a sphere is also a battlefield, since the hierarchy produced by the sphere (all social spaces contain dominators and aspirants) would not be accepted by all even if it possessed an ensemble of consecratory mechanisms designed to legitimize it. Bourdieu thus distinguishes between two types of action: *strategies of succession* and those of *subversion*. The first amounts to accepting the "laws" governing the functioning of the sphere, appropriating them for itself, until eventually being able to benefit from them when the day comes.... Other social agents..., perhaps because they realize that time is not on their side, may have an interest in subverting the rules of the space in which they evolve: they promote a kind of symbolic "overthrow" by trying to impose other criteria of appreciation and at the same time to sap the legitimacy and authority of those holding high positions.[20]

It is easy to comprehend why the logic of a return to the foundation is the only one that will guarantee the widest possible reception of orthodox ideas by the other Muslims. The support provided by public institutions to certain cardinal Islamic actors in France or the encouragement given by a part of public opinion to certain Muslim thinkers proposing to reconcile Islam with modernity under the auspices of human reason are just so many arguments to be rejected by the Salafists:

This is why the strategy par excellence is the return to the sources as the guiding principle of all heretical subversions and all literate revolutions because it allows turning against the dominators the weapons with which they have imposed their domination, to wit, asceticism, daring, rigor, and detachment. The one-upmanship of demands that presume to bring the dominators back to respecting the fundamental law of the universe, the denial of the "economy," can only succeed if it attests in an exemplary manner to the sincerity of the denial.[21]

We can paint a sociological picture of Islam in France starting with the degree of integration of the Islamic norm and the manner in which it is perceived as compatible or not with French society, and in this way attempt a

---

[20] Riutort, *Précis de sociologie*, 227–228.
[21] Pierre Bourdieu, "La production de la croyance: Contribution à une économie des biens symboliques" (The production of belief: Contribution to an economy of symbolic goods), *Actes de la recherche en sciences sociales* (Proceedings of social science research), no. 13 (1977): 12.

typology. In doing so we detect four ways of living the Muslim reference within French society. If the first two, properly speaking, do not structure identities whose calling is to act in the Islamic sphere, the other two cannot conceive of staying on the margins of hammering out the discourse over Islam in France and in the world.

The Traditionalists and the Neotraditionalists

We will call the first form of identity "traditionalist" or "neotraditionalist." To claim to be Muslim is lived as obvious, and constructing this identity is not the object of a distancing. The family circle being strongly attached to the religious norm, even if only on a formal level, to think of yourself and live as a Muslim is synonymous with appropriating a cultural and confessional heritage after parental intermediation. As sincere as faith and belief may be in transcendence, the norm is almost exclusively invoked by the best known religious acts, such as prayer. Islam constitutes a credo but does not deliver a "one thought fits all" for everyday life. The interaction with the French context is marked by the entry visa stamp, with the traditionalist circles seeking to perpetuate the legacy structures. Islam without question is the fundamental item but rarely results in an alignment of all behaviors with the religious injunction.

The children coming from these families, for which religion and tradition are so intertwined that they can no longer be distinguished in practice, present different profiles. We have opted to define them as neotraditionalists because the traits transmitted by the parents live on but at the price of a certain adaptation to the French context. The legacy traditions are the object of critical scrutiny without always being replaced by French habits and customs, due to a rapport with Islam still thought of as allogeneic in the French context.

The Private Muslims

The second profile is the private Muslim, for whom Islamic morality constitutes neither a formal heritage identified as such nor the source of positioning in the social space. Applying primarily to the descendants of immigrants from Muslim societies, it signifies not the disappearance of the Islamic referent but the refusal to put it foremost in the definition and presentation of the self. Paradoxically, belonging to the Muslim religion is mobilized with the aim of expressing oneself in favor of not having the Islamic referent play a role in the public debate in France.

The Militant Muslims

The militant Muslim identity takes an opposite course. It is more Islamic than Muslim, since it rests on the idea that there is beyond the simple religious reference a path inspired by this morality that allows translating the appropriation of the sacred into real life. It is militant because the believer who remains stuck in simple ritual obligations would deny one of the essential characteristics of Islam: the calling to govern horizontal relations (*al-mou'amalat*) between individuals in addition to the vertical link that connects the human being with the Creator (*al-'ibadat*). Militants seek to insert Islam's values into French sociopolitical debates. The leading figure in this movement is the Swiss preacher-intellectual Tariq Ramadan, for whom the spheres of religion and citizenships are complementary, thus authorizing militant Muslims to be uninhibited in demanding religious rights. The demand for the right to wear the hijab in public secondary schools in 2003–2004 was one of the most widely covered instances in the media. Young Muslims wearing tricolored Islamic headscarves, showing their identity cards during demonstrations, and carrying banners bearing slogans like "Don't touch my veil!" and "I'll remember this at election time" offered a good example of this state of mind. Citizenship and faith intertwine in a positive-sum game: militant Islam seeks to fulfill morality with means offered by the condition of being a citizen of the republic. While religiosity is superior to all other forms of identification, the fact remains that practicants see no conflict between French citizenship and Islamity. A demanding Islamic norm is presented as compatible with the exercise of a full and complete citizenship.

The Exclusive Muslims

Finally, we have the exclusive type; for them, the norm would by no means tolerate a competing system as a guiding principle of life. It is Salafism that, in theory, does not recognize any other form of allegiance but to God and to the *'oulama* that are the interpretive vectors of His word. A monodimensional identity, it invalidates the state, the nation, social class, or country of origin. Dividing Muslims from others and dividing orthodox Muslims from deviant Muslims, it is ontologically binary. Certainly the quietists are not the only exclusives (the Tablighis and the jihadists[22] are just as much), but they have been in the spotlight ever since the debate over the full veil in 2009. They

---

[22] Although the latter are also militants because, for example, they are seeking to irrigate the political terrain with the religious reference formulated in an intransigent manner.

define themselves as structurally resistant to change, for then Islam would no longer be central to regulating human societies. The religion looks like a closed and jealously guarded system, the filter for interpreting everything. In contrast to the militants who integrate other elements with the Islamic referent that are judged as positive, stressing that the faith's appeal is universal, the Salafists see these compromises as threatening alterations to moral integrity. But while they share with the militants the idea that they are the only Muslims who promote a religiosity of "raised awareness," they nevertheless differ from them: Islam represents the unique prism through which the exclusives conceive identity and action in the social sphere.

The ʿ*Alim*: The Maker of Salafist Meaning

The *ʿalim*, Islam's religious cleric or scholar, is the person engaged in the study of sacred references with the mission of interpreting the religious message to enunciate norms and prescriptions that let the faithful draw nearer to the most complete religious realization.[23] As the key figure in the intellectual and epistemic edifice of Salafism, he is the guarantor of Islamic legitimacy and, indeed, the theorist of the rupture, personified by his embarking on a career of advocacy for the religion's preservation. Through mastery of values and norms, he justifies the positions and actions of practicants who see him as the interface between their times and that of the Pious Forebears. He thus has a dual function. By anointing a sociopolitical order, he justifies the right to live in such a society; by contrast, by reference to religion, he legitimizes the duty to withdraw from an impious land that does not respect the fundamentals of Islam. Moreover, in a given society, he offers the believer the guarantee of safety by demarcating a framework of possibilities that, if respected, will assure him of the condition of pious contemporary here below and final success in the other world. To know the authentic logos and be versed in its interpretation without ever leaving the sphere of claimed orthodoxy is the faculty of an Islamic scholar, as distinct from a deviationist theoretician. As the backbone of the Salafist logocratic system, the scholar is the producer of meaning who establishes and develops the religious norms around which the social actors align themselves.

---

[23] Nabil Mouline, *Les clercs de l'Islam: Autorité religieuse et pouvoir politique en Arabie Saoudite, XVIIIE–XXIE siècle* (Islamic clerics: Religious authority and political power in Saudi Arabia, 18th–21st century) (Paris: PUF, "Proche Orient," 2011), 9–10.

The Daʾwa Salafiyya as Exclusive Islamic Paradigm

Deviance and Deviationism

Mastery of the ʿilm[24] confers notional power in Islamic society; however, for the Salafis, not every person who proclaims himself "learned" merits being listened to. Behind an apparent mastery of the Muslim logos, the deviant theoreticians and/or deviationists give an erroneous reading, and hence a dangerous one, of the norm. They fall into two categories: they may be deviants when they teach a false version of Islam but without being called into line by the clerics of authenticity, and they become deviationists if they have been warned by the upholders of true Islam but persist in their positions and continue to dispense religious teaching that runs counter to this path. This is how a traditional imam from the Maghreb, for example, becomes the object of a reformist discourse by the Salafis; cadres in other offers who promote rapport with an Islam disfigured because it deviated voluntarily from the right path will be treated differently. The imam being meant to incarnate the keystone of the micro- or macrosocial edifice based on the sacred norm, the Salafis see in the Islam of proximity a degenerated form of Islamic practice, explainable by a lack of education of the parents as well as the deleterious effect of acculturation with a system of values and morals drawn from an agnostic moral referent source that is atheistic, secular, even Islamophobic.

The situation of believers who claim they have been called to extemporize as cadres of the Muslim faith or Islamic theoreticians in our era is quite different. These are deviationists because they have the intellectual fire power to verify the soundness or not of actions that they prescribe. However, this leads them to the exact opposite of that which pure preaching is supposed to result in: they extol sociocultural integration, think about the reference to Islam in a private context because of secularism, or, more fatally, lay claim to redefining the religious injunction by believing that it must free itself from its frame of reference—Islam's early times. Examination of certain quietist websites permits us to note the systematic presence of a warning rubric pointing explicitly to tendencies to preach a message that contradicts the original spirit and letter of Islam. The true message conforms to an interpretation that is the monopoly of clerics who think

---

[24] ʿ-l-m is the root for "knowledge" and, by extension, for "science."

of Islam only within the strict limitations imposed by the religious vision of the first generations of Muslims, or Salaf. The paradigmatic position of the Salafi clerics is summed up in the words of one of its contemporary eminences, Sheikh Al-Albani:

> And we cannot know the truth about [the] questions [relative to religion], except by referring to the manner in which the Pious Forebears (*as-Salaf*) and among them, in particular, the Prophet's Companions have understood religion....
>
> In my courses and conferences, I repeat unceasingly that it is not enough to "call people to follow the Koran and the *Sunna*" but to this must be added the phrase "according to the understanding of the Pious Forebears" or something similar, in order to establish the religious proofs in this meaning. This is mentioned elsewhere.
>
> It is an obligation that must be met, the more so because, in our times, calling on people to follow the Koran and the *Sunna* has become fashionable; all the Islamic groups and preachers do it—despite all the essential and secondary divergences that confront them—so that it can happen that there are enemies of the *Sunna* among them in practice, or others that say inviting people to the *Sunna* sows division among them! May Allah preserve us from them.
>
> I ask Allah to let us live in the *Sunna* and that He lets us die in respect for the *Sunna*.[25]

A Scientific Religiosity: Rational-Legal Legitimacy

Studying the links existing between the body of orthodox scholars and the body of the faithful authorizes us to see in the legitimacy conferred on the former the product of the three forms of domination identified by Max Weber, with the rational and legal dimensions being essential. The authority argument between an offer of Islam presenting itself as "scientific"[26] and the claim of an "authentic" Islam places in the center of this system of meaning the administration of the Islamic proof. Salafist

---

[25] Sheikh Muhammad Nāsruddin Al-Albāni, *La description de la prière du Prophéte: Du premier Takbir aux salutations finales. Comme si tu la voyais* (Description of the Prophet's prayer: From the first takbir to the closing salutations. As if you were there), 1st edition (Riyadh: Al-Maaref, 2003), 8.

[26] When it comes to their religiosity, the Salafists love to evoke the Salafiyya 'ilmiyya (scientific Salafism), which lets them claim a rational dimension.

prescriptions rest on a form of Islamic reason, a scientific methodology. If this epistemic framework is not respected, the cleric, even if he thinks of himself as Sunni, joins the ranks of the "innovators of religion."[27] Thus it is possible to see in the dominance exercised by the Salafi ʿoulama the interaction of three types of legitimacy, each referring to a specific mode of authority:

> These three types of legitimate dominance do not uniquely rest on sentiments but also are wrapped about with beliefs by their members regarding their smooth functioning. Thus the traditional legitimacy functions on the model of customs and traditions. Equally, there is legitimacy by virtue of law (laws and regulations) as well as of norms. Whereas charismatic legitimacy is based entirely on the personal value of the leader; around his qualities of an exceptional, almost abnormal order, maybe even an otherworldly one. His simple word is law.[28]

According to traditional authority, the Salafis are the inheritors of the legacy left by the blessed generations of Islam. The traditions bequeathed by Muhammad and the first believers form the Tradition: Islam as a religion that "descended on Muhammad" and the calling for it to be reproduced until the Day of Retribution (*youm ad-din*). The faithful have no choice but to take this inheritance, the Koran and the Sunna, as their authority. Only one group of Muslims stayed on the straight and narrow path. The Tradition is carried on only by this "saved group" (*al-farquat an-najiyya*), which explains the the ethic of initiation at the heart of Salafist socialization. This is equally true for the Salafi theoreticians whose traditional legitimacy is derived from the intermediation of the preceding generation of scholars that anoint the new clerics.[29] This passing of the baton corresponds to the passing on of capital that sustains and reinforces the sphere.

---

[27] As opposed to "people of the Sunna and the Consensus," believers who do not subscribe to the Salafist methodology become "people of deviation and bewilderment" (*alh al-bid'a wal-dalala*). Religious innovation (*bid'a diniyya*) must not be confused with worldly innovation (*bid'a douniayouiyya*), which involves objects and attitudes without direct relevance for the religious rite (driving a car instead of riding a she-camel, for instance).

[28] Xiberras, *Les theories de l'exclusion*, 66.

[29] In the Salafist scholar communities prevail the principles of intermediation (*wasta*) and of recommendation (*tazkiyya*). A cleric known for his faithfulness to the authentic teachings and recognized by his peers is in a position to make a recommendation to another (often one who was his student). who in turn is known as a "scholar of the Sunna."

Going back fourteen centuries, the Tradition, however, also defines itself by another form of legitimacy, one that grows from religious reasoning based on Islamic proof. Charismatic authority remains attached to the fact that preaching cadres have integrated the key dimension of the proof, or *dalil*. They command the power of the proof. Thus this kind of rational and legal authority constitutes the pivot of adherence: the cleric knows how to derive an orthodox response from the sources to every problem and can give a proof as the reason for his decision. Theorizing a scientific Islam and thus putting at the heart of socialization the necessity to learn your religion, the Salafis promote a demanding identity that resists the minimalist reading practiced by certain tendencies. No conduct, no word of religious vocation will find grace unless it is based on a proof.[30] The normative and demarcated Islam that ensues from this must secure for the believer the feeling that the religion is a coherent, logical, rational, scientific, and exclusive system. No longer belonging to himself, the believer becomes the individual expression of the Salafi sphere whose calling is to standardize the religious practice of all.[31]

Obedience to the religious logos therefore offers a more dynamic reading of the terrain than one might think. The importance of the rational and legal character of Salafist socialization explains two dynamics.

The first is that *Homo salaficus* is on a constant quest for the most purified Islamic practice possible. Lending allegiance to the logos as interpreted by the clerics induces recognition of the principle "Knowledge is not the Truth." If the clerics formulate the most refined codes of authentic religiosity, it is common during discussions with practicants to stipulate the existence of a certain principle of reality. To sacralize the positions taken by scholars would be to indulge in a grave innovation since in essence only the teachings and example of the Prophet are sacred. Hence, to the extent that authentic Islam has a vocation of putting the purified logos in the center of the believer's life, it is possible to challenge a norm promulgated by some 'oulama, signifying that anyone's preeminence at a given time may find itself transformed. On an individual level, the practicant can therefore relativize, even break with certain Salafist norms by a reading that is also orthodox. On a sociological level, this allows nuancing the sectarian dimension of Salafist society, such an intransigent phenomenon not tolerating structurally the possibility of

---

[30] The only thing demanded by the practicants for eventually accepting the opponent's opinion is that "the proof is established" (*iqamat al-hujja*).

[31] This way, upon the believer's entering the deviant career, "the pole of his conduct is [henceforth] located outside of him." (Xiberras, *Les theories de l'exclusion*, 45.)

loosening the hold of a norm generally established by an authority that is charismatic in nature. It is nonetheless true that this dynamic may just as well explain, *a contrario*, the multiplying of groups even within the Salafist communities, since the disparity in interpretations then leads to religious quarrels that has actors who all claim the same norm for themselves facing off against each other.

The second is that the field may find itself contested or even deconstructed from inside. Under the effect of dynamics perceived as heterodox, the norm finds itself in a position of weakness when its vocation is to be hegemonic. If the condition for positioning oneself is a methodology based on the administration of the proof, the field becomes contestable in its very structures. The goal being to orient preaching always toward more orthodoxy, the actors occupying a dominant place must seal the interpretation of the norm, at the risk of the Salafist sphere's imploding or being contested by new clerics also brandishing arguments of authenticity. The quietist scholars today are dominant if we go by the size of their audience, which is larger than that of the protesters; however, since the end of the twentieth century, they have faced competition from other actors who question their authority. To repulse potential competitors, the legitimist clerics can thus declare them to be deviationists. The Salafist way certainly envisions a space for discussions of possible points of divergence, but if they become too strident, they can constitute a threat of sedition (fitna). "Refer to the scholars" may be considered a consequence or cause of the state of anomie and of division which many Muslims have had to confront. The pretension of enacting an imperative of purity that is ever more demanding and scrupulous runs the risk of seeing certain scholars making the sphere implode with orthodox preaching to ensure a rigorous balance between two fundamental duties: to promote the Islamic notion of the good and to preserve the faithful against fitna. The most important movement of the contemporary era designed to destabilize the quietist Salafi sphere is that undertaken by the enemy brothers who lay claim to a combative, revolutionary vision of Islam. Structured around jihadist figures like Osama bin Laden or religious men like Sheikh Abu Muhammad Al-Maqdisi,[32] this alternative Salafist sphere makes it its mission to obliterate

---

[32] A scholar of jihadist Salafism, who espouses among other principles the need for combating those who oppose a puritan takeover of Muslim societies by granting himself the right to cast anathema on Muslims who do not judge according to divine laws. See "La religion démocratie" on a jihadist website of this excommunicator-theoretician: http://tawhid-wa-al-jihad.over-blog.com/article-28818716.html.

the work of politically legitimist Salafism practiced by the majority in Saudi Arabia or in France.

The Sociology of the Salafist Sphere: Rupture as an Effect of Historical Preaching on a Global and Local Level

Required to return[33] to the great scholars under all circumstances, the practicant is duty-bound to refer to them for his religious, political, and social conduct. He delegates to them the tending to the commandments of his existence and makes his life a quest to conform to their injunctions. The desire to follow in their wake corresponds as much to the search for an authenticity by way of a teacher-student relationship as a doing away with history. The physical or intellectual closeness with the ʿalim is synonymous with a leap back in time in reference to the age when Muslims knew and practiced. The cleric is a trace of the past, a living legacy of the true[34] way to be followed. To go meet a scholar is like traveling through history to reconnect with the Golden Age of Islamic purity.

The sphere, insofar as it is represented by French virtuous contemporaries, must be regarded as the interweaving of four levels of scientism and authority. The appearance during the second half of the twentieth century of a globalized Salafist sphere essentially attaches to puritan Saudi-centric preaching, with other phenomena explaining the organization of a French Salafist sphere. It is determined by the identification with four categories of clerics whose legitimacy is presented here in descending order. The values are carried by successive generations of scholars of righteousness sharing a common adherence to the demanding vision of an intact Islam. The prevalent logic in these Salafist epistemic communities[35] is the transmission of

---

[33] The lexical field of "return" sees frequent use. See the article taken from a Salafist website addressing the "need to return to the experts" to convince us of the latter's "focal" character: http://kitab-wa-sounnah.over-blog.com/article-la-necessite-de-revenir-auxgrands-savants-en-ce-qui-concerne-les-questions-importes-45452681.html.

[34] The Salafists are attracted only to "the transcendental order" structured around the norm delivered by the ʿoulama. See Gilles Kepel, "Les oulémas, l'intelligentsia et les islamisted en Égypte: Système social, ordre transcendental et ordre traduit" (The ulemas, the intelligentsia and the Islamists in Egypt: Social system, transcendental order and translated order), Revue française de science politique, Passage au politique 35, no. 3 (June 1985): 424.

[35] It is possible to see in the Salafist communities of scholars "epistemic communities" defined as "spaces for reflection on the problematics from disciplinary references held in common." See Peter M. Haas, "Introduction: Epistemic Communities and International Policy Coordination," International Organization vol. 46, no. 1 (1992).

a cognition and a feeling of initiation. Every blessed generation co-opts the next one so as to erect an orthodox genealogy, a puritan lineage as the vector for sustainability and of propagation of authenticity.

The Historical 'Oulama: Ibn Hanbal, Ibn Taymiyya, and Ibn Abdul-Wahab
During the period of troubles and sedition, three main Sunni figures who represented as many opportunities for a return to Islam's sources reaffirmed the authentic rules. To preserve the unity of the umma while not remaining silent about the blows against the truth of dogma, they had to hark back to the norm, all the while protecting the believers against political and religious anarchy.

The first of these clerics, Sheikh Ahmad Ibn Hanbal (780–855), is the incarnation par excellence of the principle of resistance by the spoken word, or "the great test" (*al-mihna*) that he had to pass in his time in confronting the theoreticians of a rationalist Islam that tended to renounce the absolute divinity of the Koran, saying that it was created in this world and not created in the hereafter. Under the Abbasid Caliphate, whose head sought to reform the religious creed around a vision influenced by the Mu'tazilism School,[36] Ibn Hanbal led a counterreform movement with the goal of restoring the original purity of Islam and of the Tradition[37] in the face of a conception that put reason first.

Opposing the "objective sources"[38] of Islam to the Muslims of innovation who notably integrated elements of Aristotelian philosophy, he entered into conflict with the caliphs favoring the Mu'tazilist vision. However, if this puritan opposition focused on dogma (*al-'aqida*), the conflict between the scholar and the politician never turned into a formal contest. The passion of Ibn Hanbal did not become a confrontational political project, and he never issued an excommunication against the prince, forbidding the turning against the governors except in case of manifest

---

[36] Appearing during the eighth century, this theological school of Islam posits that it is possible to access knowledge of God by exercising reason and logic. Influenced by Aristotelian thought and integrating speculation on being and matter, the Mu'tazilist theoreticians considered hardly credible the idea of "an uncreated word of God," meaning the Koran, because this would mean that the Holy Book would in essence be divine and therefore worthy of veneration. Concluding that in fact the Koran is a divinely inspired book but *created* on earth, this approach was not slow in attracting sharp critiques from partisans of an orthodoxy of a "great test" that would formulate in a more coherent manner the confrontation with heterodox tentative definitions of Islam.

[37] The believers siding with Ibn Hanbal thus becoming the "people of the Tradition" (*ahl an-naql*) contrasted with the practicants of Mu'tazilism as the "people of reason" (*ahl al-'aql*).

[38] Laoust, *Les schismes dans l'islam*, 383–387.

atheism on their part. While he remained an ardent partisan of the authentic dogma during the period of the "State inquisition"[39] launched by the caliph Al-Ma'moun, defender of the Mu'tazilist creed, Ibn Hanbal never formulated the obligation to revolt against him—a perfect illustration of the attitude to be adopted in case of conflict between the ʿalim and the secular power.[40]

The second cleric, Sheikh Taqi ad-Din Abu Al-Abbas Ahmad Ibn Taymiyya (1263–1328), is the greatest of the great for many Salafis. Ibn Taymiyya, inheritor of the Hanbalist School and its most famous *faqih* (specialist in Islamic jurisprudence, *fiqh*), is equally presented in the Salafist literature as an ardent defender of the Sunna. In an era when the religious truth had to face the diplomatic conversions on the part of the new Muslims, the Mongols,[41] as well as numerous initiatives to assume power emanating from the Shiites (whom he would fight physically himself at Karawan in Lebanon), he took up the torch of the Salaf Salih for illuminating the night the believers found themselves in. Presented as the incarnation of religious courage in facing persons preaching a false or lukewarm version of Islam, he popularized the concept of *tawhid* in the form that today is the Sunni Islam consensus. Dividing this principle into three categories, Ibn Taymiyya distinguished:

- Uniqueness of lordship (*tawhid ar-rouboubiyya*), by virtue of which He is the Lord of all things and no Master of the Universe would know how to be separate from Him.
- Uniqueness of worship (*tawhid al-ʿuluhiyya*), in which no being or thing outside of Allah could be the object of veneration.

---

[39] Robert Mantran, *L'expansion musulmane: VIIe–XIe siècle* (The Muslim expansion: 7th–11th century) (Paris: PUF, 1995), 231.

[40] The Hanbali experience of the *mihna* prefigures a modern vision of the state and politics. Formulated in anachronistic terms, it postulates the dangers of a "flawed Leviathan" (a state lacking a strong prince as ruler). This prefiguration of the philosophy of Thomas Hobbes makes of "The Passion of Ibn Hanbal" the example of a certain modernity in Salafist thought, with the difference that the latter's approach is "naturalist" (security is a natural right and not imposed by God). See http://www.islam-al-haqq.com/article-l-attitude-a-avoir-vis-a-vis-du-detenteur-de-l-autorite-38835878.html.

For Hobbesian thought and the development of his vision of the "survival contract," in whose name the people give up a part of their sovereignty to a political authority, see Thomas Hobbes, *Leviathan* (Paris: Vrin, 2005).

[41] Ibn Taymiyya produced his most famous fatwa (Hunt Janin and Andre Kahlmeyer, Islamic Law: The Sharia from Muhammad's Time to the Present (New York: McFarland, 2007), 79) in which he cast anathema on the Mongols (Tartars), whom he reproaches, despite their "nominal" conversion to Islam, with continuing to make law based on the Yassa (secret legal code dealing with commerce and criminal law) established by Genghis Khan. In the eyes of the legal expert, this constituted a grave breach of the faith and was comparable to a return by these Muslims to the pre-Islamic era.

– Uniqueness of the number of attributes (*tawhid fi al-asma wal-siffat*), starting from which it is impossible to affirm that human attributes are exactly the same as those of the Creator (His grandeur, for example, having nothing in common with that of humans). Thus, one of the divine names, *Al-Kabir* (the Exalted), does not lead to any possible comparison between the Creator and the created.[42]

This conception of the *tawhid* furnishes an illustration of the internal cleavages in the orthodox sphere, when the jihadists oppose the legitimists: their doctrine counts a fourth form of *tawhid*, "uniqueness of sovereignty" (*tawhid al-hakimiyya*), in whose name it is advisable to guard against the application of legal precepts of Islam and never to evolve in a judicial-legal framework that borrows from other references.

The third cleric, Sheikh Muhammad Ibn Abdul-Wahab (1703–1792), was also a legal expert of the Hanbalite rite in the Arabian peninsula of the eighteenth century who showed himself to be even more rigorous in his approach. Intent on revitalizing the essence of Islam in a profoundly deviant society, he tried to restore the purity of dogma by condemning and combatting the ways of the times, such as tomb visits and the soliciting of benedictions from the deceased, God alone being the Recipient of human invocations. To see his preaching take hold, the '*alim* in 1744 concluded a politico-religious alliance with Muhammad Ibn Saud, the village chief of Dir'iyya near Riyadh, to whose project of unifying Arabia and its populations he proceeded to lend religious legitimacy. Beyond the historic dimension of the event, the founding pact concluded in 1744 in the Najd[43] is emblematic of the social compact that is supposed to prevail in an authentically Islamic society. As a result, the Saudi state and society are perceived as the social, religious, and political modes of organization closest to the Muslim norm. The fact that this country would be, in principle, governed by a body of righteous scholars[44] contributes to its prestige and to its being placed by all practicants at the head

---

[42] http://3ilm.char3i.over-blog.com/article-25992462.html.

[43] Hamadi Redissi, *Le Pacte de Najd: Ou comment l'islam sectaire est devenu l'islam* (The Najd Alliance: Or how sectarian Islam became Islam) (Paris: Seuil, 2007).

[44] As represented by two Salafi networks of theorization and application of the norm: the Représentés par deux réseaux salafi de théorisation et d'application de la norme: The Council of Senior Scholars (*hayat al-kibar al-'oulama*) headed by the grand mufti of the kingdom, who almost always is descended from Muhammad Ibn Abdul-Wahab (called "Al-Sheikh" from the name of the family of inheritors of the cofounder of the Saudi Kingdom) and the Standing Committee for Scholarly Research and Issuing Fatwas (*lajnat ad-daiyma lil-ifta wal-bouhouth al-islamiyya*). See Mouline, *Les clercs de l'islam*, 192–222.

of the countries that are most respectful of the Islamic heritage, so that the majority of Salafists want to live or study in the the nation of the *tawhid*.

The Salafi social compact may be pictured as a tripod. Human beings by nature are religious animals; their behaviors, sociality, and duties must be regulated within a societal framework ruled by the sacred. The ultimate end of the collective life is to facilitate the salvation of its members. In this respect, the idea of an Islamic society as a theocratic construct has relatively little justification, since power belongs to God, whatever may be the social or cultural configuration in which the individual finds himself.[45] The celestial dimension[46] of the society of Islam is guaranteed by the intervention of scholars. By a mutually beneficial work, the political holder of authority (*wali al amr*) assures himself of the enlightened counsel (*nasiha*) of the ʿ*alim*, who, in turn, is going to guarantee the religious legitimacy of the political power before the common people who are invited to follow the head of the community possessing the monopoly on legitimate violence. The latter, in order to claim his temporal power as enduring and perpetuate this structure of allegiance, must integrate the Islamic norm of which the ʿ*alim* is custodian when preparing to take an action. He is therefore the keystone of the social edifice constructed from the sacred reference. Situated in the lineage of the Prophets, he possesses the highest degree of knowledge of their work and their message, of the religious, social, and political engineering that characterizes the history of Islam after the death of Muhammad, and this makes him the religion's backbone. Arbiter of potential tensions between the people and the individuals vested with political authority, the cleric[47] is the key interface in the mode of Islamic control. Occupying "the two polar positions of religious work,"[48] the ideal Salafist system is defined as a "scientocracy," a "logocracy," or an "epistocracy"[49]: it is the privileged interlocutor between a people that complains of certain shortcomings in the spirit and the letter of the religion on the part of the rulers and the moral conscience of a power that must not permit itself to lose the anointing by the ʿ*oulama*. With the

---

[45] Jean-Paul Charnay, *Sociologie religieuse de l'islam* (The religious sociology of Islam) (Paris, Hachette Littérature, "Pluriel," 1994).

[46] Saint-Augustin, *La Cité de Dieu* (City of God), volumes 1–3 (Paris: Seuil, "Points Sagesses," 2004).

[47] This is what we call the person with responsibility for "the management of salvation goods." See "Salvation Goods and the Religious Market," *Social Compass* 35, no. 1 (2006): 5–108.

[48] Pierre Bourdieu, "Genèse et structure du champ religieux" (Genesis and structure of the religious sphere), *Revue française de sociologie*, no. 12 (1971): 295–334, quoted in Kepel, "Les oulémas."

[49] David Estlund, *L'autorité de la démocratie: Une perspective philosophique* (The authority of democracy: A philosophical perspective) (Paris: Hermann, 2011).

source of authority being religious and not political, it is normal for the secular power to be exercised within a framework limited and controlled by the clerics. But the political sphere, just like all others, being subject to and irrigated by the religious sphere, within which the Salafist norm is supposed to have the upper hand, the true wielder of authority is the *'alim* and not the *hakim*.[50] The permanence of the *hakim*'s position depends on the *'alim*, religion being represented foremost by those who perpetuate the prophetic message. In the Salafist construction, the *'alim*'s political power—except for the primary function of interpreting the religious norm—relates to the fact that the authentic Islamic system must rest on the experiences of the Revelation. The values introduced by the Prophet into the framework of his apostolate, such as justice, equality, and the quest for salvation, are just as much moral finalities that political action has to guarantee. This is why the organization of society is not so much theocratic as scientocratic.

Studying the nature of the social compact permits relativizing the fundamentalist reach of Salafism in the political sphere, since the vision of the tie between cleric and prince does not obey the same logic as that which unites the *'alim* and the people. The people owe obedience to the religious and political powers in return for the scholar's lending an attentive ear so that he can then bring the people's expectations before the prince. As for the secular leader, he must accommodate to the greatest extent possible the advice of the *'oulamas* through which they try to expand the domain of application of the religious norm at the summit of power. This means, therefore, that the prince's religious autonomy is greater than that of the common people, who must watch the correctness of their practice, while the wielder of political authority—given his position and function as protector against sedition—is subjected to a less strict religious control by the scholars. This dissymmetry linked to the nature and functions of each of the three components of society justifies our seeing in the Salafist vision of politics a secularizing fundamentalism to the extent that the prince's and the people's religious control regimes wielded by the clerics are not subject to the same considerations. The secular leader is first of all characterized by his duty of guaranteeing the physical security and the sustainability of the Islamic order; this is why the scholars impose minimalist religious control on his practice but maximalist religious

---

[50] "He who wields power" (here political). The root *h-k-m* is that for "wisdom" and "governance," the political power expected to be exercised in the measure that it is conferred by religion.

control on the common people. This differentiated judgment thus plays a part in constituting a political space obeying separate rules with differing sanctions for deviations from religious prescriptions. Thus there exist two orders of judgment in the Salafist construction of politics that allow seeing in it a secularizing modality by which the weight of the religious is weaker in circumscribing the political agenda, even in the name of a fundamentalist conception of Islam. This is crucial for understanding the reactions of jihadi Salafis who cast anathema on political leaders who have largely exceeded their right to deviate from the norm, to the point where their policy is criticized as no longer having in it anything Islamic. The jihadists also take on the legitimist scholars, whom they blame for these deficits, which, moreover, earns them the name of "palace scholars" (*'oulama al-balat*) or "scholars of the prince" (*'oulama as-sultan*). This secularizing fundamentalism also explains why the Salafist sphere is more dynamic than it appears and why it is possible to call into question its structures in mobilizing the orthodox reference to its advantage.

The Clerics of the Second Half of the Twentieth Century and the Albano-Saudi Connection: "Salafism Goes Global"

The second half of the twentieth century saw the emergence of a new pole in global geopolitics: Saudi Arabia, one of whose levers of influence, in addition to oil, is the export of what is called "pristine" Islam. This globalization movement is buttressed by the financial power derived from "black gold" revenues, the combination of the two having favored the Saudi preeminence in the space of Islamic meaning. The purified preaching was the doing of numerous theoreticians, but in particular of three figures linked to Saudi Arabia who represented the principal contemporary producers of Salafist meaning for practicants. They are the subject of widespread consensus within the quietist Salafi sphere, and they structure the orthodox paradigm.

The cleric Sheikh Abdelaziz Ibn Baz (1910–1999), the only figure not descended from Ibn Abdul-Wahab to have occupied the office of grand mufti of the Saudi Arabian kingdom, was one of this country's most influential religious functionaries.[51] If the historical scholars of Salafism are characterized by geographically conditioned preaching because of the clear-cut separation, during their time, between "the house of Islam" (*dar al-islam*) and "the house of unbelief" (*dar al-koufr*), the generation to which Sheikh

---

[51] Mouline, *Les clercs de l'islam*, 202.

Ibn Baz belonged was the first to touch the global space during their lifetime. Taking advantage of the Saudi state's changed political dimension during the second half of the twentieth century, this *'alim* (blind since adolescence) gains recognition as the "global mufti" since his works, his legal rulings, and his courses had a planetary reach. Author of religious opinions with decisive impact,[52] he was considered the key driving force in the Salafist sphere until his death in 1999. Siding with the House of Saud, the guarantor along with the scholars of respect for Islam in the "land of the two sanctuaries," Sheikh Ibn Baz represented the archetypal palace scholar or sultan's scholar in the eyes of the jihadi Salafis. These, although they supported Saudi policies until the 1900–1991 Gulf War, began to reproach the kingdom for its alliance with the American enemy and the official clerics for having given an Islamic anointing to the apostate heads of this state. The latter having betrayed Islam, it became legitimate to fight them and launch an armed and violent jihad against them. The religious aspect of this reaction was concretized by the disqualification of *'oulama* who continued to support the preaching carried on in Saudi Arabia, such as Sheikh Ibn Baz.

The second great figure of the Da'wa Salafiyya of the second half of the twentieth century was Sheikh Muhammad Nassirdine Al-Albani[53] (1914–2000). An ardent advocate of reintroducing the term "Salafi" and an erudite connoisseur of the prophetic hadith whose importance in the rediscovery of the original Islamic heritage he theorized, he is considered by the quietist Salafis as the "reviver of the Islam of his time."[54] An adversary of the militant movements that seek to invade the political realm in the name of the Islamic referent, he was a supporter of abandoning politics[55] in favor of the activities

---

[52] Noteworthy are the fatwas that he rendered in 1979 to consecrate an Afghanistan invaded by the USSR as land of jihad for Muslims, then, in 1990, the one authorizing the Saudi Kingdom to call on the American military power after the Iraqi Baathist Saddam Hussein invaded Kuwait and so threatened the security of that state. See Gilles Kepel, *Jihad: Expansion et déclin de l'islamisme* (Jihad: Expansion and decline of Islamism) (Paris: Gallimard, "Folio," 2003).

[53] He was born Muhammad Najah Hanouti, in Shkodra, the capital of Albania, in 1914. After his family immigrated to Syria, his advanced religious studies convinced him of the necessity of returning to the original Islam and developing a methodology based on rediscovering the Prophet's words as the best complement for the Koranic text. His authorized biography portrays him as predestined to become the "master of the hadith." See Ibrahim Muhammad Al'Ali, *Biographie de Muhammad Nāsir Al-Dīn Al-Albāni: 1332–1420 H.* (Lyon: Médine Éditions, 2007).

[54] The Tradition teaches that in each century a person appears to guide Islam back on the way of truth and so triumph over the deviants that have diluted the Message. This is a controversial element, the object of symbolic battle, with each enterprise of re-Islamicization elevating its tutelary figure to the era's *muhi ad-din* (reviver of the religion).

[55] One of the theoretician's famous formulations being that "he subscribes today to the good policy of not engaging in politics."

of purification and education (*tasfiyya wa-tarbiyya*). This translated into his involvement in the study of scriptural sources to the detriment of political action and his maximal distancing from sources of perversion of the faith.

The third member of these people of the consensus was the cleric Sheikh Muhammad Ibn Salih Ibn ʿOtheimine (1926–2001). A student of Ibn Baz, from whom he inherited his vision of Islam and his relationship to politics, Ibn ʿOtheimine was a member of the Council of Senior Scholars and an imam of the Mosque at Mecca. During his life he was considered the second to Sheikh Ibn Baz in that he was his closest student, anticipated by the rest to become grand mufti of the kingdom after the former's passing. Being one of the most popular teachers in the country's Islamic universities, he was considered to be one of the most authoritative voices in religious matters after Ibn Baz and Al-Albani.[56]

The Contemporary Inheritors: Between Bureaucratism and University Networks, Sheikh Salih Al-Fawzan and Sheikh Rabiʾ Ibn Al-Hadi Al-Madkhali

The contemporary ʿ*oulamas*, socialized in institutions of religious learning created during the second half of the twentieth century in Saudi Arabia, when the preceding generation had benefited from the precarious puritan education system on the peninsula (Ibn Baz, Ibn ʿOtheimine) or in Syria (Al-Albani), come off more as stakeholders in the Wahhabi-Saudi social compact. By virtue of a "routinization of charisma"[57] and an "institutionalization of religion,"[58] we can distinguish two profiles here.

The first has the hallmarks of the bureaucratic scholar. Sheikh Salih Ibn Fawzan Al-Fawzan (born in 1935) studied with the preceding virtuous generation but stood out for a religious career marked by the official Saudi predication apparatus. We learn from studying the quietist Salafi websites[59] that he is a graduate of the Shariʾa department in Riyadh and that he subsequently practiced at that city's Scientific Institute and at the Supreme Institute of Justice, whose director he became. He is today one of the most

---

[56] Lacroix, *Les islamistes saoudiens*, 260–262.
[57] Max Weber, *Économie et Société* (Economy and society), volume 1 (Paris: Plon, 1971), 249–258; Samuel N. Einsenstadt, *Max Weber on Charisma and Institution Building. Selected Papers, Edited with an Introduction* (Chicago: University of Chicago Press, 1968).
[58] Fuse Toyomasa, "Les institutions religieuses à la lumière des théories des institutions religieuses" (Religious institutions in the light of the theories of religious institutions), Concilium, no. 36 (1968): 129–147.
[59] http://salafway.free.fr/fawzan.html.

famous members of the Standing Committee of Islamic Research and Issuing Fatwas. If his work hardly contrasts with the principles defended by his predecessors who sang his praises, the place he occupies in the Saudi and globalized Salafist sphere attaches to his institutional position. Faithful to the teaching of Sheikh Ibn Baz, his preaching is corseted by his functions in the state's religious establishment, in contrast to his master, whose charisma and influence were essentially the product of a stronger personality.

The second representative of this generation, Sheikh Rabi Ibn Al-Hadi Al-Madkhali[60] (born in 1934), falls within a logic of scholarly university socialization. In contrast to Sheikh Fawzan, he is not part of the institutional state fabric. Even though he took a religious university course from the Shari'a faculty at Riyadh and then at the Islamic University of Medina, where Sheikh Ibn Baz was among his professors, as a cleric Al-Madkhali never took part in the highest instances of religious preaching of the Saudi state. However, he held various important posts at the University of Medina, where he taught the sciences of the hadith and was director of the Department of the Sunna. In 2011 he took the permanent chair of professor at the university. His progress and his rather more universitarian than bureaucratic influence are distinguished by a logic that is more intellectual: his output and his research work and teaching earned him a global influence. Taking advantage of the opening of Saudi religious universities in the 1970s, when the country started to build a Saudi-centered sphere of Islamic meaning, the influence of certain scholars like Madkhali is based on a reticular logic. To the extent that the Islamic university field became internationalized starting in the 1970s, the state-sanctioned official preaching is no longer the only one to be taken into account in the study of the globalized Salafi sphere.

Two Figures of the Local Salafi Preacher: The Transplanted Imam and the Student Who Returned to the Country

The passage from global Salafist sphere to national Salafist sphere and even to local is explained by the encounter between an offer and a demand for re-Islamization. The principal trait of this category of preachers relates to the fact that their work is geographically conditioned in the French Islamic fabric, as contrasted with the globalized clerics.

A transplanted imam, Sheikh Rajib, officiates at the mosque of the Indes subdivision in Sartrouville. This category of cadre is characterized by a

[60] http://www.alminhadj.fr/modules/news/article.php?storyid=94.

primary socialization in the country of origin and arrival in French society as an adult. As a transplanted cadre,[61] he remains wedded to the unifying and homogeneous dimension of the Salafist sphere. Originally from Mauretania, he is known for having studied with scholars who studied under the great clerics mentioned earlier, and for having dispensed with an education that is orthodox based on the Koran and the Sunna. An interface between the doctrine developed by the internationally renowned cadres of the Salafiyya 'ilmiyya ("Scientific Salafism," another way of calling quietist Salafism) and a population whose majority is ignorant, he is the producer of a norm with local reach. Benefiting from the aura surrounding all the men of science, Imam Rajib, whose slender, agile figure is emblematic of the scrupulous respect for Salafi sartorial custom, develops relationships with his students that are simultaneously hierarchical and cordial. This forty-year-old with a sparse beard, dark skin, and plain manners cultivates closeness with the town's young Salafis and those in the vicinity that affords him moments of complicity, even camaraderie with his disciples; he nonetheless remains the master who sets the correct interpretation of the scriptural sources. It is when he puts on his preacher's garb that the true nature of the connection with his disciples emerges, revealing one of the foundations of Salafist Islam. Down here on earth being by definition the domain of testing, which induces the imperative to remain constant throughout life in the face of the risks of deviationism that the world harbors, from this follows the obligation to remain attached to the Men of Righteousness, Constancy, and Faithfulness to the original oath. For several years he has been the keystone of the Salafi micro society that inhabits Sartrouville.

The second profile is that of the endogenous student born in France who left to study the religion in an Islamic land and then came back to teach his coreligionists. Nou'man, from a Moroccan immigrant family and a train driver with SNCF (the French national railway company), represents one of the first Salafi preachers to experience success during the 1990s. Nearing forty when interviewed in 2009 and the father of a large family (five children), he lives in southern Morocco, where his parents hail from, in a framework of a family *hijira*, but he delivers the ritual Friday sermon at the Salam (Peace) mosque in Maisons-Alfort. He is known for straight talk and for being one of

---

[61] Felice Dassetto, "L'Islam transplanté: Bilan des recherches européennes" (Transplanted Islam: State of European research), *Revue européenne des migrations internationales* 10, no. 2 (1994): 201–211.

the first to have preached the Salafi message in Nanterre, in several mosques in Seine-Saint-Denis and in Maisons-Alfort.

AUTHOR: When were you born, and where are you from?
NOU'MAN: I was born in '72, in Bobigny.
AUTHOR: Kindly explain to me how you became a *daʻi* [preacher].
NOU'MAN: [*Thinking*] In fact, you could say that I became a *daʻi* by accident, yes. I became *daʻi* without wanting it. . . . I became interested in religion and learning the Arabic language. I was young and starting my schooling. I really had no plans to become whatever. It's just that I had the chance of learning Arab very early in my childhood and adolescence and to become interested in religion.

. . .

AUTHOR: And so from that, how did you come to the Da'wa Salafiyya?
NOU'MAN: Let's say that the one who taught me got me to love it. I went to Paris, to a school for learning Arabic. I liked it a lot. But afterwards I studied on my own. With that professor I got into discussions—on Islam, about life and lots of things. I reached a good level of Arabic. . . . At that time also, I was continuing to learn Arabic, during the week in school, then also on the weekend. There was lots of noise about Islam. There were some Shiites. You have to remember that in '88, Khomeini was still alive. Me, I didn't know much, but thanks to the Arab school, I started to meet people. I even got acquainted with someone, a Shiite, who had a magazine whose name now escapes me.[62] But he was a Shiite. Me, I didn't know really what that was, but okay. . . . Later I met others, notably with my Arab teacher whom I mentioned, who explained to me things about Islam. He filled me in on their reality.
AUTHOR: That's how you became interested in Islam?
NOU'MAN: I'm saying that I did not attach myself blindly. I've never had a blind attachment. At the time, the Shiite Da'wa was stronger. The magazine I was talking about was published in three languages. The one who was in charge, I recall, was Abu Farid Al-Kabtani [Gabténi],[63] a

---

[62] The magazine in question was *La voix d'Islam* (Voice of Islam). See Gilles Kepel, *À l'Ouest d'Allah* (To the west from Allah) (Paris: Seuil, 1994).
[63] He is best known for having participated in organizing demonstrations against Salman Rushdie after the publication of his scandalous book, *Satanic Verses*.

Maghrebian, at the time of the Salman Rushdie fatwa. There were even some Maghrebian Shiites, but we didn't know.... Anyway, me, like I told you, I've never been impressed by people, even if an individual says things well, in the end I'm always looking at a human being like me.... I started to gravitate toward people I thought were educated.

AUTHOR: And then?

NOU'MAN: I made up my mind to go study abroad. So I went to Mauritania in '92, to Nouādhibou, but I did not take compulsory instruction from Da'wa scholars. Actually, they were not all that strongly Salafi. I also went to Syria in '94. I took some courses in mosques. I progressed. After that, I came back to France.

AUTHOR: So then how was it that you joined the Minhaj Salafi?

NOU'MAN: It is a godsend from Allah who blesses whom He wants. Really, no one came and talked me into it. I've always been independent-minded. It helped me during my journey. So, with my research, my knowledge of Arabic, I made my choice, and there you are.

AUTHOR: But more precisely, how was it you told yourself, "This Da'wa Salafiyya is for me"?

NOU'MAN: Here's the thing. Let's say that I always took people who make sense seriously. For example, when people talk about the Sunna, I saw that they were dressed according to Sunna, and no other way. I evaluated. There are people who say one thing but do another. It's how I look at things, I really like this way of acting. Already, that's a strong point for me.

. . .

AUTHOR: And how did you become a *da'i* then?

NOU'MAN: I began to teach classes at the Mosque of the Acacias in Nanterre. They called me, the people in the mosque knew I was available, so then I accepted. Then, later, I gave courses at Longjumeau, also at Bobigny. Today, at Maisons-Alfort, same principle, the people at the mosque knew I had been available for some time. They also proposed that I do some course here.... There's another thing, and that is that I always loved teaching. It interests me, even more so in religion. This is what I like.

The Salafi Habitus: Convert the Epistemic Rupture in the Social Arena

Call to Order: The Salafi as Guardian of Dogma

The first organizing principle of this habitus consists in the strong reminder of Salafis' moral engagement with the Creator: the worship of God in a pure and unchanged way. The matrix of all social practices,[64] venerating Allah translates in an empirical manner in a binary mode of the licit and the illicit. He who follows the true way becomes a vector for broadcasting the Truth. The armed force of an active proselytism without concession, the Salafi is the figure by which humanity is called back to its original duty to devote an exclusive worship to the Unique, inseparable from the wish to bring back others to the ways of moral righteousness and orthodoxy. This call to order participates in a process of symbolic elevation, thanks to which the Salafi is ahead of history, knows the true meaning of life and how to succeed here on earth.

The daily pursuit of blameworthy innovation by coreligionists not strong enough to break with what Islam disapproves of sets the Salafi up as guardian of the dogma, as the measure of all things Islamic. The moral prism by which a social practice, an individual, or a group is cataloged as orthodox or deviant, the Salafi, having mastered the administration of Islamic proof, has enthroned himself as the judge of an era that has strayed from the way of the original Islam. In his life, gestures and words are marked by a scenography of the sacred and an aesthetic symbolizing its moral distinctiveness. This is accompanied by a teleologic vision of human history into whose center he places himself. The Salafi appears when Islam is in the grip of the forces of evil: political sedition, social division, and religious heterodoxy. He enters the fray in order to restore a religion that is on the road to disintegration. The protesting dimension of Salafist preaching is clear here, because it is by venturing into the space of Islamic meaning that it takes on a reactive dimension structured around the idea that the religion has been betrayed. Practicants of "the Islam of the return to Islam," the upholders of the Da'wa Salafiyya think of their religiosity as a consequence of the doctrinal and sociological disruptions that endangered it.

---

[64] Rémy Puyuelo (ed.), *Les pratiques sociales: Une utopie utile* (Social practices: A useful utopia) (Toulouse: Erès, 2001).

History, consisting of a succession of cycles that are in essence challenges to the true faith, can engender only a sole legitimate posture: that of guardian of the dogma calling humanity back to its first vocation—allegiance to the principles of authentic Islam.

Orthopraxy

The second principle structuring the Salafist habitus is orthopraxy. Since Islam constitutes a complete system of values and practices whose purpose is to govern the ensemble of the believer's actions, he must perform daily rituals and gestures as faithfully as possible. At stake is the sincerity and quality of his belief. The appropriate practice also has a statutory finality, for it is this objective quality that authorizes the Salafi to call his coreligionists to task. The search for the most legitimate form of religious expression furnishes its daily program. This morality moreover justifies a differentialist ethic based on the irrefutable proofs of its religious superiority. The psychological dynamic, a permanent self-hypnosis phenomenon, functions as if inscribing his religiosity in everyday life ends up giving him the proof of his ability to be a guide. Sanctifying the routine and routinizing the sacred furnish the substrate of the mechanism of self-persuasion in whose name he attains the quality of pious contemporary. Conforming to the ritual framework prescribed by the clerics permits a Salafist sphere to appear in an Islamic sphere that is perceived as incapable of resisting modernity. Practicing Islam with rectitude as a microsociological resource in parallel with the macrosociological resources furnished by the Saudi state makes possible a positive differentiation.

The Noah Syndrome

The third axiom pertains to the vision of salvation. In theory this is reserved for the Salafis, for it is accorded only to someone who has pursued the road of Truth. However, in reality, this problem is more complicated. A dual reality is discernible when discussing this subject with practicants. They see the best chance of garnering divine approval for being admitted to Paradise (*jannat an-naʾim*) in their religious practice, but when questioned if they know whether their coreligionists are eligible for the same reward, their replies are vague. The hadith of sixty-three sects, the pivotal element of Salafist doctrine, is key in the discourse of practicants. This text in large part explains the relationship between a monopoly on expressing Islam truthfully and salvation in the afterlife. With the Tradition according a choice place to the authenticated prophetic sayings, the Salafis overvalue them by reason of the justification that it seems to give them. The majority of those we were in contact with therefore knew of this hadith:

> The Jews are divided into seventy-one factions and the Christians are divided into seventy-two factions. And my community will be divided into seventy-three factions, all will go to hell except for one.
> They say: "Who will they be, O messenger of Allah?"
> He says: "All those who are my companions and myself today." And in another version: "They are the Djamā'ah" [Community].[65]

The term "sect" is utilized in the Tradition as a synonym for "group" or "faction." By this hadith the Prophet specifies that religious division, which the Salafis loathe, perverts the message. A menace like this justifies clinging to the sacred texts.

If division has fractured Judaism as well as Christianity into seventy-one and seventy-two sects, respectively, all of them destined for perdition in the beyond because they were led astray by their clerics, Islam will not be spared fragmentation into seventy-three sects. However, while the near-totality of deviant sects is also condemned to failure in the same way, one only is destined for eternal salvation for having chosen to stay constant on the road of Truth and orthodoxy. The Muslims who belong to this saved group (*al-firqa an-najiyya*) or this victorious faction (*at-taifa al-manssoura*) are the true People of the Sunna and of the Consensus/of the Assembly (*ahl as-Sunna wal-Jam'a*), the only Muslims to have embraced the model established by Muhammad and next adopted by the Companions and then the people following in the footsteps of the first Muslims. The identification of a group saved by its constancy explains why many Salafis develop a Noah syndrome, or exclusive salvation complex, like the prophet by that name who, heeding the divine call, could save himself from the deluge and the scant few who joined him.

---

[65] The true hadith pivot of Salafist thought, this prophetic saying generally benefits from an explanation of choice on the Salafist web: http://www.manhajulhaqq.com/spip.php?article225; http://www.al.baida.online.fr/les_reglesbasesmanhaj.htm; http://www.sounna.com/spip.php?article16.

Resistance and Persistence

The fourth characteristic trait is the principle of resistance and persistence. To be the guardian of the dogma and to be called to an exclusive salvation implies cultivating the determination not to succumb to the world's variability. Bearers of a project of liberating others, the Salafis credit the conversions to their religiosity for their moral uprightness and resistance to social change. This ethic sets the Salafi up as a beacon in the night of modernity.

A Stranger among His Contemporaries

The fifth and last axiom refers to the figure of the stranger. Incapable of generalizing the norms for all of society or even for a significant part of the faithful, the Salafi becomes a stranger in his country and his era.[66] Intransigent, he contrasts sharply with the accepted sociocultural codes. In the name of an exclusive allegiance to the authentic precepts, he develops a perception of himself that approaches religious stoicism. He incarnates the figure of the Islamic virtuoso, and his existence is strictly extraordinary in a society overcome by the profane and by hostility toward the Truth. His strange mores in the dominant system of French society lead him to positivize his exteriority with regard to the world. Assuming that he does not belong to the era, he claims that he is in fact not of this country. Stranger in a society whose principles he does not share, he sees his habitus of rupture reinforced by the belief that his future does not lie in the land of unbelief, from which he cultivates a heroism that springs from his aptitude for cutting himself off from the world in the name of superior values. He can therefore not realize himself except by leaving a country seen as a prison for his puritan aspirations. His status of stranger comes to reinforce this intransigent attitude stripped of all complexity. Extraordinarily ordinary because he does nothing but reproduce a forgotten norm, and ordinarily extraordinary because he cultivates a sociality inspired by the sacred that is overlaid on a commonplace way of life in the midst of fellow men astonished by so much moral rectitude and religious constancy, the Salafi incarnates a frustrated serenity.

---

[66] It is therefore no wonder that many Salafist websites in French take the name of www.alghourabaa.free.fr. In Arab, the term *al-ghouraba* means "the strangers" and is the title of a Koranic sura.

2
Pyramidal Socialization

Salafi Militant Apoliticism and the Control of French Islam's Political Agenda

Pyramidal socialization deploys first of all in the arena of politics. Viewed properly, the position of the Salafis is a demobilization and disengagement with respect to militancy, with the theorization of political challenges past, present, and future taking place in a moralizing and radical mode.[1] Salafist sociality in matters of political morality harks back to the example of alternative groups in the United States in the years 1960–1970: the Salafist way of life and socialization are comparable to the countercultures in vogue during that era and are built on opposition to the dominant culture in the form of a moral radicalism.[2]

Politicization is the aspect of the socialization process that impacts the political arena. Salafis embrace a moralizing and militant apoliticism that characterizes their relationship to the politics of the humanitarians. Viewed as the domain where man's passion will push him into forgetting the orthodox worship of God, the political sphere is regarded negatively, with disengagement and demobilization the chosen rules of conduct. We can compare the political offer of the Salafis to that of a nongovernmental organization in which, in fine, the individual and collective welfare will guide an eventual politicization.

---

[1] According to Hirschmann's template for interpreting mobilizations, which is formulated in terms of defection, voicing opinions, and loyalty, the Salafist viaticum appeals to a "defectionist" posture in relation to the "godless" spheres of power, to a "speaking" posture in order to counsel other Muslims in a moralizing mode to not integrate in a society opposed to the Muslim norm, and to a "loyalist" strategy vis-à-vis the Muslim powers established de facto at the top of majority-Muslim societies. See Albert Otto Hirschmann, *Face au déclin des entreprises et des institutions* (Confronting the decline of enterprises and institutions) (Paris: Les Éditions ouvrières, 1972), 10–11; Lionel Arnaud and Christine Guionnet (eds.), *Les frontières du politique: Enquête sur les processus de politisation et de dépolitisation* (The frontiers of politics: Inquiry into the processes of politicization and depoliticization) (Rennes: Presses Universitaires de Rennes, 2005), 14–15.

[2] Marie-Christine Granjon, *L'Amerique de la contestation: Les années 60 aux États Unis* (The United States of dissent: The '60s in the United States) (Paris: Presses de Sciences Po, 1985), 23–24.

Salafism Goes Global. Mohamed-Ali Adraoui, Oxford University Press (2020). © Oxford University Press.
DOI: 10.1093/oso/9780190062460.001.0001

In Salafist militant apoliticism, the militant expert finds himself supplanted by the scholarly expert in defining and interpreting the political stakes. The scholarly expert is tasked with reminding Salafis to worship Allah (among others, a *political* mission) and to deter them from activism in the classical sense. The example of the debates that preceded the vote on the law of March 15, 2004, on the wearing of religious symbols in public schools showcases Salafis' slight propensity for joining the throngs of militants that demonstrated in the streets of Paris for the right to wear the hijab (Islamic headscarf) in public institutions of learning. Several years later, the ban on wearing the niqab (full veil) did not impel Salafis to mobilize in the public square. Bilal (a young convert from the Southern suburb of Paris) gave us his analysis of the debate concerning the hijab and its ban in French primary and secondary schools. He also brought up the debate about the niqab:

AUTHOR: Would you say that you can practice Islam fittingly in France? Especially when seeking to follow the ancients?

BILAL: In France? . . . [*Brief moment of reflection*]. In France you can practice Islam, but . . . someone who wants to work, to practice his religion while trying to meets his needs, he will have difficulty joining [*sic*] the two: keep the religion and make a living. . . . Most companies refuse to allow acts of religious devotion during working hours. What to do in that case? When it comes to prayers, for instance? You can't hear the *adan* [call to prayer] when it matters. In the Muslim countries, you hear the *adan*. . . . But above all, they want to change the laws of Islam, for example with regard to the veil. In France they want to lift the obligation of the veil. You understand . . . while they talk about liberty for anyone. Picture the suspicion with which they regard Muslims. A girl who undresses has the right to do it, but a girl who wants to protect her modesty . . .

AUTHOR: But tell me, did you think of going into politics to defend the rights of Muslims?

BILAL: Politics in this country? They would never accept my going into politics. They need to adapt their society to Islam, but they do everything they can to make Islam adapt itself to their society. You want an example? The veil. Their politics and Islam are separable.

AUTHOR: Yes, but let's take the vote, for instance. You don't plan to vote to tip the balance toward the side of Islam? For that matter, what do you think of the scholars' advice on voting?

BILAL: There is a split about voting. Some scholars forbid it regardless of circumstances. For them, it's clear, you do not vote even if it supposedly would turn out to be useful in certain cases. For Albani, it's the rule of the lesser evil. When you are in a Muslim country, and if there is the choice of whatever lesser evil, one would be permitted to vote.

AUTHOR: And you, if they authorized you to vote in France, who would you vote for?

BILAL: In France I don't feel drawn to anyone. My position is that it's necessary to leave this country. How do you expect me to accept the dissoluteness, the pornographic images plastered all over the billboards? There are serious things that must not be accepted. If some want to accept them, fine for them, but me, no.

AUTHOR: And do you feel attracted to one party rather than another? On the left, for example, as opposed to the right? You know, they say that, generally speaking, people from the suburbs feel closer to the left. In opposition to Sarkozy (considered to among many French Muslims as antiIslam and antiimmigrants), for example.

BILAL: Like socialism and all that? It's all the same. These are laws made by man. These are no good laws, because they are from societies known to be deviant, and that is where they have more murders, more crime. This very well proves the uselessness of these laws.

AUTHOR: And you think that it is better in some Muslim countries?

BILAL: In Saudi Arabia they have the least number of violations. The people in the West criticize the Shari'a as something barbaric, inhumane, when you find only a few thieves, fornicators, and no drugs; this is a pure society. While it is in the most developed countries that you find the most evil.

AUTHOR: And, just for the sake of example, between Nicolas Sarkozy (French President from 2007 to 2012) and Jacques Chirac (French President from 1995 to 2007), which one would you prefer?

BILAL: Sarko is worse! It's been under his government that they tried most to infringe on the Muslims. That law against the *sitar* (a type of full facial veil)[3] . . . that one's the enemy! I won't say Chirac is good, but he doesn't do that.

. . .

AUTHOR: What's your opinion of the vote on the law of 2004, banning the veil in schools?

---

[3] Later I provide a more in-depth definition and analysis of the *sitar* phenomenon.

BILAL: That 2004 law is no good. It's done a lot of harm to Islam. It opens a door to temptation, it encourages intimate relations at an early age, and it favors coeducation.

AUTHOR: And why not organize demonstrations to protest the proposed law while it was being debated? Certain individuals in the UOIF (Union of the Islamic Organizations in France, main movement related to the Muslim Brotherhood) did it, for example. In other currents they did as well.

BILAL: But the scholars prohibited demonstrations, because it leads to disorder and also because of the resemblance to nonbelievers. For all that, it also implies mixing of men and women in the same place, the disorder that can cause. But as I said, the degradation in public places, the authentic Islam has formally forbidden havoc and stirring up strife.

AUTHOR: And what do you think of banning the niqab?

BILAL: It's a bad law. It's because it lets the sisters who wear the niqab show that they are different. They feel attacked for being different. I don't understand it. I don't see where it's bad. The person who wears the niqab, she's not forcing anyone to adhere to her convictions. As long as we don't proselytize, it shouldn't cause any problems.

AUTHOR: And how would you answer those who bring up the question of the niqab from the aspect of women's dignity and the relations between men and women? You must have heard about the debate concerning the women of Islam.

BILAL: Careful! We are mixing everything up. Islam advocates equality between the man and the woman insofar as rights are concerned, but not the same functions. They educate themselves, they inherit, they study their religion, et cetera. But the functions are not the same. The man has his functions, the woman has hers. The man has rights where the woman is concerned, the woman has rights vis-à-vis the man. For example, the woman must remain at home to look after her husband's property and the children. If she is a pious wife, she looks after things while he is traveling, for instance.... She must not show herself in the street because the frequency with which women go into the street is a factor in adultery. Mixing creates opportunities that can end up in adultery.

AUTHOR: And if they ever pass a law that bans the wearing of the niqab, how will that affect you?

BILAL: If they implement that law, it will lead to numerous problems, like, for example, resistance to the forces of law and order.... It might even come to clashes, to riots. Those inclined to revolt will say "We're being attacked!," and in response to the attacks they'll destroy things in that country, they'll burn cars. . . . But that is bad behavior. For the Salafi, he will fault them but also himself. He will say, "If I were not in this country, they could not do me this harm." If he has no way of leaving, he'll plead with Allah to take care of the problems. He'll make *dou'a* [invocations], he'll ask for patience, but the *takfiris* [excommunicators], those who have misunderstood Islam [*raises his fist and physically contorts his face, which we interpret as his way of describing* takfiri *morals*], they'll respond to it with reprisals. We Salafis . . . we can defend ourselves. If someone strikes our wife, for instance, it is normal to defend your relatives and property, but do so without going on the offensive. The best way of responding to this attack is to leave the country, the *hijira*. Just like the prophet left Mecca . . . they left Mecca for Medina and were free to observe Allah's commandments. Because the Prophet and his Companions furnish the best examples to follow. It is by following the Sunna that we win. Strictly observing the Sunna will make all problems disappear, all the inconveniences.

We can draw three lessons from this. The first attaches to the vampirization or demonization of the political and religious alterity incarnated in French elites. Thus we note the frequency with which the pronoun "they" occurs in Bilal's statements. Bringing the deciders into it (without ever employing a precise designation), he insists on the relationship between domination and French society's opposition to the Muslim community, especially when the latter appears inflexible, defending and promoting values from another era that it judges to be ontologically superior to contemporary values. This vindictive aspect reflects a principle of resistance as well as a sentiment of being divinely chosen. The more "they" go after the manifestations of religious purity, the more the Salafis are sure that they are on the right path, so long as they are never called to wear the yoke of a foreign iniquitous power or influence. The essence of the link that makes them oppose French institutions resides in conflict, at least symbolically. In contrast to the Islamic currents that preach negotiation within the republican framework based on moderated demonstrations of piety in the public square, the Salafis would not know how to abandon their pretension to totality. Their reading of society's challenges comes close to the "radical fundamentalism" conceptualized by

Jean-Marie Donegani,[4] who utilizes this concept to describe the behavior of certain Catholic groups in reacting to secularism and the separation of church and state. The accommodating ethic of militant Muslims or the refusal to make Islam the center of daily life, especially among private Muslims or traditionalists, eventually will compromise the faith and reinforce positions that are hostile to Islam. Intent on preserving religious authenticity, the Salafis end up eschewing all engagement with the political debate, even when it is likely to lead to an attack on Muslim rights. According to the typology developed by Nancy Venel, the followers of Tariq Ramadan or the UOIF are "accommodationists" because their Islamity finds its meaning in fertilizing the social field with religious morality. They combine "integral religious affiliation and anti-authoritarian citizenship," since their relationship to society is characterized by "a dual civic and religious belonging."[5] Their religious practice nonetheless remains characterized by a form of subordination to the French context.

As for the Salafis, they are "neo-communitarians," characterized by an "introverted assertion of identity and [an] anti-authoritarian citizenship."[6] Living in a "perception of territorial exclusion," "[they] have the sense of evolving in a diffuse climate of hostility. They say they are subjected daily to discrimination, lack of respect, and a delegitimization of their presence. The way they are regarded, be it in school or in the professions or simply in the street, is intolerable to them. They are continually reminded of their origins."[7] In particular:

> The neo-communitarians decline the invitation to share the ensemble of the characteristics of a collective national identity, favoring instead the promotion of a differentiating identity. . . . They know themselves to be in a space that belongs to them and that supersedes the (artificial in their view) borders of states: the *Umma*, the extraterritorial community of believers . . . whose existence stems more from a mental construct than reality. The place of residence is immaterial. It engenders neither allegiance nor affectivity. Identifying with France is not possible (or desired).[8]

---

[4] Jean-Marie Donegani, *La liberté de choisir: Pluralisme religieux et pluralism politique dan le catholicisme français contemporain* (The freedom to choose: Religious pluralism and political pluralism in contemporary French Catholicism) (Paris: Pressed de Sciences Po, 1993).
[5] Venel, *Musulmans et Citoyens*, 77, 59.
[6] Ibid., 165.
[7] Ibid., 174–175.
[8] Ibid., 247.

This exclusive Islam upholds a contradictory posture of moralizing indifference: its followers reserve the privilege of harboring as many value judgments as necessary to warn Muslims against modernity, all the while staying on guard against ever engaging in or actively opposing the French political arena. Their posture can be compared to that of someone who turns away from a brawl, judging that it does not concern him and that the parties involved are on the wrong path no matter what the outcome, yet he keeps an eye on the fight and his coreligionists who want to intervene in the dispute. Discourse that combines democracy and secularity leaves no room for faith. The identities of *citizen* and *believer* are mutually exclusive. The faith that the integrationist Muslims of the UOIF or those close to Tariq Ramadan practice is the fruit of an *isomorphism*: here the context has shaped the definition of the Muslim condition and religious practice. This renders unacceptable certain strategies that do not take into account the dominant sociopolitical norm in the definition of the individual or of the group. Secularism in France, in the same way as sustainable development or environmental protection, is subject to a quasi-consensus that impacts both the perception that a social group has of itself and its political or social agenda. The manner in which the law of 1905 (French Law on the Separation of the Churches and the State) was integrated into the discourse of organizations representing militant Islam symbolizes a dynamic of isomorphism. In this case, we even speak of an "institutional isomorphism"[9] (the norm adopted by an entity proceeds from societal, media, and political pressure). Among the Salafis, the opposite is the rule. What they are after is saving differentiation, not integration (voluntary or forced) of a system of values and practices emanating from a society that is implacably foreign and iniquitous. Interaction with the French environment is a negative-sum game: that which is *given* in France represents something *taken away* from the true Islam. Thus a refusal to vote indicates the militant depoliticization that typifies the relationship to politics of the upholders of the true way.

A second point concerns the politicization of the *hijra*. As Bilal told us, "the strategy of departure" from the French social space is conceived of as a self-preservation solution that is religiously justified. Although the majority of Muslims have consented to tolerate the perversity and iniquity of nonbelievers, the Salafis do not plan to remain in hostile territory. And this

---

[9] P. J. Di Maggio and W. Powell, "The Iron Cage Revisited: Institutional Isomorphism and Collective Rationality in Organizational Fields," *American Sociological Review*, no. 48 (1983): 147–160.

plays a role in a political understanding of the *hijra*: a salutary migration takes on a protective but also pyramidal dimension, since the positive differentiation that typifies it turns the practicants into beings capable of physically breaking away from France solely by force of will. Going to a country where the names of Allah and his Prophet are not trampled on, Salafis emerge into the light, awakening[10] to the realization that only an ersatz Islam can survive in France. We asked Bilal where he would hope to live if he had the chance to leave France:

AUTHOR: In your view, which are the best countries for living in as a good Muslim? To make the *hijra*, for example.

BILAL: [*Our question barely finished*] Saudi Arabia... Yemen, Egypt. Mali, in Africa. Mali is better than Senegal because there have been many *toulab al-ʿilm* [students (seekers) of science] who did the Daʾwa there. There were also scholars there. Me, I'd like to go to Saudi Arabia and, if not, to Yemen, *inchʾallah*. But I'd like to finish my life in Senegal. If they don't grant me a visa to Arabia, I'll go study in Egypt, where I was already, but it will be Africa for finishing my life, in Senegal [his family's native country].

AUTHOR: And what about Afghanistan?

BILAL: Afghanistan before was good. There was a real jihad. People studied their religion. There was a Daʾwa Salafiyya. The believers practiced true jihad. Then came bin Laden. He took the reins. He arrived with his money, he's a rich man, and he turned the people's heads around. There used to be a great scholar in Afghanistan, Jamiʾou Rahman Al-Afghani,[11] he had a real Daʾwa and people practiced the real Islam. Afghanistan was Daʾwa country.... Like Sheikh Fawzan said, there are two types of jihad:[12] defensive jihad for repelling an attack, like when the Russians entered Afghanistan. Jamiʾou Rahman Al-Afghani united the Muslims on the basis of *tawhid*.... He talked with a jihadist and told him that for a jihad they needed an emir, but he [the jihadist] answered, "What does it take to have an emir?" He [the sheikh] responded that if the Muslims united

---

[10] The Salafists have a Platonic view of life in France and the religious practice that it engenders. Reduced to evolving inside the "French cave," Muslims are lied to and made to believe that the Islam they are following is good.

[11] A cleric educated in Saudi Arabia who returned to preach an intact Islam in his country of Afghanistan, where he was killed: http://as-salafiyyah.overblog.com/sheykh-djamil-our-rahman-al-afghani.html.

[12] See "La parole de Shaykh Salih Al Fawzane sur les conditions du jihad," Scribd, http://www.scribd.com/doc/10970131/La-Parole-de-Shaykh-Salih-Al-Fawzane-Sure-Les-Conditions.

according to *tasfiyya wa-tarbiyya*,¹³ after that they could do jihad. You can do it on the basis of uniqueness. Strategic unity would come from uniting around the credo.... That is what the Prophet did: First, he preached to the Companions against associationism, and so on. The factor behind unity is *tawhid*.... Where *tawhid* is lacking, like in Palestine or Iraq, the enemies benefit from it. Why do you think the Palestinians have to be *'ammar*?¹⁴

AUTHOR: Where, in your view, is jihad legitimate in the world? The talk is of jihadism, but no one knows where it is ultimately legitimate. For example, is Iraq a territory for legitimate jihad? About Afghanistan too, along with Pakistan, there's been an enormous amount of talk. What do you think?

BILAL: There was a jihad in Afghanistan, also in Chechnya. Not in Iraq, not in Afghanistan today. Whenever there is no emir, there's no jihad. The Taliban, before, they were Salafis, but not now. They've become ... bizarre. Bin Laden arrived with his Da'wa of *takfiri*, when they'd stopped cultivating opium, they were in *tasfiyya wa-tarbiyya*, Shari'a applied, there was no injustice, and the women were veiled. Bin Laden, he called for jihad; he enticed them, without passing through the *tawhid*, without adopting this methodology. The scholar I mentioned to you [Jami'ou Rahman Al-Afghani] was killed by the Northern Alliance, by Commander Massoud, an *ikhwan* (a Muslim Brother). He allied himself with the Westerners because he didn't like the Taliban. It was one of his followers that killed that scholar, when all the scholars had spoken well of him. He was a Salafi, but bin Laden, he oriented them toward hating the West. People reverted to being what they had been. They went back to worshipping graves and cultivating opium. It was the return of Muslim decadence. The Americans came, they turned against the governor. Bin Laden fled. That story we know.

AUTHOR: And as for jihad in Islam?

BILAL: For us, it's the *jihad al-talab* [defensive jihad]. Before, people saw how Muslims behaved and they converted like that. That is truly the light of Allah.... It is wrong to say Islam is violent. If there were wars, there must not have been that many. It's false to say that Islam is violent and calls

---

¹³ Bilal here repeats the famous saying (justification of militant apoliticism) of Sheikh Al-Albani, according to which "it makes for good politics these days to leave politics behind" (see chapter 1 in this volume).

¹⁴ A modern word meaning "to fill," "to fulfill," "to make oneself," *'ammar* also conveys the sense of "receiving blows," an expression used in the present case for describing the situation of the Palestinians.

for war. Muslims before were engaged in commerce, that's how they got people to convert.

Finding a substitute product for best quality Islam, especially in Saudi Arabia, the Gallic way is bound to be unsatisfactory. Where a majority of Muslims seem to accord importance to legitimate mechanisms of political participation, such as electoral participation, the Salafis "vote with their feet," in the sense Hirschmann employed when he analyzed the emigration from Eastern European countries to Western European societies.[15] Salafist socialization therefore is to be understood as an obligation to teach contemporaries in the religious domain (*voice strategy*), while, in the political field, only an ethic of loyalty toward the Muslim states is justifiable if life in a non-Muslim society makes a moral and physical departure imperative (*exit strategy*).

In the third place, the practicants reject political engagement in favor of a radical and soteriological moralism; this makes Salafist militant apoliticism postmillenarian, whereby the wise practice of religion prevails over the infantilism of wanting to precipitate an uncertain political revolution. Such postmillenarianism discredits any enterprise with that aim. According to the doctrine of salvation, the sole posture grounded Islamically is to rely on God in the face of a given social problematic. This does not mean that Salafist apoliticism will never resort to a large-scale mobilization to defend the Muslim religion if the time is ripe. Yet regardless of circumstances, such an action will be up to the scholars to approve. Even though they deny it and consider it to be a pure moral religious issue, what we have here represents a question of a political thought. Indeed, the problem of how a city should be ruled has clearly been tackled and theorized. What is targeted and denounced is the fact that this matter usually divides people, not that how best organize a city.[16] On the other hand, the Islamic state will someday materialize, if for no other reason that its arrival is predicted in Koranic times. Engagement is possible, on the condition that there is proof of the relevance of the moment of assumed politicization, when quietism must give way to militancy.

The Palestinian question without doubt best illustrates the greatest gap between the Salafist position and that of numerous militant Muslim organizations agitating for this cause. Between December 27, 2008, and January 18, 2009, the Gaza Strip was the subject of an intense barrage by the Israeli army

---

[15] Hirschmann, *Face au déclin*.
[16] Gilles Kepel and Jean-Pierre Milelli (eds.), *Al-Quaida dans le texte* (Al-Qaeda in texts) (Paris: PUF, "Proche Orient," 2008), 313.

under Operation Cast Lead, during which more than fourteen hundred Palestinians perished, including several hundred children. This impassioned conflict is the one that most impacted the Muslim world during the years of my research on Salafism, not to mention the numerous crises framed by antagonistic relations with the West that called out to the planetwide Muslim conscience. At a time when masses of people demonstrated in protest and demanded a halt to the massacres, the contrary movement in the Salafist communities has to be noted. The Salafis aligned themselves with fatwas issued by the clerics, particularly the one promulgated by the grand mufti of the kingdom of Saudi Arabia, Abdel Aziz Al Sheikh, while the fighting in Gaza was in full swing and the streets of the great Arab cities (Cairo, Damascus) and London, Paris, and Madrid regularly filled with demonstrators. This fatwa[17] qualified the act of demonstrating in the street as a "senseless act" and ordered a stop to the "bedlam" in favor of donating blood or money to the victims. The grand mufti finds an echo in Saudi Arabia, in the person of Sheikh Saleh Al-Luhaydan, the head of the kingdom's Supreme Judicial Council, who characterizes the demonstrations as "corruption [*fassad*] on earth" and individuals who call for expressing anger in the street as only "[diverting] people and [preventing] them from invoking God."[18] Where many Muslims see duplicity by the Saudi elites allied with the Western nations, the followers of the true way have developed a policy position that is radically different from that of militant Islam. Abdelsamad, formerly named Francisco (he is a convert in his 30s of Portuguese descent), provides us with the example:

AUTHOR: How did you experience the events in Gaza? Were you thinking about the fatwa by the grand mufti of Saudi Arabia, who came out against demonstrating?

ABDELSAMAD: Bah, he's right. Frankly, what good will it do? You think it will change anything? Did the people who took part stop the Israelis from firing on the Palestinians? No. Well? He was right in issuing this fatwa. You think the Muslims should make noise in the street? No, what they really need is to learn their religion, believe me. It's not by making noise that you'll instill fear, on the contrary. That is far removed from Islam.

---

[17] For a fatwa by Sheikh Fawzan on the legal status of participating in demonstrations, see "Demonstrating Is Not Good Behavior," https://salafislam.fr/organiser-rassemblements-manifestations-sheikh-al-fawzan/

[18] https://www.islamsounnah.com/les-revoltes-et-troubles-politiques-sheikh-al-louhaydan/.

AUTHOR: And what do you tell those who say the sheikh is remote-controlled by the king so as not to call on the people to show their discontent?

ABDELSAMAD: That's plain ignorant. In Saudia [sic], it's like this. The officials and the scholars, they get together to decide what to do. The people who say that, they don't know what happens and they criticize. They're ignorant.... How many billions has the king of Saudia sent to the Palestinians? How many? Well, let those who demonstrate keep demonstrating.

AUTHOR: Do you think he tries to help them secretly?

ABDELSAMAD: Why not? It is written in Islam that when you do good, don't talk about it, keep it to yourself. The ignorant people just talk. [*His tone hardens slightly.*] The scholars know better than them what needs to be done, they see things that the others don't see. And then they criticize the scholars. Can you imagine? It upsets me, people who talk out of ignorance. It's always emotions. People do things without thinking.

AUTHOR: What do you think is going on with the Palestinians? Why are they oppressed?

ABDELSAMAD: To start with, they ought to stop fighting among each other. Stop dividing themselves and fighting each other, because it helps their enemies.

AUTHOR: What are you suggesting?

ABDELSAMAD: Bah, shouldn't you know, of all people? You specialize in politics, right? The Palestinians haven't been beating each other up, for how long? Hamas and Hezbollah haven't been killing each other?

AUTHOR: Not always. What do you mean by that? Hamas and Hezbollah? They've never fought each other.

ABDELSAMAD: [*Ironic tone, a bit condescending*] They never fought each other? A year or two ago, they didn't fight each other?

AUTHOR: Oh, you mean Hamas and Fatah?[19]

ABDELSAMAD: That's it! Hamas and Fatah, sorry. Hamas and Fatah. Hamas and Fatah didn't fight for power?

AUTHOR: Sure, sure. And that, as far as you're concerned, explains that they are oppressed and occupied by the Israelis?

ABDELSAMAD: What else? They're not united, they wrangle over power, and they ignore their religion. It's no wonder they beat each other up.

---

[19] Our interviewee is referring to the bloody clashes in the Gaza Strip in the summer of 2007, one year after the electoral victory of Hamas.

AUTHOR: And so you, during the Israeli strikes on the Gaza population, you did not think about taking part in demonstrations in support of the Palestinians? Not even once?

ABDELSAMAD: Nope. Anyway, how would I have? The fundamental rules of Islam are not respected. I didn't make up the mixing that goes on in the demonstrations. I have a brother who works at Renault with me, in Guyancourt [site of the car maker's Technocenter], who took part in the demonstrations.... He's a practicant, but he is more *ikhwan*, you see. He told me I should participate in the demos, but I told him, "How to do it in the presence of sisters? You'll touch them, hear their voices. They will raise their voices, when that's not allowed." He didn't answer me, he just told me you have to express your anger, you had to do something and not stay on the sidelines. And you know what?

AUTHOR: What?

ABDELSAMAD: The day after the demonstration, I told him, "Well, how did it go?" He told me, "Good." But in talking to him, I asked him if he said prayers when he was demonstrating along with the others. And get this, he said no. He couldn't do it because, you know, he was busy demonstrating. He missed a prayer, he skipped a prayer while he was demonstrating. When you say that, you've said it all.

...

AUTHOR: In your opinion, what impels some Muslim countries and non-Muslim countries to fight?

ABDELSAMAD: It's nothing new, it's always been like that, the wars against Islam. They don't want the Truth to spread. It doesn't suit them. We know very well if the true Islam spreads, it will destroy them.

AUTHOR: And what do you say to people who maintain that Islam is a violent religion that seeks to dominate? There are, for example, the extremists who only see things their own way. Some of them, for instance, cast the *takfir* [excommunication] on other Muslims, also on those in power.

ABDELSAMAD: [*In a didactic manner and a tone that is both moralizing and professorial*] Oh, not at all! Those are the *ikhwan* that do the *takfir*! Render unto Caesar the things that are Caesar's! No, we appeal for respect for religion, it's the *ikhwan* who call for rebellion against the governing elite. We never do that. Did you ever see a Salafi cast the *takfir* on a government leader? Believe me, if he did that, he would be a strange Salafi, with a weird *'aqida* (creed), a Salafi with his head screwed on backwards.

The Quest for Status through Economic Independence

If the political arena is an object of defiance, it is different in the economic sphere, which enjoys a positive image because it constitutes the domain for realizing the Islamic self by pushing the believer onto the way of the Prophet and the first Muslims. As long as it respects the prohibitions prescribed by Islamic morality, the economy is the object of a veritable strategy (religiously and socially grounded) of engagement (in word *and* deed), for two reasons. The first has to do with the political vision of economics, by which Salafis strive to escape from the godless society. The second resides in the accomplishment of the commercial and entrepreneurial vocation of the religious ethic. Where the other Muslims "are bent"[20] and placed under the heel of the repressive state, the commercial dimension recovers status and political scope. The economy is in the service of Salafist desocialization in relation to the norms and standards of French society. Since earning a wage leaves no room for respecting the imperative of worshipping God, it leads to a resocialization in an economic area structured around the principle of independence and symbolic opposition. Here are the remarks made by Othman (a young convert and an entrepreneur from the city of Athis-Mons), whom we asked about his profession and how he conceived the economic ethics bearing on his projects. The scene takes place after a course taught by Yassir, a young Salafi imam, in early 2008 at the Red Cross Mosque in Athis-Mons. Othman suggested picking us up at the RER train station in Juvisy-sur-Orge. He drove a Peugeot commercial vehicle behind whose backseat was piled a lot of material for use in assembling kitchen furniture. Seeing these items, we asked Othman what he did for a living:

OTHMAN: [*While driving*] I install marble for private customers in their kitchens. I'm self-employed and I work with some brothers.
AUTHOR: You only work with brothers?
OTHMAN: Yes, a long time already, more than a few years. At times, when the work load is not so heavy, when there are fewer contracts, I can't call everyone, but it works out, *al-hamdoulilah* [God be praised], there's nothing to complain about. . . .

---

[20] We quote the words with which Othman, a Salafi having taken up Islam, situated for us the believers living in France who want to play the integration game.

AUTHOR: What did your father do?

OTHMAN: He did a variety of things. He was on his own. He worked hard but made a good living. Me, I think he did the right thing. He paid a lot of taxes to the state, but at least he had a real business, he was his own boss. [*Here we sensed a moment of sincere admiration for the entrepreneurial father, a native of Spain.*] He was also very intelligent. So I thought that that's the way to go. I didn't wait around for someone to give me a job.

AUTHOR: So how does it go, day by day? An example: when your clients see that you have a beard and that you wear the *qamis* (Islamic dress for males)?

OTHMAN: No problem. People can see I'm not trying to put one over on them. . . . I do good work. The work is clean, and they say thanks. Some even refer our name to other people, and that's how one thing leads to another. There are no problems. I observe my religion, but I work normally. Most recently, I installed a kitchen for . . . [*slight hesitation*] Anyway, I'm not going to tell you how much, but the money isn't bad. The clients were very satisfied.

AUTHOR: I imagine so. I'm not surprised. But you won't tell me how much? It embarrasses you, or?

OTHMAN: [*With a frank, sincere laugh*] No, not at all, but good money, you know, people don't like to talk about it to just anyone. Anyway, I made good money, *al-hamdoulilah*. Don't worry about it.

AUTHOR: Okay, so how much do you gross? Ten thousand euros? Five thousand?

OTHMAN: [*Another frank, sincere laugh*] Bah . . . ha, ha, ha. . . [*slight pause while he holds the smile*]. Well, the gross isn't far off from what you say, maybe even a little more. When the work is plentiful, it's about that. That should do it.

AUTHOR: Do you have any complexes about money?

OTHMAN: Pfff! No, why? Look, you work, it's to earn money, help others, not to get stepped on, it's normal. Why do you think people work? *Allah Zawjel* [God almighty]. He says it: "Work, apply yourself, and make an effort." What do you expect? The young people today, for example, they wait for it to happen, for it to fall out of the sky. No. You've got to take charge. That's what I do.

AUTHOR: But tell me. So, you also do it to "be at ease"? So you don't have to depend on anyone? For example, some non-Muslims?

OTHMAN: Bah, well, yeah. For me, it's like the *hijra*. You know, because you're a researcher, you know the *hijra*. The brothers here in France, they wonder why they are bent. They don't do anything. They stay in France and then they wonder why the state controls you. It's abnormal. Don't wait to get out. The Muslims in France complain, but then what do they do? They do nothing. They don't move. They need to take their head out of the sand. There are other things to do. For your religion, your life, your family, et cetera. As for work, if you don't find what you are looking for, or if you don't find a good career to do your prayers, bah, change. Listen, guy, it does no good to complain if you stay put and let yourself be bent.

AUTHOR: In your case, for example, that means you wouldn't hesitate to leave France?

OTHMAN: [*Renewed smile*] Ah, but it's already happened! I have a deal in the Gulf with some brothers.[21] In Sharjah [one of the United Arab Emirates, known for being the most scrupulous when it comes to respecting Islamic morality] we have a real estate sales business. It's totally different there. The people, business, commerce, nothing like France. You can work, you can open your business, not like in France, where they put obstacles in your way, for example.

AUTHOR: You find that they make it difficult in France for people who want to start a business?

OTHMAN: Are you kidding me? You're joking, right? In France they put obstacles in your way at the drop of a hat. If you want to build a dossier, when you put in a claim, when you want to do something useful. They say, "Take charge! Invest!" But, look, if you want to work, you can't, or you really have to be damn strong. My father had it the same, he worked, but he gave, I don't know how much, to the state. Do you think that's right? For instance, they make some laws, I saw it under Sarko, it goes without saying, he wants to make it easier for business [*heavily ironic*], but you'll see every time in France, there'll be talk, blah blah blah, and they'll debate and they'll pass a law that will come into effect months later or I don't know when. And just now you talked to me about Dubai and all that, and, bah, you know that one of the reasons why they're strong and become richer all the time, it's because when they do business they mean business. If they have a problem there, they pass a law and apply it in not even

---

[21] Here Othman is referring to the company that he founded with two of his peers, Mokhtar and Christophe (Antillean converts who chose Abdallah as their Muslim given names), both of whom hail from Essonne like he does. The company is called Gulf Properties.

a month, not like in France. Yes, there, that's how you get ahead, not like they do here, where it's meaningless.

Othman's description is representative of the Salafist conception of the economic playing field. Mobilizing a strategy of speaking out in a quest for status, the practicants show the rest of society that they depend on themselves and put their confidence in God. They promote depoliticization by economic means:[22]

OTHMAN: I never have voted in all my life. I don't think I'll ever vote. It means nothing to me. I don't know in the name of what I should elevate a man: he's just a man. It's not that I'll believe him just because he says he'll do things or that he has some incredible qualities. A man stays a man. Those who vote, they have confidence, but I don't. It's useless. . . . And then, let's not forget one thing: what are people seeking power for? Always more power.
AUTHOR: [*Laughs*] You're quoting from *The Matrix* there, quite a remove from the hadiths.
OTHMAN: [*Laughs*] Bah, yes, he's right in that film. Let's be frank: what are people who govern looking for? Always and again, more ways of gaining greater power. I don't see why I would go back in there and why I would give them my vote.

Besides the pacifying dimension of the economy, the Salafist conception manifests empathy for the libertarian ethic. Convinced of the fact that, by taking charge, the individual on his own avoids being subservient and retains the self-respect that is lost when expecting subsistence from another, the Salafi here offers a vision of society and the market economy. This perception, wedded to a consumerist spirit, offers a much less negative conception of the Occidental heritage; here free enterprise and mass consumption are perceived as constitutive of the ethos of a sincere orthodox Muslim. The Salafist approach to the economic field is symbolic and prosaic. Its political message: that economic independence makes it possible

---

[22] Taking up Carl Schmitt's concept, he invokes a "depoliticization through ethical-economical polarity." Carl Schmitt, *Théorie du partisan* (Theory of the partisan) (Paris: Flammarion, "Champs," 1992), 114–130.

for one to avoid the godless system's yoke. Also, it lets the Salafi take a stand vis-à-vis his coreligionists who lack sufficient resolve to put an end to what is lived as a relationship of alienation between French society and its Muslims.

Rising in the socioprofessional hierarchy by breaking with the classical integration circuits on the labor market is perceived as the empirical consequence of the principle of spiritual, psychological, and sociological rupture from unbelievers and deviant Muslims. Unlike those who choose to play the cooperative game with society in their quest for resources and status and who expect society to reward their individual efforts, Salafis choose socioprofessional careers that permit both material and religious accomplishment. In the manner of the first Protestant sects studied by Max Weber,[23] Salafis experience economic and material success as a sign of divine predestination, of God enjoining the pure to persevere in saving up for an "entrepreneurship of salvation" whereby capitalist success will give pleasure to the divine. The practicants believe that Allah traces an invisible line between those He fills with His grace and those He does not call to success in the beyond, prefigured by a worldly victory here below.[24] But they go further than the Protestant communities, who seem to understand the course of their economic affairs by trial and error, since the assessment of their possibility of salvation after death depends on the success or failure of their investment. The Salafis cross over into a supplementary stage by interpreting their economic success as the evident sign of the benefit engendered by breaking with the social codes and political contract that too many Muslims subscribe to. It is no longer about seeking, like the Protestants, signs of a next victory in the by-and-by prefigured by success in the here-and-now; it is about proving to yourself as well as your coreligionists that the—true—way of Islam is that of dignity regained by an ambitious economic ethic and of breaking with a labor market that is hostile to Muslims.[25]

---

[23] Max Weber, *L'éthique protestante et l'esprit du capitalisme (suivi d'autres essais)* (The Protestant ethic and the spirit of capitalism [followed by other essays]), trans. J.-P. Grossein in collaboration with F. Cambon (Paris: Gallimard, 2003).

[24] Olivier Bobineau and Sébastien Tank-Storper, *Sociologie des religions* [(The sociology of religions)], (Paris:, Armand Colin, 2007), p. 34.

[25] By the idea of *Beruf*, Weber means "profession-vocation" (ibid.). This concept refers to the "carrying out of duties within secular professions" and constitutes "the highest content that an individual's moral activity can take on" (Weber, *L'éthique protestante*, 71).

Social Rupture: Between Elitist Religious Practices and Cultural Desocialization

A Counterculture in Retreat and in Collision with the Dominant Culture: The Full-Body Veil

"The dress code"[26] yields one of the best illustrations of the Salafi will to rise above the cultural habits that are dominant in French society.[27] Among these codes, the most controversial garment is without doubt the full-body veil: the niqab, which covers the entire body except the eyes, and the *sitar*, a niqab that also hides the eyes behind another veil. While the Salafis make it a point of honor to dress according to the habits and customs of Islam's first believers,[28] the *niqab* or *sitar* also perfectly represent the symbolic and practical break sought by women practicing the true way in an environment they judge to be oppressive and iniquitous.

Moreover, wearing the veil, considered *moustahab* (religiously recommended),[29] signifies the moral force of the female believers who thus reproduce the original norm while not submitting to an allogeneic or anti-Islamic standard. Abdelwahid's wife wore the *sitar* for several years and still does on occasion, especially when she attends certain mosques. Oum Daoud[30] explained her motivations and the journey she took to wearing the *sitar*:

---

[26] Quentin Bell, *Mode et société: Essai sur la sociologie du vêtement* (Fashion and society: Essay on the sociology of clothes), trans. I. Bour (Paris: PUF, 1976), 13–24.

[27] The "counterculture consists of . . . political ideas, a lifestyle, and of philosophical conceptions that above all define themselves by their opposition to the modes of thought of the great majority of the population." Christiane Saint-Jean-Paulin, *Le contre-culture États Unis, années 60: La naissance de nouvelles utopies* (The counterculture in the United States in the '60s: The birth of new utopias), Memoirs no. 47 (Paris: Autrement, 1997), 9.

[28] The beard, *qamis, taqiyya* (skullcap), *izhar* (never having your garment reach down to the ankle), and the *siwak* stick (used to clean up the teeth as the first Muslims used to do) are indispensable parts of the Salafi kit. The *qamis* is the principal distinguishing mark of men who want to recognize each other and cultivate a clothing aristocratism. Although some Salafists in the French market offer *qamis* brands as Sunna (managed by Salafists), it is Saudi Arabia and the Gulf states that occupy the top rank, with brands like Ad-Dafa, Al Asil, and At-Tiyaf. Pilgrimages to Mecca and travel to this area of the world are as much occasions for purchasing these clothing items at lowest cost.

[29] The Tradition distinguishes between gestures that are licit (*halal*), forbidden (*haram*), advisable but not required (*moustahab*), to be avoided although not subject to punishment (*makrouh*), and permitted without being obligatory (*moubah*).

[30] This is her *kounya* (the way a Muslim can be called by referring to the name his/her child). This can be translated into: "Father/Mother of . . ."

AUTHOR: May I ask you to please introduce yourself? Your age, your educational level, your profession if you have one?

OUM DAOUD: My name is Oum Daoud. I was born in 1986, and I'm twenty-four years old and married. I'm originally from Algeria. I come from Constantine, but I grew up in Paris. I came to France as a baby, but grew up in Paris. I have a secretarial vocational diploma, but I don't work.

AUTHOR: And how old were you when you started wearing the niqab? And what were the reasons that persuaded you to wear it?

OUM DAOUD: In fact, I wore the jilbab[31] starting at eighteen, nineteen years old. Prior to that, I didn't wear the niqab. Also, I never wore just the niqab, since I wore the *sitar* right from the start. I always covered my eyes. It was part of my understanding right from the start.

AUTHOR: And just how did you arrive at this understanding? On which arguments did you base your decision to wear the *sitar*?

OUM DAOUD: To be honest, it's hard to explain. It's more of a feeling. I was interested in my religion: why we pray, why we fast.... Then I asked myself questions about the veil, and I understood that it was *fard* [obligatory]. I was not influenced by anyone.... I read a lot, I read the scholars like Ibn Taymiyya, Ibn Baz, and Albani. And then I also saw the sisters in the jilbab, I was with them. I told myself, "It's not possible. I'll never have the strength to wear it. It's impossible." I only wore the hijab at the time, but I was asking myself questions. I admired them.

AUTHOR: And so how and when did it click?

OUM DAOUD: One day I went into a clothing store owned by a Pakistani, in some bazaar in Ménilmontant, where they sold everything. He sold long veils and shawls. I went in and I bought one. It started like that, so I started wearing the jilbab.

AUTHOR: And then?

OUM DAOUD: Then, two months later, I put on the niqab. I started wearing the niqab, and then more the *sitar*. I didn't know any girls who wore it, but I decided to wear the *sitar*. I also hid the eyes. I wore it for a long time, but one day I took it off.

AUTHOR: But why?

OUM DAOUD: Bah, when you start working and going out. Anyway, I was pushed around, they spit on it.

---

[31] A shapeless robe or coat designed to hide the feminine form, with the goal of respecting the imperative of modesty. This clothing type conforms to many Salafists' expectations.

AUTHOR: Oh really, and who did that?

OUM DAOUD: Mostly it was women who told me . . . They were even Muslims . . . They said to me, "You bring us shame, you're infringing on women's freedom, we fought for that," et cetera. One time even, at a store cash register, I was with a friend, a French woman, and I no longer wore the *sitar*. A woman came to the register that started saying, "Why don't you go back where you came from if you want to do that." So then my friend lifted her *sitar* and told her, "It's you who should go back to your country. Look at my face, here's my ID card." And everyone in fact saw that she was French, while the other one was a foreigner. . . . Sometimes it also was men who spit in front of me, like it happened with a man over by Gambetta. I was walking, and a man came, looked at me, swore at me, and spit in front of me just like that.

AUTHOR: And today you no longer put on the *sitar* because you are afraid since that time?

OUM DAOUD: No, I no longer put it on because I told myself it's not obligatory. But I still put it on occasionally when I go to the mosque on Fridays. . . . I feel good when I put it on. When you wear the *sitar*, it's a sign of faith, you feel good, and you feel protected. I started from the principle "If I mind people, I won't get ahead." If I pay attention to what they say, I'll never do anything. So I decided to put it on, and there you are. When I wore it, it was out of modesty, no one ever made me wear it.

AUTHOR: What was the reaction from your relatives, your parents, for instance?

OUM DAOUD: My mother didn't agree with it. My father was also against it. Even [though] they are Muslims, good Muslims, but as far as they're concerned it has nothing to do with Islam. They say it's not required. Still, unlike other parents, they never made me take it off, even though they were afraid of aggressions in the metro or the RER. It worried them.

AUTHOR: Can we go back to the reasons that made you decide to remove the *sitar* one day when you said that you felt good wearing it? How did you change your mind about it?

OUM DAOUD: It wasn't obligatory, I decided. Just on the spur of the moment, it wasn't a requirement. Also, I saw how it created problems for sisters. For example, they stepped on their *sitar* and it embarrassed them. For me, it was okay, because I worked in the store [her husband's bookstore]. . . .

But because I was often at the ASSEDIC (French Job centre dedicated to paying unemployment allowances), the mayor's office, they asked me questions.

AUTHOR: You encountered problems in these administrative offices?

OUM DAOUD: Sometimes they asked me questions that were a bit harsh. But I stood my ground, I didn't let myself be pushed around. I answered that I didn't make anyone do like me. . . . Sometimes they tried psychology on me, where they would say, "But, madame, if you want to work in the chic neighborhoods, it's going to be difficult. This is not how you succeed over there. Moreover, your head looks fine. It's a bit of a waste." I just answered, "But I don't have to justify myself." But I didn't try more either, because afterwards it goes too far.

AUTHOR: And as you see it, if there's a law against it, how will the *moutanakibat* sisters [those who wear the niqab] react? What will they do if they can no longer wear the niqab?

OUM DAOUD: If there's a law, it won't do any good. There will just be problems. If they enforce it, the sisters take off the niqab. That's how it always is. I have a friend, when she is driving and is stopped, she removes the niqab. . . . If there's a law, some of them will take it off automatically. After they spend a week or two at home, they won't have a choice. Others will stay home and not take it off. After that, the others, the fighters, they won't take it off and won't pay the fines. Then there are those who will leave France, who'll go to England, like some that I know. Some are already. I know two sisters getting ready to leave and join their husbands.

AUTHOR: And in your opinion, why to England and not a Muslim country?

OUM DAOUD: For lack of means. Foremost because they lack the means. They'll choose England before thinking about going elsewhere.

AUTHOR: And according to you, why is it that certain politicians today want to prohibit wearing the niqab or *sitar* in public? Are you among those, for example, who view it as Islamophobia?

OUM DAOUD: [*Smiles*] It would be a lie to say it's not Islamophobic. People fear Islam, its advance, the conversions. I listen to the debates and sometimes hear that there are ten thousand Kabyles who converted to Christianity, but when people convert to Islam, it's a problem. People are afraid, they are afraid of the unknown. . . . It's vicious on their side, it's calculated. They know where they're heading. They don't do things haphazardly. It's like when you build a house, you need an architect.

For instance, there's a clear connection between the law of 2004 on the hijab and today. One is building on the other. . . . And then, frankly, I don't like to say it, but we, we are not united. When they say to the sisters, "Come on, organize," they say no. Or if not, they complicate things and sleep.

AUTHOR: So, as far as you're concerned, it's truly an anti-Muslim project?

OUM DAOUD: Well, sure. For example, my younger sister wears the hijab. She says things, sometimes, she forgets. She says, okay, all this, it's not really obligatory. And then, in school, they do everything to teach her things that are contrary to the religion. For instance, they tell her things so they will forget it. They say to her, "Why don't you just put on a bandanna? Look, this piece of jewelry, why don't you put it on? But you're pretty, why do you dress like that?" If your faith is weak, you are weak. I tell her, "Look out, we're Muslims." But the problem is that we're still asleep. Out of ten people, nine are asleep while one is awake. . . . They say, "France is a secular country, a free country," but when a woman wants to wear the niqab, they forbid it, it's a catastrophe. But when they put up a nude woman to sell yogurt, they don't say anything. There's confusion between liberty and libertinism. Forty years ago Coco Chanel created a scandal because she wore a miniskirt, but nothing like today, still not as short. They talk about integration, but they don't forget to say that it was used during the era of French Algeria to get Muslims to forget themselves. Sure, there's a problem of suffering, I don't say there isn't, but why fixate on Islam? . . . And then, when you see who defends the Muslims, really? Last week, for example, I saw a broadcast with Copé and Ardisson,[32] the one they brought on and who wore the niqab. Sometimes I wonder if it's just to gain viewers. The sisters who go on television, I get the impression they want to denigrate men, their husbands, for example, in saying that they don't do it as an obligation and that they decided on their own to wear it. My impression is they do it to show who's wearing the pants in the family. I just wonder if it's not on purpose, all of it.

---

[32] Here Oum Daoud is referring to the broadcast *Salut les terriens* on Canal+ on Saturday, January 9, 2010, presented by Thierry Ardisson, who staged a debate between Jean-François Copé and Dalila, a girl wearing the niqab and wanting to defend her point of view against one of the most mediatized proponents of banning the full-body veil.

Elitist Proselytizing: A Conversion in a Mosque Attended by Salafis

Salafist religiosity does not sustain itself by mass preaching, as in the Tabligh, where the potential believer is preached to in a diffuse fashion and without regard to his progress or individuality. Whether or not he comes from a Muslim background, the Tablighi practicant is concerned with faith, spirituality, God's existence, and the need for conforming to His demands. The important thing is to bring the individual to the path of Islam, while ignoring the dogmatic quarrels or legalistic debates. Besides, this type of Da'wa is more active the more the preacher seeks out others. It's the sense of "embarking on the way of God" (*al-khourouj fi-sabil ilah*). The goal is to shrink as much as possible the distance between the Truth and the individual who is estranged from God. Seeking to bring the message to all of humanity, Tablighi proselytizing, through which many non-Muslims and Muslims have been resensitized to the sacred, advances this expansive aspect.

The religious socialization that follows is demanding but is characterized by the refusal to divide the practicants with dogmatic quarrels. Among the Salafis, the problematic of the credo represents a casus belli on a symbolic level. Certainly Muslim unity is important, but it should not be achieved on the basis of a false conception of the '*aquida* (dogma, doctrine). Virtuosos of Islam, they are a source of imitation since they themselves imitate the only Muslims whose authenticity cannot be challenged. As such, their convert model focuses on the individual's potential. Embracing the Salafist career amounts to entering a community of the saved; it would therefore be out of the question to bring others to Islam without socializing them in the true framework, without furnishing them with the knowledge backed up by a rigorous methodology of Sunni sources. This structures a more introverted approach to preaching. Conversions to quietist Salafism are not the outcome of a mass enterprise that, for example, has taken Tabligh preachers into bars to ask individuals who were born Muslim to go to the mosque for their salvation. Salafist communities are magnetic poles; potential Muslims are drawn to them, in contrast to Tablighi socialization in which the *khourouj*, exceptional symbol of a more extroverted posture, occupies a central place. Salafist preaching is more elitist. Hence the most diligent and the most receptive individuals coming into the places of worship are priority targets. This is where the adept, alone or in a small group, can try to deepen his connection to Islam, on condition that he shows himself worthy of receiving this superior word. Muslims already showing puritan potential are favored. Preaching pays attention to serious but disengaged religious profiles. Mobilizing an ethic of conviction, the orthodox preaching builds like a logical approach, focused and thought out in a way to get the receiver to admit that giving allegiance to Salafist precepts is natural. One of the principal consequences of this approach is that the number of people sensitized to their religious view is, ultimately, less important than in other currents, such as the Tabligh.

In the Montreuil mosque, the Saturday service ends and the question-and-answer session is over. Before the call to prayer, Abdeljalil, the young Salafi imam, asks for the congregation's attention. There is good news in the offing for the faithful: a young man has embraced Islam, and as Tradition prescribes, he must give his statement of faith before at least two witnesses at the mosque, although it is recommended that the maximum number of persons attend the officiating of his entry into the religion. After the prayer, a young man, age sixteen, of African origin comes forward to join Abdeljalil. Before the faithful who have stayed to witness this scene, the one henceforth to be called Walid attentively listens to the words that brother Abdeljalil says to him. The young man, tall and slim, formerly named Michel, is timid, and his tone of voice shows that he is impressed by the dozens of people waiting to hear his responses:

ABDELJALIL: [*His tone is warm but grave.*] Walid, you are here, having chosen to become Muslim. You must know what that means and which road you must take. I'm told that you chose to become Muslim because you keep company with some brothers who attend the mosque and who talked to you about Islam. They told me that you became interested in Islam and that you made your own discoveries. You chose to embrace Islam. That's good. I am now going to tell you what the principles are, and you will tell me what you think about them. Are you still prepared to become Muslim?
WALID: [*In a reedy voice*] Yes.
ABDELJALIL: Good. I already told you that few people embrace Islam. If you are here today, it means that Allah has guided you. Good. Before, you followed a different religion, that of your family, therefore you were not a Muslim. But God showed you the right way. Therefore, so that you know the importance of it, I tell you one thing. Now that you are Muslim, it's as if you never committed any sins. You start from zero [*laughter*]. And even all the bad acts you committed since you were born, bah, today they

turn into good actions. You realize that Allah transforms all your sins into good deeds. You start over again from zero. Good. Do you understand?

WALID: Yes.

ABDELJALIL: Now, know that Islam does not simply mean "I am Muslim." You are going to begin your religious apprenticeship. You will pay attention, come to the mosque, and continue to talk with the brothers. There are books that you are going to read. Also, I take this opportunity to say to the brothers [*turns to face the audience of the faithful*], "Brothers, I repeat, there are books. Look around at the walls of the mosque [*points to the bookshelves along the walls*]. Take advantage of these books, don't let them just stand there without paying attention to them." So you see, now you will start your apprenticeship in religion. Islam means faith and prayer. You will learn about paradise and hell. Now I will say to you, now that you know all that, do you still want to become Muslim?

WALID: Yes.

ABDELJALIL: *Ma cha Allah* [Glory to God], now you are Muslim, and be on the alert because now the Devil, he will be after you. You just saved your soul from the eternal fire.

AUDIENCE OF THE FAITHFUL: *Ma cha Allah* [*repeated several times*].

Muslim Worship, Restorationist Practices with Elitist Effect: The Example of Prayer

The ensemble of worship practices constitutes many spaces of differentiation that result in producing a two-pronged effect of Salafist sociality in the French context. This duality—identifying with and reproducing the practices of early Islam and then putting yourself above those who have not made the effort to rediscover their religion in an orthodox mode—is the key to understanding the aristocratic dimension of the Salafist identity.

More than any other Salafist worship practice, prayer is what recaptures the first norms: it represents the demarcation line between believers and nonbelievers. Indeed prayer erects the practice of Islam's second pillar as a "fervent obligation": on a fixed schedule in congregation at the mosque and according to the most authentic prophetic ritual. The condition of being Muslim is arguable for any believer who neglects prayer, so that a large number of Muslims in French society see a soft faith in Allah as the dividing line between individuals authorized to call themselves Muslim and those who are not.

We reconnect with Abdelsamad. In contrast to a number of his coreligionists, he dates his effective conversion from the moment he began regular and purposeful observance of canonical prayer. The part of the interview that deals with the perception of his progress explains the Salafist principle that belonging to the religion should translate not only into a spiritual belonging but also into a practice:

AUTHOR: How did you come to Islam? Can you tell me the story of your coming to Islam and what reasons you had for choosing this religion? And also, of course, why you chose the Minhaj Salafi?

ABDELSAMAD: I was born in '74, I'm thirty-five years old. I work in a research department for Renault, but for the past several months, I live in Casa in Morocco. I made my *hijra* and had the opportunity to get training and professional experience that made it easy for me to find a job in Morocco. So I left Guyancourt by the sea for Casablanca.... In fact I have the BAC +2 (two years of undergraduate studies after the baccalaureate), I have a BTS (undergraduate degree) in industrial product design that I earned from the Corbeil Technical College. I got that in '98.... I converted ten years ago, and to answer your question, I chose the Da'wa Salafiyya right away. Why? It was clear to me from the start, no muddle, no ambiguity.... It seemed obvious to me, there was no mistaking it. Nothing, for example, but to follow the last of the Prophets, that's logical. You only need to read the *The Bible according to Barnabas*,[33] who writes that a Prophet would come after Jesus and that he would be called Muhammad. Also, I could show you this book. You can find it in Couronnes, in Ménilmontant. My parents are Portuguese. They are believers but not practicants. In the outback. [*speaking of Portugal in the way many Maghrebians evoke Morocco, Algeria, or Tunisia. We underline this Arabization of the lexical field employed by the Salafis.*] Sometimes we said prayers in the evening, we went to church, but I had a problem on my mind. It seemed to me that who we prayed to, God, was not Jesus. Then why say it's God? It jarred me, there was a contradiction. Sure, I believed in life, death, and what comes

---

[33] Here Abdelsamad is referring to a lesser-known version of the Jesus story that many Muslims, foremost the Salafists, cite as clear proof that Jesus announced the coming of a Prophet who would bear the Seal of God's Messengers and who had to be obeyed. See Luigi Girillo and Michel Frémaux, *Evangile de Barnabé* (The Gospel of Barnabas) (Paris: Beauchesne, 1999).

after, but there, no, I told myself, "No, this isn't possible." I never believed what they told us in school: Darwin, the monkeys, Cro-Magnon. . . . It's all bullshit. We're descended from monkeys, and this, that, and the other. Aside from that, the little I knew about Christianity, even if, as you can see, I didn't agree with everything, I was more attached to it than anything I learned in school.

AUTHOR: And so? The Da'wa Salafiyya?

ABDELSAMAD: It was thanks to someone I met. [*Laughter.*] I always met the one who kept apart. At age eighteen or nineteen, I met someone who did the prayer. I fell into the LEP (professional-skills based learning high school) at Nadar, in Draveil, in the 91st (Department 91 in the South of Paris) . He was doing *salat* [prayer], and it was me who covered up for him. I hid him in the facility when he did it. I watched so no one would come and disturb him when he prayed. I wasn't Muslim, but I already had stopped eating pork. . . . By the way, you know that even in the Bible, eating pork is forbidden? But they don't know, they don't talk about it. Anyway, I went with him to hide him while he prayed. . . . Afterwards, in the Bac pro (type of baccalaureate based on the learning of professional skills, not general knowledge), I again met someone else who did the prayer and who I hung around with. Then the same in the BTS.

AUTHOR: [*Noting that he was still in high school at over twenty years old*] But tell me, when did you get your BAC?

ABDELSAMAD: Yeah, I'll admit, I had a rough time. I had to transfer quite a few times.

AUTHOR: And there, based on what you just told me, you still did not call yourself a Muslim at that time?

ABDELSAMAD: No, I converted at the age of twenty-four, during BTS in '98. That's where I started praying. I think it's with the prayer that you really convert.

AUTHOR: But you just told me you found that Christianity didn't make any sense and that you felt drawn to Islam even well before that. Also, you just told me that you'd stopped eating pork for quite a while. . . .

ABDELSAMAD: [*Hesitates*] I was in the Muslim faith, but I think that I became a full-fledged Muslim with the prayer.

AUTHOR: And what about the Da'wa Salafiyya?

ABDELSAMAD: When I was doing my BTS, I worked as an instructor at Morangis, still in the 91st. There was a brother there who knew Islam very well. He was twenty-six. I fell in with him. He was a supervisor. His name was Farid and he did the *khotba* [sermon at the Friday collective prayer] in Corbeil, and he was also the imam at Longjumeau. He was a young Moroccan. It's from him I learned the prayer. I observed Ramadan but, as I said, didn't do the prayer. It was really him who taught me Islam, the prayer, the basics, and the obligations.

AUTHOR: And so, without the prayer, you didn't consider yourself a Muslim?

ABDELSAMAD: Bah.

3
Immunological Socialization

Justification for abandonment and migration, whether interior or exterior, derives from the principle of "alliance and rejection" of what God accepts and condemns in the faithful. The Salafist view of this principle in particular determines the relations that are supposed to unite Muslims concerned with orthodoxy and infidels. On the political level, according to Salafist doctrine, the only possible connection between the believer and the governing authority in Islamic territory is obedience, the goal being the preservation of the umma from fitna, while the pious Muslim who finds himself in an environment that rejects Islam's message can only opt out. This approach is accentuated by a geographic division of the world on behalf of a religious dichotomy between Islam and the *kufr* (the ungodly). Hence two systems offer themselves to believers: "the world of Islam" (*dar al-Islam*), which is contrasted with the part of the world that refuses to accept Islam's revelation, "the infidel world" (*dar al-kufr*). Judging a Muslim's buying into an environment resistant to the Islamic norm as incompatible with exercising an authentic religious faith, the Da'wa Salafiyya differentiates itself from most other offers of Islam for whom living in France is sometimes even presented as a privilege relative to Muslim countries that do not guarantee freedom of religion. By way of illustration, for some theorists of the Muslim Brotherhood heritage[1] physical departure from the ungodly society is by no means required. It is actually construed as giving up an opportunity for promoting Islam in a framework of predicative activity to a continent insulated for centuries from the Prophet Muhammad's apostolate. Counter to this logic of compatibility, the relationship that the Minhaj Salafi fosters between believer and French society resembles

---

[1] Tariq Ramadan, *Dār ash-shahāda: L'Occident, espace du témoignage* (The Domain of the Testimony: The West, space of witnessing) (Lyon: Tawhid, 2002).

a medical treatment. The Muslim must search for a place where he can pursue a true practice because what comes from the ungodly society is intrinsically bad. In the manner of people endangered by exposure to an unhealthy environment, Salafis perceive their presence in France as inimical to their "believing body." Refusing to submit to the ruination that is characteristic of the contemporary era, the ungodly French experience causing believers to hide their faith, the *hijra* takes on both a liberating and a prophylactic aspect. Conceived of as a rite of initiation through which the practicant gains a higher status in the orthodox field, the salutary migration represents the principal distinctive sociological feature of quietist Salafism in France. This ethic of *hijra* explains why, as long as a physical departure is not acted out, the practicant effects a partial rupture with his environment. No longer belonging to an ungodly society, because of the impossibility of appropriating its values as his own, he promotes a sociality of substitution.

Among the texts most studied by Salafists is the French translation of the synthesis by the *ʿalim* Sheikh Fawzan on the subject of "allegiance to and rejection of Islam." In it, the cleric presents what it means to lead the Salafist life in terms of relations with others, what principles to accept and which to reject. The physical and moral rupture with France thus registers as the duty of renouncing that which is un-Islamic in order to renew a strictly religious view of the world:

> Emigration (*hijrah*) means leaving the land of the ungodly for Muslim countries with the aim of flight in order to safeguard [the] religion.
>
> The emigration defined above and for the cited goal will remain an obligation until the day the sun rises in the west and the Hour is nigh. Moreover, the Prophet . . . dissociates himself from any Muslim residing among polytheists. Consequently, Muslims are forbidden to live in countries of the ungodly, with exception of those who do not have the means for emigrating or whose residence presents a religious benefit such as the call to the religion of Allah and its diffusion.[2]

---

[2] Sheikh Sālih ibn Fawzān El Fawzān, "Alliance et Désaveu en Islam" (Loyalty and Disavowal in Islam), translated by Abu Talha Said El Djazairi, revised by Abu Ahmed, https://d1.islamhouse.com/data/fr/ih_books/single/fr_Loyalty_and_Enmity_in_Islam.pdf, 10.

Internal *Hijra*: Between Psychological Withdrawal and the First Fruits of Departure

Rupture in Time and Space: The Logic of Religious Rationalization and Attendance at Mosques

Analyzing how many Salafis relate to time also sheds light on the process of a physical or symbolic exit from French society. They cultivate a relationship to France that leads to a rationalized view. As a result, socioreligious practices end up being redefined by virtue of a dynamic of optimization. Salafist socialization engenders a desire not to succumb to a passive vision. On the contrary, every day, week, and year that passes must witness a moral progression. Because the Salafi is the authentic keeper of the Islamic norm, the way he takes advantage of passing time registers as an intensive logic to the extent that it is the religious benefit of a dislodging, of an action, or of a withdrawal that conditions the way he behaves. Each unit of time must be put to use in a way that reinforces the puritan ethic. The practicant rationalizes each period available to him with the aim of maximizing *hassanat*.[3] In specific terms, besides the spatial rupture, this translates into an intensive approach to religiosity since there should be no time elapsed outside the religious prism. The benefit that this could procure in terms of good actions becomes the Salafi's objective; this is why, regardless of whether it means dropping certain practices or taking up new ones, time becomes the vector for a willingness to cut oneself off from the world of the infidel in order to concentrate on that which will *bring something*. With the practicant becoming the agent of his individual development, time must constantly contribute to gaining divine approval in the form of *hassanat*. An actor and no longer just a spectator, he does not perceive time as the moment dedicated solely to consumption or to earthly work but as a challenge and a resource for his puritan project.

The time spent in the masjid (mosque), the cardinal place for Salafist sociality inasmuch as it is supposed to be the most immunized and the least contaminated, illustrates this dynamic very well. It reflects the piety acquired by the practicant as well as his refusal to give in to certain social niceties. Where he presents himself as an obligant of the mosque, he sees his coreligionists subject to passions that drive them to leave places of worship. This is why Salafis evoke this place as the one symbolizing best their rupture from the

---

[3] Plural of *hassana*. This term designates the good coming from an action, a speech, or a thought.

rest of society. "Attending the mosque" thus becomes in their mouths a formula symbolizing their distance from the rest of society in an inversely proportional relationship. The refusal to go to venues like political meetings is argued for by the differential gain from frequenting places blessed by God. This explains how a mosque becomes an agitated place when a cleric known for his knowledge is on tour in France. The gain the faithful can draw from such a presence in places of worship is that much higher when they can welcome a renowned person from the Da'wa Salafiyya. Time then stands still for the persons present at the *dars* (course or lesson), the theoretician as well as his audience moving about in a bubble, neither entrapped in the French sociocultural tissue nor in the present. Salafis speak of their participation in a course taught by an *'alim* as a privileged experience allowing them instantly to escape a society they are trying to emancipate themselves from. The *hijra*, defined here as an interior escape from an oppressive world, takes on not so much a physical as a mental dimension, the proximity to the *'alim* being interpreted as an exit factor from a tentacular society determined to corrupt the devotees.

The scene described here is the visit by a quietist *'alim* known for regular sojourns in France that are occasions for his making the rounds of numerous mosques with the aim of right and authentic preaching. He is Sheikh Fayçal Al-Koweïti, known especially within the *tazkiyya* (sanctification) principle for having studied under Sheikh Ibn 'Otheimine. On this Friday the end of midmorning congregant prayer is unusual: Sheikh Rajib of the Sartrouville mosque concludes his speech by telling his audience that those "lucky ones present" that very evening will be able to attend a *dars* given by an individual wearing the "badge of honor" of having learned at the side of Sheikh Ibn 'Otheimine. We were there to observe the reactions as well as what the practicants said on receiving this news. The agitation of the young Salafis was genuine. On hearing of Sheikh Fayçal's visit, everyone broke out in smiles and praised the Master of the Universe for allowing them to benefit from the "lights" of an *'alim* who spent his religious apprenticeship close to a pinnacle of "unaltered Islam."[4] This is what we heard: *Ma cha Allah* (God's will be done), *Soubhan Allah* (Glory to God), *Allah Akbar* (God is the Greatest). We observed lots of eye contact, hinting at a real emotional complicity among the practicants; hands went into pockets to pull out cell phones, followed by

---

[4] http://www.3ilmchar3i.net/article-biographie-du-cheikh-mouhammad-ibn-salih-al-outhaymine-123317707.html.

sending text messages or making calls once the pious contemporaries had filed out of the mosque. Some of the most hyped up of the Salafis discussed the need to immediately spread the word in diverse forums about the arrival of the Kuwaiti scholar. The smiles were frank, the giving of thanks to God sincere, and the exchanges concerning the good news brotherly.

Come the evening, the mosque was jammed; many new faces not present that morning were now seen, the text messages evidently having resonated among Salafist communities in other cities. Seated at the foot of the minbar from which Sheikh Rajib had delivered his sermon to the faithful of the Indes housing project a few hours earlier, Sheikh Fayçal, in a thick Kuwaiti accent, recalled once more the axial character of the *tawhid*. The substance of the preaching that evening is rigorously the same as that of convocations led by other clerics that we attended in other mosques. Bringing up the Prophet's never ceasing to speak of "unicity," of the necessity of hunting down all forms of associationism (*shirk*) until his dying day and even after the end of Koranic revelation, the *'alim* put his public on guard against associationism of whatever kind: many Muslims today, particularly the young, he said, grow up not knowing the true *tawhid*. Once more taking up the example of the Prophet continuing to preach unicity even at the point of death, he criticized those who made objects of worship out of the Messengers before him or venerated their tombs. He called for respecting the principle of divine unicity and the necessity of holding on to the Sunna to keep from erring and "falling into the *bid'a* that corrupts the Sunna like vinegar spoils honey" (a reference to a celebrated hadith). Not for a second did the cleric deviate from the typical Salafist line of preaching. He broached no political subjects or social issues; the expectations uniquely concerned that which the light-skinned, corpulent cleric had to say on the manner of practicing certain rites and how a Sunni Muslim is to comport himself in daily life. The questions posed to the face of the "Salafism of teaching" showed no interest in current political issues or even a religious curiosity about an Islamic morality of politics.

As the time for the last prayer of the day approached, pieces of paper and pens moved through the crowd, signaling that the scholar's *dars* would soon give way to a question-and-answer session, when one interrogatory after another would be presented to him as he knelt, finishing the last traditional invocations.

After the scholar had spoken at this conference of sacred science (religious knowledge) (*majliss al-'ilm*), the questions were read out loud in French by a Salafi, who then translated them into Arabic for Sheikh Fayçal.

The answer, in literary Arabic, was translated into French and Arabic dialects for the faithful. The course ended with a more direct exchange between the cleric and his audience, a large part of which included young people in full agreement with him. The call to order then proceeded in a more interactive manner. The practicants present in the mosque, so numerous that many had to stand at the entrance, silent, knit their brows at every question posed, reflecting their impatience at having to wait their turn. The questions mostly dealt with worship and how to perform the ritual. The slips of paper read to Sheikh Fayçal bore the following questions: "Is it possible for people at work to pray while seated?" "Who has the priority in getting the *zakat*?"[5] "What to do when your daughter has chosen a husband? What to do?" "Is it possible to group the prayers at day's end when working with non-Muslims who do not accept prayer at work?" "Is cooking with alcoholic vinegar permitted?" "Does a disabled woman have the right to an abortion?" "Is it permissible to pray behind an imam whose way of dressing does not conform to the Sunna?" "Noble Sheikh, can you explain the hadith in the end times?" The questions from the patriarchs essentially concerned daily life, and those from the young contemporary pious, primarily revealed an interest in dogma and knowledge of God.

Protection against an Islamophobic Society: Media Discourse about Islam

Analysis of the media discourse about Islam conducted by academics, journalists, intellectuals, and others, including in the context of the post–September 11 world, reveals another facet of Salafi immunological socialization. Perceived as a flagrant illustration of the structural hatred that Western society nourishes toward this religion, the arguments of persons authorized to talk about Islam is subjected to an ontological interpretation. The pronouncements by the majority of observers on the subject of the Islamic way demonstrate the need to flee a French and, more generally, a Western collective that is nothing less than a contemporary manifestation of the ongoing mythical conflict between the defenders of the Truth and its detractors since the earliest days of humanity. The historical progression that authorized

---

[5] "Ritual, legal, and purifying alms" in the Muslim religion. Constituting the fifth pillar of Islam, they amount to 2.5% of income spent by the faithful.

a greater freedom of expression concerning Islam and Muslims in the wake of the September 11 attacks was experienced as Islamophobia,[6] convincing the contemporary pious to cut off all relations with France.

An interesting example of this fear inspired by the discourse on Islam was provided to us by Mekki, in Montreuil-sur-Seine. He was born in 1982 to a family of Algerian immigrants with a traditional relationship to Islam. His speech is laced with the distrust of all that revolves around "the Muslim problem" in France today. Mekki works in the Pompidou Center as an official in the library, which leaves him lots of time "for reading and keeping [himself] current on what is being said about Islam." His perspective is representative of the pious individual whose final departure for "the land of Islam" is on his horizon in the medium term and who cultivates a negative view of the intellectual production linked to this subject since the banalization of the debates on Islam in the media after September 11:

AUTHOR: And so, for you, what problems would you say confront you in France?

MEKKI: Bah, already, here we have a state that has a big problem with Muslims already.

AUTHOR: Oh, really? What exactly do you mean?

MEKKI: Bah, I mean the media campaigns, the attacks, all of it. Someone who practices his religion, someone who practices his religion, you get the impression that they think he's somebody violent, who is going to lapse into violence. If they don't want Muslims, let them say so! I have the impression that the state won't accept *al-Haqq* [the Truth].

AUTHOR: The people and the state are the same thing, in your view?

MEKKI: Regardless, I think they view Muslims in the same way. . . . For example, I had a professor when I was at the Rene Cassin high school in the 16th. He was a professor in computer science. He came right out and told me that for him Islam was the problem, that there was a problem with it. He didn't hold back in telling me what he thought. I told him I didn't agree with him, but he just laughed about it.

AUTHOR: And when you talk about media campaigns, to be precise, what are you referring to? Are you thinking about particular people?

---

[6] The debate about the body veil, for example, was interpreted as an entire system's hate for the Salafis. See the article "La Burqa! La Burqa!," http://www.convertistoislam.fr/article-33199509.html.

MEKKI: Let's say I was well acquainted with the authors, the intellectuals, all those writing about Islam, geopolitics, all that. I was working for several months at the Centre Pompidou, I took advantage of it to read, to hit the books, and, frankly, what interested me most was what they said about Islam. I read, I saw. . . . Also, the debates, the debates I watched on TV quite a bit, even though, frankly, it was more and more catastrophic. I really want to . . . When I hear this stuff . . . Well, never mind.

AUTHOR: You no longer watch?

MEKKI: When I get a chance. Less, but when I can. But the others, the brothers, no, frankly, they are disgusted. People are turned off by what they hear. There are people, when they open their mouths, they can only say "Islam! Islam! Islam." But the worst is they know absolutely nothing. I wonder what gets them invited.

AUTHOR: What do you reproach them for? Are you thinking of any particular persons?

MEKKI: I blame them for being know-nothings, for hating, for being way off the mark. And yes, I have quite a few people in mind.

. . .

AUTHOR: Are there any shows that you like watching?

MEKKI: [*Slight pause*] Yeah, Taddéi (French journalist who for many years was I charge of one the most popular talk-show on French TV) I like; his show is less hateful. He hosts interesting debates.

AUTHOR: Such as?

MEKKI: Such as? [*Reflects a moment*] Not long ago, a few days ago, I think . . . yeah, several days ago I saw a show about Al-Qaeda. . . .

AUTHOR: Who was on the set, do you remember?

MEKKI: Yes, Dominique Thomas.[7] I finally saw what he looks like.

AUTHOR: Meaning what?

MEKKI: Like I told you, when I was in Beaubourg, I read books on Islam, topical books. I like reading books that insult us. I found that very interesting. There's no sense saying "They insult us, so I won't touch them," not at all. And so one day, I read a book by someone named Dominique Thomas, about Islamists in London. What he wrote surprised me.

AUTHOR: What do you mean? In what sense? Are you talking about his book on Londonistan?

---

[7] Expert on radical Islam and author known for Dominique Thomas, *Le Londonistan: La voix du djihad* (Londonistan: The voice of jihad) (Paris: Michalon, 2003).

MEKKI: There, that's it. Yes, that one. Yeah, the Londonistan. And bah, in fact, it was not hateful. What he wrote . . . well, I don't know how to put it, but . . . how to say it, he was precise without being sensational, and besides, one thing is that in his book he thanked the people he interviewed. He said thanks to the Islamists that he met there. That surprised me. I told myself, "Wow that is very rare."

. . .

AUTHOR: Gilles Kepel was also on the show. What do you think of him? You know who he is?

MEKKI: Yes, sure, I know him. Yeah, he was on too.

AUTHOR: And?

MEKKI: He really speaks good Arabic, I already had seen him on TV. He speaks Arabic well, it's true. He's intelligent, but when he talks about Salafism, he doesn't know what he's talking about. He says, "Salafism . . . jihadism," "Salafism . . . terrorism." What they say about Salafism shows they don't really know it . . . just, that's impossible, terrorism. We condemn terrorism, severely even, for us it's very serious. But them . . . they . . . But when you study Salafism like they say you come to understand that Salafism isn't violent. It has nothing to do with it. You see very well that there's no connection.

AUTHOR: So as far as you're concerned, Gilles Kepel. . . ?

MEKKI: Ah yes, you also know him, you told me, you told me you know him. . . .

AUTHOR: Yes, I know him, I do.

MEKKI: What's he like?

AUTHOR: He is . . . in what respect?

MEKKI: Is he rich?

AUTHOR: Is he rich? Let me see . . . I don't really know. I think he is more likely to own his house than rent. . . . At least, I would hope so. Why, is money important to you?

MEKKI: No, but since he writes books, I wonder how much that brings. I don't know if going on TV pays well.

AUTHOR: Ah, that I can't tell you, I don't keep track. I think it depends on the individual. And otherwise, you know some other persons?

MEKKI: Other people. [*Reflects a moment*] You make me think of with Gilles Kepel . . . there was one whose name was . . . Bruno, Bruno Étienne.[8] He

---

[8] Expert on the Muslim world, known for Bruno Étienne, *L'islamisme radical* (Radical Islam) (Paris: Hachette, 1987) and *L'islam en France* (Islam in France) (Paris: CNRS Éditions, 2000). He died in 2009.

too astonished me, that day I saw him on TV. He was defending Tariq Ramadan. What he said surprised me. In front of Mohamed Sifaoui,[9] who did a segment on him. He answered him that Tariq Ramadan was a decent... guy. That he wasn't like what he said, that he had interesting ideas. That surprised me....

AUTHOR: And so, in the end, in your view, what explains all this intense activity concerning Islam?

MEKKI: In my view? [*Pause*] In any case, today it's simple. If you want to stand out, write a book about Islam. You write a rag, it will sell no matter what you write.

AUTHOR: And as far as you're concerned, all that shows what? What does it say to you? For example, does it worry you or not?

MEKKI: [*Thinks a moment*] Honestly, I will tell you, yes. Yes, because no one knows or can tell you how it is going to play out. We know where it starts, we don't know where it will end. Yes, I do think about it, and this is why I'll tell you one thing: it gets me thinking, to figure out how I can react.... For me, sure, one day, I tell myself, okay, there will perhaps be a time for drawing conclusions. An ounce of prevention is worth a pound of cure, as the saying goes.

The *Hijra* to the Land of Islam: Leaving, Rebirth... and Fulfillment

Egypt, or the Erasmus *Hijra*: Go East, Learn... and Return

Egypt is among the most popular destinations for Salafis on a quest for scholarly socialization. Land of ancient Islamic tradition, best known as the home of celebrated Islamic universities, of which the most famous is Al-Azhar,[10] as well as multiple mosques where important Companions of the Prophet preached.[11] The city of Cairo is especially sought after because of the presence of the Markaz Al-Ibana (Al-Ibana Center), known to Salafis

---

[9] A journalist known for his works on Islamism, such as Mohamed Sifaoui *La France malade de l'islamisme: Menace terroriste sur l'Hexagone* (France sickened by Islamism: The terrorist menace over France) (Paris: Le Cherche-Midi, 2002).

[10] Renowned institution of Sunni Islam, Al-Azhar University, founded in 988, is celebrated for having represented over the centuries a citadel of Islamic knowledge and education.

[11] One of them, for example, being 'Amr Ibn al-'As, conqueror of Egypt and Companion of Muhammad.

the world over and which every year attracts hundreds of individuals wishing to perfect their religious apprenticeship. Founded many years ago by Afro-American practicants who embraced Islam, the school is known for attracting French Muslims, mostly from the suburbs. This in fact is why the Americans elected to have the center operated by French brothers, the religious affiliation not erasing the economic reflex. Promoting the primacy of the *tawhid* in its educational offerings, the Center's pedagogical project attracts the interested faithful looking to find themselves and guarantees them the opportunity of getting fresh ideas in an orthodox place of learning.

Of the several dozen, mostly francophone individuals encountered in the Center, all wore beards and the typical Salafi garment (the *qamis*) but said they were there in order to resume studies abandoned earlier. The basic Ibana experience is revitalization of a heritage that they perceive a majority of their coreligionists have sacrificed.

We visited the Markaz on June 25, 2009. The school is located in the popular Madinat an-Nasr (City of Glory) district. Situated close to the Al-Houda mosque (the Guided One), its mandate is relatively clear-cut: offer to interested individuals courses in Arabic and a religious education with an orthodox foundation. We stayed in the Center for several hours in order to observe the thinking in a place for religious teaching in Muslim country and to cast an outsider's look at a society in theory sharing the same system of values as these expatriates of salvation. Only a two-minute walk from one of the principal thoroughfares of the Cairo megalopolis—the grand avenue Makram Ebeid[12]—the Markaz is architecturally ordinary and not instantly recognizable. Housed on the ground floor of a two-story apartment building typical for the Madinat an-Nasr quarter, the education center at first glance appears to be a boarding school specializing in Arabic-language courses for a religiously motivated public. The mood is cheerful, and people coming to attend class or to get information are received warmly, always with fitting Islamic greetings. Religious brotherhood is emphasized, the guests being seen as equals seeking an orthodox haven in the midst of a world lacking true meaning.

Idriss is eager to say that he is not the owner; that is an American Salafi woman who seldom asks for an accounting, knowing that the majority

---

[12] An artery that is itself located just a few minutes from another famous avenue, named 'Abbas al-'Aqad, after the celebrated Egyptian writer (1889–1964). Makram Ebeid (1879–1961) was an Egyptian Copt politician and member of the Wafd Party.

of students are French, which explains her willingness to let individuals from that country run the institution. He most often adopts a friendly tone, so that everyone feels at ease in the school. The part of the institute by the main road facing Makram Ebeid Avenue is reserved for the women, which explains why we had to wait a long time before a young man invited us in.

The school's sociology emulates that of French Salafis: everybody is young (twenties and thirties), many come from Maghrebian families, and all are there to study their religion. Following a practice of temporary *hijra* in this country, almost all tell us they are in Egypt for some time (from months to, in very rare cases, one or two years) for religious and education reasons. Many live close by in the neighborhood. Several hours of lessons are scheduled each day. Several options and different levels are offered (approximately seven or eight in Arabic, for instance). The students, usually a handful per class, together with Idriss, choose the course of studies that suits them best. The teachers have been recruited by the Center's owners, but not all are Salafis. Some of them speak a very solid French, mastery of Molière's language unquestionably constituting an asset in the eyes of the Center's operators. The classrooms are few and small. Two of them, accessible from the backyard, are set aside for the administrative team; Idriss occupies one of them. It has a fax, a computer, a table and some chairs, as well as a minimum of office furniture for keeping school records.

We questioned Idriss about different points regarding Salafism and the functioning of the Markaz. For instance, we had no idea about the various course fees. In this regard, he told us that they are highest for the language courses, but we learned that several hundred euros will pay for a basic course (a good twenty hours of elementary Arabic before going on to more advanced studies). On one wall are the house rules, including a stipulation that, pursuant to the state of emergency in force in Egypt since the 1980s, it is forbidden to gather (especially in large numbers) around mosques outside the hours of prayer or around religious schools, which includes the Center. A short time later, when we accompanied some Salafis to the Al-Houda mosque, the practicants went there by twos or individually to keep from attracting attention.[13]

---

[13] Since 1981 Egypt had been under a state of emergency imposed following the assassination of President Anwar Sadat on October 6 by an Islamist commando and the taking of power by Hosni Mubarak, whose fall would mark the end of this device.

Algeria, or the *Hijra* of Origin: Go East... and Stay?

"Algerian-style" emigration is a movement to return to origins. The Salafi leaving behind French ungodliness for Algeria is acting on a different logic than the migrant heading for Egypt. Salafis of the origin are primarily believers from the Algerian immigration in the process of definitively leaving France, while Erasmus Salafis are from more diverse origins (Antillean, Maghrebian, etc.), and their first objective is scholarly salvation in Muslim territory, not the abandonment of a despised society.

Salutary emigration to Algerian soil can be classified as a double reversal of the symbolic and sociological order. The rupture represented by the upending of a South–North traditional migration for reasons not found in the material and economic domain relates to two different ways of looking at a global space, both read according to a religious grammar.

The first rupture relates to tendencies generally observed among entire categories of young people in Arab countries, starting with the countries of the Maghreb, from where a large number of French citizens with Muslim heritage originate. Indeed the Salafist *hijra* can be understood as the exact opposite of the emigration habitus typical for many Algerian and Moroccan youth, of heading to Europe (or other destinations), a resource they capitalize on the most. Repository of an imagined modernity and material well-being for the individual barred from the entry mechanisms to the native country's consumption economy, Europe enjoys real prestige because its economic and political systems are supposed to guarantee more civil rights and justice. Counter to this desire to "leave,"[14] Salafis adopt a logic of a return home. If the geography of their migration is supposed to reproduce a continental divide of salvation (some regions of the world being farther from it, while others are closer), the direction of the ultra-minoritarian migration of practicants (from the West, land of godlessness, to the Muslim world, land of belief and piety) is radically different from the much larger numbers of modern young people (from Arab countries like Algeria, world of injustice and hypocrisy, to a civilized, democratic Europe, land of human rights and the welfare state). Seeing their coreligionists leave a country where they should in fact be staying in order to preserve their religion and avoid becoming victims of the illusion of modernity and progress, the Salafis once again assume this ultra-minoritarian status. The geographic and mental migration, counter to what

---

[14] Tahar Ben Jelloun, *Partir* (Leaving) (Paris: Gallimard, 2006).

is happening before their eyes, is all the more convincing in that is signifies a journey in time to connect to the original codes. This effective, symbolic rupture equally distinguishes Salafis from other offers of Islam that see in the presence of its faithful in Europe so many opportunities for preaching on this continent, the cultural uprooting representing in reality a windfall for Islam.

The second rupture has to be fit into a longer historical timeline. The dynamic of return to the country that one's parents should never have left in the first place—to push the Salafist argument to its logical conclusion—can also be apprehended as a reversal of the logic of the original family immigration. Poles apart from the Salafist migration is this migratory ethic of a generation of workers that came to France in order to earn a living in the old metropole, then to start a home and raise their children. Because it signifies the refusal to sink roots in a country judged to be harmful to exercising a true Islamity, the *hijra* can be understood as a rejection of being incorporated in a profoundly alien social, cultural, and political fabric. Substantiating in a sense the position of some political parties or certain intellectuals that view the Muslim faith as an element preventing identification with a symbolic corpus that will not be the umma, the *hijra* should be seen as closing the extra-Islamic parenthesis. Because the parental project of living their faith in an environment that is not majority Muslim is frowned on by the very people this migration into well-being was undertaken for, the *hijra* passes beyond the simple religious dimension. This phenomenon of the return to the point of departure therefore can be interpreted as a settling of accounts with a French society held in contempt for not respecting the injunctions of a religion that commands departure to its faithful rather than integration.

Nassim is a Parisian Salafi who turned into a "roi" (king) in contrast to those who are "rien" (nothing). This is how a humorous difference is drawn in Algerian parlance between the "Algé-rois" living in the capital and those living in the rest of the country, the "Algé-riens." With a calm disposition and endowed with a great religious determination, Nassim is divorced and the father of a boy. At thirty-five years old and an émigré in Algeria for two years after a career as a taxi driver in Paris, he settled in the Bab el-Oued quarter. The interview takes place at his home, a family dwelling of several stories belonging to his parents, who still live in France, where he periodically returns to make money to live on for the rest of the year in Algeria. Nassim thus pioneered a kind of periodical or commuter "counter-*hijra*" with the goal of accumulating financial capital during a few weeks of work in Paris and then return to the country. This is how the interview began:

NASSIM: You see, your watch, for instance....
AUTHOR: Huh ... yes.
NASSIM: Eh, bah, you see, as we know, everybody in general wears their watch on the left hand or rather wrist. All right, because we know that's what the *kouffar* [ungodly] do, we try to be different from them. We know that we need to distinguish ourselves from the *kouffar*. So, as a result, when it comes to the watch, we put it on our right wrist. That's how we revitalize the Sunna. We do the Sunna, for example, by following this principle "Be different from the infidel."

From there, he goes on to explain the reasons for his departure. He recalls driving his taxi in Paris:

NASSIM: Well, let me tell you what happened to me. Let's see ... Good, I already asked myself some questions earlier. I said to myself... As a matter of fact, one evening I picked up three people, three...
AUTHOR: Three men?
NASSIM: [*Laughs*] That's right, indeed, three... how to say [*still laughing heartily*] some ... some homos. There were three. I took them, and one of them sat in front next to me, he said nothing. The other two, they sat in back and started to talk. They were dressed like, well, you know? You know, you can tell, a little bit.... Right, after one of them talked to his [*laughing openly and a bit embarrassed*] friend. He had a high voice, he was, how shall I say, mannered, he had mannerisms. I know what they were thinking. They saw I had a beard. I must not have been what they wanted as driver, but anyway [*once again loudly laughing*]. The one next to me didn't say a word, he just looked at me kind of strangely. I thought he was looking at me from the corner of his eye. Anyway, it was especially the ones in back who made small talk.
AUTHOR: And what were they saying?
NASSIM: They carried themselves, let's say ... they sat close to each other. They wanted to know what I thought of them, you might say. When they saw me, they were intrigued, it was obvious. The one who talked the most, he said to me, "Excuse us. We're talking too much, it must be bothering you." I told him no. They asked me to take them to the 10th. For the entire drive, I saw very well that they were.... That's it.
AUTHOR: And how did it end?

NASSIM: Nothing special, I took them to their address, and I said good bye. The talkative one wanted to ask me questions during the trip, but after a short while, I stopped talking.

AUTHOR: What sort of questions?

NASSIM: Like I said, you could tell, they were ... how to put it, curious, it surprised them. They were looking for a taxi, it was me who stopped, and so they asked themselves, "What did we get?"

AUTHOR: So? Then what? This encounter between two worlds?

NASSIM: [*Laughs*] Like you said, a meeting between two worlds. No, well, no ... well, okay, I never asked anything of anybody ... but after, it's true, I asked myself some questions, I kept asking myself some questions, rather. [*Brief silence, then laughs and looks down*] Allah mous'atan [Lord help us].

AUTHOR: And the second experience? You mentioned a second experience when you were a taxi driver in Paris?

NASSIM: Yeah, that was a different thing. You'll laugh, because that I found it to be even more serious.

AUTHOR: Meaning what? What was more serious?

NASSIM: I say that because it was a woman, as it were.... One of us. You could easily see that she came from the Maghreb. I picked her up in my taxi, not far from Saint Lazare train station, and so.... Bah, in no time I saw that she was beginning to be annoyed. She looked at me, she stared at me. She looked at me, especially the beard, as if she'd seen ... I don't know, as if she'd seen, I can't really explain....

AUTHOR: And tell me, a small question, out of curiosity, in your cab ... how to say it, are there religious things, is there the Koran?

NASSIM: Yes, sometimes, I put the Koran there.

AUTHOR: And so, what irritated the lady?

NASSIM: Then she started making faces when she saw me. She made these little noises.... Me, I didn't say anything, but I knew that, well, she was uncomfortable. I could see I was bothering her. All right, it's a fare, you don't say anything, you take them where they want to go, and that's that. That's all. But as it turned out, she was the first one to talk.

AUTHOR: What did she say? She said what?

NASSIM: She said, "Can I ask you something?" Me, bah, I said sure. She told me, "Why do you do that? We're in France. I was in Algeria, I came to France; why do you do that? I left Algeria, not to see bearded ones, people who ... Religion, religion, religion."

AUTHOR: What then? What did you answer? It upset you, did it?
NASSIM: Nooo, why? In fact, I was . . . It made me laugh, in fact.
AUTHOR: Why?
NASSIM: Because I'm accused of being the integrationist [*Laughs openly*].

. . . .

AUTHOR: And so it's this sort of reason that made you quit France? Is that why you're telling me this?
NASSIM: Yes and no. As I told you, yes, it made me think. How can you live in a place where they talk to you like that? However, paradoxically, we are the ones accused of being killjoys, and we, we are the ones being attacked verbally. Good, there you have it, this has to be made clear.
AUTHOR: But otherwise, do you think you would have done the *hijra* regardless, no matter what?
NASSIM: Yes, I'm going to tell you, there's a rule. When you live in a *kufr* [infidel] country, if something happens to you, you can only blame yourself. Allah is not responsible for you. If something happens to you, you've been confronted with situations that you didn't look to avoid. You placed yourself in a situation . . . how to say it, of difficulty. On the other hand, if you make the effort to go live in a Muslim country, there the one responsible is the *wali al-amr* [wielder of authority]. He is responsible for what happens to you. You have to put yourself under Allah's protection. People say that the Salafis are only interested in what the rulers do. Bah, maybe, except that we don't question the *houkam* [rulers]. We know what's going on but don't say anything. There's nothing you can do unless the ruler gives a sign of unbelief.
AUTHOR: And, for example, what would be such a visible sign of unbelief?
NASSIM: For example, it would be no longer respecting the laws of Allah. For instance, if a ruler gives a sign of having accepted another religion, like if he put on a cross.
AUTHOR: And does the king of Saudi Arabia, for example, obey the laws of Allah?
NASSIM: There you'd have to revert to the scholars. It's for them to tell us. Why do you ask that?
AUTHOR: Because I already saw it on the internet, some people reproach him for having been decorated by a Western head of state, and that he received a cross. That's why some persons said that they submitted to another religion's symbol.
NASSIM: [*Brief silence*] I have no opinion. That's for the scholars to say.

....

AUTHOR: And, for instance, here in Algeria, do you feel close to the scholars?
NASSIM: Yes, in Algeria, there are *macheikh* [scholars]. There is Sheikh Ferkous, to name one, who you met at Masjid Qoba.

Mohamed-Ali Ferkous is indeed one the best known figures in predicative Salafism in Algeria today.[15] This *'alim* is celebrated especially for having called back to order a number of believers some years ago in the matter of the Orascom company, which sells telecommunications-related products[16] under the Djeezy brand, highly prized by Algerians. In fact, circles around Sheikh Ferkous in 2008 were roiled when rumors circulated implying that the head of Orascom, an Egyptian Copt, had slandered Islam and announced his intention to attack this religion. Another rumor accused the businessman of financing evangelical groups in Algeria with the goal of Christianizing as much of the world as possible. It was why the *'alim* took the lead in a campaign warning against an "enterprise of corruption" (*machrou' al-fassad*) by announcing a fatwa encouraging all believers who wanted to preserve the religion to boycott this company and its products.

Sheikh Ferkous is also known for praying in the mosque of the Qoba district in Algiers, where, during the month of Ramadan, including after the *fajr* (morning) and the *'asr* (afternoon) prayers, a crowd of faithful follow the cleric to a library adjoining the place of worship, where he spends part of his day. There he answers questions from believers seeking an Islamically based solution to a problem. The rules are simple. Sheikh Ferkous answers no more than ten questions and gives precedence to ones from visitors from far away. We tried our luck in the morning, without success; after being presented to him and having explained our academic initiative, he suggested that we return in the afternoon. Still, we remained throughout the morning to find out what questions the faithful asked. These were typical: "When it rains during the evening prayer, as is the case in our area, is it possible to have the women pray inside while the men pray outside?" "What should a person who fasted and vomited while kneeling in prayer do?" "Is it possible to perform the ritual ablutions before prayer by resorting to the *taymoun* [touch a natural stone instead of the usual water] in case of illness, and when would a wall known to

---

[15] Owning a website where snippets of his biography can be found (http://www.ferkous.com/fra/A1.php), the cleric is also known as a professor of Islamic sciences at the Algiers Faculty of the Arts.
[16] http://www.ferkous.com/rep/Bb27.php.

be constructed of stone suffice?" In the afternoon, after the prayer, we joined the ʿalim in his library where, seating himself before his numerous visitors, he said that he had first to respond to questions by a researcher. We chose to ask him two questions framed by our work: What do you say about the obligatory character of a Muslim living in an unbelieving country doing the *hijra* by moving to a Muslim country? What do you say to the possibility of taking part in elections in a non-Muslim country like France? Some people take the position that this could be a way of serving Muslim interests. His responses are repeated here from memory, the author having judged it impolite to offend the imam by using a microphone. Sheikh Ferkous thanked us for these questions, which appeared sensible to him. His advice was clear and seemed at one with the interpretations he draws from reading and exegesis of scriptural sources. With regard to *hijra*, Sheikh Ferkous put forward the position that is most common among practicants in France: that it is obligatory and not permitted to prolong one's presence in a non-Muslim country if one attaches importance to "shariatic" principles. Recent trends, he said, for example in the way the French speak about Muslims, leave no doubts in this respect. From the prohibition on wearing the *hijab* to remarks by President Nicolas Sarkozy, Islam has been targeted by the French authorities for some time already. The same reasoning led the theoretician to pronounce himself against participating in the country's elections: On what basis do they legislate? Who decides what is good or bad? And who votes for the welfare of everyone and the general interest? In answer to this last question, he jovially remarked that in democracy there is one notable element that ought to stand out to any Muslim possessed of reason. Through the principle of free and egalitarian elections, you find yourself in a funny situation where the vote of one "wrongheaded" person is equivalent to that of a "person of knowledge," that of a "deviant" put on the same level as that of an ʿalim. For these reasons, the cleric condemned taking part in elections in France.

Faced with this response, we asked him to react to the argument that participation in elections can help advance causes defended by believers. His response was the same: this reasoning led Muslims to favor one policy over another, yet today they find themselves in a country that humiliates them, passes laws that deprive them of fundamental rights and exposes them to the vindictiveness of badly intentioned people. Sheikh Ferkous questioned the effectiveness of such "exceptional thinking." In a polite and empathetic manner, he asked us what we thought of his responses. When we replied that the object of our research was not, properly speaking, religious or

Islamological, he ended his talk by "reassuring" us about Muslims in Algeria today, with the following quip: Don't worry, your question is not foolish. Even in Algeria, if you were to ask many young people, they would tell you they have only one desire and that is to go live in France. And with regard to elections, if you were to poll most Algerians, they would tell you they want to return to being a French territory.

PART II
THE MEMBERSHIP GROUP

Analyzing the different forms of Salafist socialization tells us nothing about the macrosociological reasons that may motivate embarking on the Salafist career. The sole explanation furnished by the actor is linked to the attraction exercised by a discourse presenting itself as objective and orthodox in the religious sense. Yet the ambition to restore a morality abandoned by all nourishes a shared feeling that cements the relationship to a world of individuals united, on a sociological level, by certain weighty or primary characteristics. By way of examples, we can cite the youthfulness of the practicants, the fact that the majority come from the suburbs and from families strongly stamped by the migratory epoch, and the serious difficulty they have calling themselves French. (This also goes for the converts.) This background is in turn linked to a sincere empathy for their parents' native country, the search for an extraterritorial identity, an attraction to material success, open disdain for political affairs, and deprecation of engaging in the public sphere. The mobilization of a different epistemology is needed to shed light on this career choice. To the study of the resocialization which the identification with Salafism ultimately results in must be added the analysis of conditions that explain the adoption of certain ways of thinking. Therefore, when it comes to interpreting the relative success of the Da'wa Salafiyya, it is important to establish an epistemological distance that allows us to shift away from the actor's own perspective on his course. After the manner of Émile Durkheim, we need to change our points of reference with the aim of examining the individual *and* the environment from which he can or cannot innovate in identity terms as he forges a place in a social world he judges to be dangerous. Socialization no longer is confined to an assimilation of norms and ways of being; it is equally a form of communication addressed to a reified society, a sort of debate, an exchange, or, in the case of Salafism, a conflict by which the individual defines a new space in a society that he despises in theory. The Salafist identity thus must be understood as an identity strategy, which means that the resource symbolized by authentic Islam is first the result of a quest for positioning in a social space. The search for an alternative and oppositional identity matrix is then understandable as the fruit of a project that aims at breaking a kind of domination by the rest of society to which an actor can or cannot belong.[1] It therefore behooves us to interrogate Salafist socialization as a response to a position in the French social space featuring certain characteristics that more or less influence the emergence of identity strategies of rupture: "Socialization invariably takes place in the context of a specific social structure. Sociocultural conditions circumscribe its content but also its measure of 'success.' In other words, microsociological or sociopsychological analysis of phenomena of interiorization must always be accompanied in the background by a macrosociological understanding of their structural aspects."[2]

---

[1] Riutort, *Précis de sociologie*, 253. We could even add that "identity, which is essentially social, is to be seen more as a 'problem' to be solved than as an explanatory concept." Roger Brubaker, "Au-delà de l'identité" (Beyond identity), *Social Science Research Acts*, no. 139 (2001): 66–85. Also see Joseph Kastersztein, "The Identity Strategies of Social Actors: Dynamic Approach of the Objectives," in Carmel Camilleri, Joseph Kastersztein, Edmond Marc Lipiansky, Hanna Malewska-Peyre, Isabelle Taboada-Leonetti, and Ana Vasquez, *Stratégies identitaires* (Identity strategies) (Paris: PUF, "Psychologie d'aujourd'hui" [Modern psychology], 1990), 30–31.

[2] Berger and Luckmann, *La construction sociale de la réalité*, 222.

4
Filtered Socialization

The Suburbs as a Symbolic Space for Differentiation and the Emergence of Counterworlds

The Suburb: A Space for Forming an Antagonistic Habitus

Quietist Salafism has its greatest success in the suburbs. Most of the practicants have been socialized in exurban areas marked by symbolic conflict with the rest of society. This point must be understood in a wider sense, because it is principally the symbolic and psychological dimension of the suburban youth identity that must be taken into account in analyzing the relationship they maintain with society. If Islam can be understood as a social fact in effect acting as a constraint on individuals, studying why certain social profiles appropriate the Islamic reference must take a finely honed approach. This religion is a brute given, a referent without any psychological, sociological, or cultural essence or its own politics. The penchant for a Salafist viaticum becomes a tendency that we can observe in persons sharing a number of sociological patterns. Principal among these is origins: of the Salafis we met, totaling more than one hundred individuals, over 90% were socialized in the suburbs. While that makes the suburbs a space for creating identities, we nevertheless find a number of traits in common with other eras when it comes to the content of a connection maintained with a center considered a dominating force.

This center supposedly acts in a hostile manner toward the denizens of a part of society that it does not consider to be like those in the center, so that it finds itself negatively integrated in the representations of many young people. These youth in turn develop a number of identity strategies stamped with the seal of defiance and structured around the overturning of the center's dominance. Knowing this, it is possible to understand the advent of a religious discourse that makes no concessions. The oppositional habitus that finds in Salafism a sacred legitimation draws in reality on the idea, anchored in the perception of many suburban youths, that they are *the other* and, as such, under attack by "the system." The inability to think of yourself as symbolically *integrated* can result in an anomic situation in which the part of your identity that is a legacy of immigration is accentuated. This dynamic of socioterritorial peripheralization and symbolic, if not cultural, marginalization explains the propensity of certain profiles to set themselves up in counterworlds. The vindictive character of the relationship between the center and the periphery spills over into the nature of the sociological careers adopted by individuals. On a religious level, the Islamic option can incorporate a dimension of the "class warfare" type, a characteristic in other eras of the relations between working-class categories and a society viewed as illegitimate. The state is regarded as privately owned and the government as a biased actor that from the start represents only part of the population. In that sense France is perceived as an abstract entity, both geographically and symbolically. It is understood as the prerogative of persons who benefit from it and the national identity as a socioeconomic affiliation, so that a pauper, for example, cannot consider himself to be French. The national is therefore someone who obtains tangible benefits from his French citizenship, while some social positions prohibit identification with the nation. These spaces, which are just as much "French ghettos,"[3] distinguish themselves by a negative integration into sociopolitical institutions and norms reigning in the rest of society. Thus Didier Lapeyronnie notes that many urban districts contain "grey zones," spaces forming ghettos in which the powerlessness of the inhabitants is institutionalized. Stripped of sovereignty, with norms defined elsewhere, these suburban dwellers suffer feelings of dispossession.[4]

The ghetto is the privileged space for forming counterworlds, the alternative meaning-making framework permitting identifications that run counter to the identity considered normal in French society. The young who embrace Salafism are therefore, on this level, children of the ghetto. While the ghetto

---

[3] Éric Maurin, *Le ghetto français: Enquête sur le séparatisme social* (The French ghetto: Inquiry into social separatism) (Paris: Seuil, 2004). In this work the author identifies the dualisms and contrasts of a socioeconomic order on which may come to be superimposed a map of the geographic division of ethnic or sectarian groups. The author thus speaks of a continuum of fissures between, for example, the central city and suburban districts.

[4] Didier Lapeyronnie with Laurent Courtois, *Ghetto urbain: Ségrégation, violence, pauvreté en France aujourd'hui* (Urban ghetto: Segregation, violence, poverty in present-day France) (Paris: Robert Laffont, "Le monde comme il va," 2008), 249–250.

cannot be analyzed apart from the difficulties that characterize it (racism, discriminatory practices, poverty, violence, etc.), the pathological dimension does not suffice as analysis. In fact it is the actor's subjectivity that is important in the emergence of antisystem identities capable of mobilizing the dominant cultural codes while contesting others as it chooses:

> The ghetto presupposes an internal and positive definition. It is not solely a poor quarter of immigrants whose inhabitants stay trapped by social difficulties. It is also a place whose population ended up putting together particular modes of life, visions of the world organized around its own values; in short, it is a form of social organization that lets it confront social difficulties and deal with the wounds inflicted by society. The ghetto is constructed from the outside. It is the product of racial segregation, poverty, and social relegation. The resident population lives there in a more or less forced manner for reasons both racial and social. But the ghetto is also constructed from the inside. It is an urban territory apart in which the population, or at least a part of it, has worked out a special way of life, a particular kind of counterworld that protects it collectively against the external society. It is the conjunction of this dual construction, internal and external, that defines the ghetto in the most descriptive and widest sense of the term.[5]

A ghetto religiosity despite its pretensions to the universal, the Minhaj Salafi in France is a reversal of the peripheralization dynamic and the practical and symbolic marginalization that touches the suburbs and the young, the children of asphalt and bitumen, there where the same religious message finds a ready hearing among other social categories under other heavens. This current of Islam is more of a middle-class religiosity in the Gulf countries, especially in Saudi Arabia, attracting practicants with a puritan religious message that is politically legitimist, socially conservative, and economically liberal. French Salafism primarily recruits suburban youth who have difficult relations with institutions. Benefiting from the security and redistribution of oil income, the Saudi middle class makes up one of the principal sociological bases of Saudi power. What Olivier Carré terms "politically moderate Islam" in effect rests on pious social groups that

---

[5] Ibid., 11–12.

are disposed to integrating a puritan religious ethic underpinning political stability and economic liberalism:

> The political Islam advocated in Riyad is more to the right than the classic ideas of the Muslim Brotherhood. . . . This right wing Islam is also more elaborate. It insists on the practical benefits of global capitalism and on the blessing that the immense oil income represents for the Muslim community. The equation appears simple, both for the religious men and the technocrats. . . : The Koran (read with Wahhabi rigor in the practices and with accommodation of the common interest in economic and financial matters) combined with the petrodollars assures the security and rebirth of this Arab and Muslim world bullied to such a degree by the West as a divine punishment for a loss of authentic Muslim piety. . . . This moderate political Islam gets a ready hearing among the middle classes, often disappointed by the Arab nationalist "revolutions" with socialist tendencies. Arab-nation loyalty has not been abolished, but favored are state loyalties and Islamic loyalty.[6]

Conversely, in French society the quietist Salafis are more widely visible than the revolutionary Salafis, who have been targeted by the security forces since September 11, 2011, and epitomize a different contestation. If the suburb and the ghetto are geographic and mental spaces of marginalization, the Da'wa Salafiyya represents the most accomplished form of delegitimization of the symbolic order on which the godless preeminence is constructed:

> The ghetto therefore is not the consequence of a natural evolution of things. It cannot conceive of itself as a pathological excrescence of society. On the contrary, it is more of a solution than a problem. It is the product of collective choices that find their expression in the urban division by social and racial groups as segregated and hierarchized. In French society today, urban segregation is a mode of distributing inequalities and managing the tensions between social and ethnic groups. Distances have replaced the conflicts between classes.[7]

---

[6] Olivier Carré, *L'Orient arabe aujourd'hui* (The Arab Orient today) (Paris: Complexe, 1990), 42–43.
[7] Lapeyronnie and Courtois, *Ghetto urbain*, 14–15.

Militant Apoliticism: Between an Anti-imperialist Ethic, Disdain for Engagement, and Unfulfilled Politicization, a Relationship to Endogenous Politics?

The Salafist viaticum inculcates in adherents the immorality of protesting and the illegitimacy of classic political participation, requiring reliance on a cleric's judgment instead.[8] The political ethos distinguishes a dual aspect of contemporary challenges: the impossibility of nourishing an activist vision and the necessity nevertheless of praising the good and reproving the bad. This double constraint results in assuming moral stances unaccompanied by any form of organized militancy. The aristocratic dimension of the Salafi positioning in a way translates into a direct progression from the state of premobilization to that of demobilization, the state of mobilization somehow having been skipped. We can therefore read in the relationship to politics two complementary rather than opposing tensions. The practicants mobilize a discourse of a political nature without embracing an activist logic. Steering toward the militant sphere in the name of praising the good without, however, biting the bullet—that is how the Salafis position themselves. This translates two ideas. The first attaches to the existence among Salafis of a political critique of French society, which, not being religiously based, is delegitimized for what it does but especially for what it is. The second is associated with the fact that they do not feel sufficiently integrated into this society to reform it by means of a religiously motivated activism. The Salafis are integrated intellectually in a political field in which they feel like strangers. The resemblance is striking with some NGOs with an interest in politics but unwilling to enter a potentially corrupting sphere.[9] If quietist Salafism is perceived as a religiosity that canonically forbids resort to the militant act, the audience that it encounters in the youth of the ghetto constitutes a reason to situate itself politically in relation to a dominant order. Placing itself in a contractual logic vis-à-vis the prevailing institutional order in France is comparable to signing a nonaggression pact, which leads to living a parallel life, eschewing any interest in an eventual mobilization against the disavowed state and society. Two temporalities are therefore key: one, protesting an antisystem inherited

---

[8] Johanna Siméant highlights the fact that moral judgment serves as a "functional equivalent" of political engagement when describing the position of people engaged in humanitarian action. Johanna Siméant, "Un humanitaire 'apolitique'? Démarcations, socialisations au politique et espaces de la réalisation de soi" (An "apolitical" humanitarianism? Dividing lines, socialization in politics and spaces for self-realization), in Jacques Lagroye (ed.), *La politisation* (Paris: Belin, 2003), 165.
[9] Ibid., 169, 173.

from socialization in the ghetto; the other, reasonable because conservative, stemming from a widely shared view of politics today, notably among young people, that is mistrustful of organized militancy and dialogue with institutions.[10] Their duty consisting solely of calling their peers to honor the principles preached by orthodoxy, they benefit from public goods (security, state welfarism, citizenship, etc.) while still conceiving of themselves as existing in an alternative space vis-à-vis society and the state. They fulfill their responsibility to reject unbelief while actually benefiting from a peaceful life in a societal framework that they despise.[11]

Salafi ghetto youth do not refrain from adopting an anti-imperialist rhetoric against the West, but in order not to heighten the risk of generalized chaos, they refuse to normalize their rejection by resorting to the classic tools of mobilization, such as strikes and political parties. They thus develop a dual, apparently contradictory habitus. On the one hand, we observe in their espousing a certain vision of politics a will to opposition, a wish to delegitimize the structures of power and authority, illustrated, for example, by the caustic view of the Islamophobia imputed to the deciders and shapers of French opinion.[12] By viewing themselves as the new "damned of the earth,"[13] that is, people at the margin of society for the sake of a blessed religious membership, they perpetuate the anti-imperialist tradition of the red suburbs characterized by a strong worker culture of social struggle. Even so, they fail to convert this antagonism into a militant project. It is interesting that the three regions once known as strongholds of social conflict framed by the extreme left—northern France (around Lille, Roubaix, and Tourcoing) and the suburbs of Paris and Lyon—are the principal zones where the Minhaj Salafi has taken hold today. The most media-hyped illustration of this evolution is without doubt the campaign waged in 2009 by the Communist mayor of Vénissieux, André Gérin, against the widespread wearing of the niqab in his

---

[10] Anne Muxel, *Avoir 20 ans en politique: Les enfants du désenchantement* (Twenty years in politics: The children of disenchantment) (Paris: Seuil, 2010).

[11] Kirstine Sinclair, a specialist in the radical Hizb al-tahrir (Party of Liberation), in researching the establishment of the caliphate and installation of an Islamic state, notes that its hardline rhetoric does not result in violent action. She thus suggests, "For [this movement], language does not function like a safety valve. Strong criticisms are leveled and violence is no longer necessary." Quoted in Jean-François Mayer, "Hizb-ut-Tahrir: L'évolution d'un parti islamiste transnational en Occident (Grande-Bretagne et Danemark) (Hizb-ut-Tahrir: Evolution of a transnational Islamic party in the West [Great Britain and Denmark]), in Amghar, *Islamismes d'Occident*, 101. This suggestion seems to fit the Minhaj Salafi.

[12] Vincent Geisser, *La nouvelle islamophobie* (The new Islamophobia) (Paris: La Découverte, 2003).

[13] Frantz Fanon, *Les damnés de la terre* (The wretched of the earth), preface by Jean-Paul Sartre (Paris: La Découverte, 2002).

town, which he saw as the clearest sign yet of the growing hold that "Islamist integrationists" had on populations with an immigrant background. This leftist or revolutionary habitus couched in religious terms informs the will of a majority of Salafis to delegitimize the French institutional order. Viewed as a crutch of imperialism in the service of anti-Islamic interests, state institutions and political personnel become objects of a stigmatizing discourse structured around a sacred perception of the world. The dominator becomes the kafir (unbeliever); the state becomes *taghout* (tyrant, idol); distancing oneself from society becomes rejection. The semantic change is no less linked to a primary reality, a synonym for a major antagonism between the losers in the system and its privileged ones.

However, this oppositional predisposition structured by a leftist habitus characteristic of heavy sociological membership in working-class categories coexists with a much more conservative and legitimist modality of institutions and political stakes. While Salafist socialization forbids political engagement, the practicants are distinct in their categorical refusal to question society's structures. However subversive its preaching may be with respect to its relationship to the institutions and values of society, Salafism rejects any undertaking of destabilization so that it ends up neutralizing the oppositional discourse that it propagates. We could describe their politicization as the superpositioning of a discourse of nonengagement on a terrain that is propitious for making demands (socioeconomic membership in the lumpen and religious belonging to the stigmatized).

If it is possible to see in the Da'wa Salafiyya a factor that anesthetizes the partisan point of view, this religiosity presents the comparative double advantage of being able to revile a delegitimized political order without having to make an effort to change the world. This last element explains why the appetite for the entrepreneurial world and mass consumer society is favored: believers benefit from an economically developed society, civil rights, and the context of an exit from politics. The religious impossibility of engaging in confrontation is explained by the simple fact that for this generation of young people politics in its militant and organized version figures in a very relative manner; besides, this position seems to justify religiously an agenda that is widely observable beyond Salafi communities.

The desire to enrich oneself and integrate in the mass-consumption society is thus multiplied by the religious carte blanche accorded the Salafi. Moreover, for some people this militant apoliticism is reinforced the more that business success is encountered, so that investment in the economic area is accompanied by rejection of political engagement. Likewise, being focused on the imperative of migrating to the pious land furnishes a supplementary safety valve for depoliticization. The decreasing identification with society, already weak before conversion to Salafism, intensifies the closer his career brings the practicant to the great departure. This doctrine thus both serves to reinforce the resentment many individuals socialized in the ghetto harbor and to dispense the seemingly paradoxical advice to eschew institutionalized protest. Salafist socialization in its political aspect therefore takes on a tribunitial dimension to the extent that the political relationship can be viewed as a win-win situation. With the pious contemporary legitimizing his stance toward society through the religious, we can observe here the diffusion of a feeling of frustration and a demand for recognition that are not called on to engender an organized conflict with the rest of society.[14] We can assume that the Salafist counterculture has an integrationist relationship to institutions that is simultaneously imprinted by defiance; the initial conditions of Salafist apoliticism have to be sought in the prior socialization of its practicants.

An Example of This Dual Habitus: The Conspiracy Theory

The conspiratorial analysis of the Muslim situation both on the French level and globally enjoys widespread popularity in Salafi communities. Acquiring an axial dimension informed by thinking themselves the favorite enemies of the more powerful civilization, Salafis count on Allah and their faith to see them through this trial. This antagonism facilitates a perception of themselves as the last resisters against a new world order. The West is presented as an impersonal figure, with the Jews, the Americans, the *kuffar* (nonbeliever), the Freemasons, and the rich vilified at one time or another. The anti-imperialist dimension underlying this analytical matrix is interpreted with a logic of religious struggle but equally a logic of class conflict. Impoverished because they are plundered by the rules of the global economy and dominated by the fact of their status as enemies of the imperialists, Salafis redress their situation by blaming an undefined group for the harm they have suffered. From

---

[14] The hypothesis of a tribunician function pertaining to some Islamic currents was formulated in the early 1980s by Rémy Leveau and Gilles Kepel at a time when preaching the Tabligh was in vogue among the first-generation immigrants, before they found a place in a French society in crisis and an often difficult relationship with immigrant populations. See Rémy Leveau and Gilles Kepel (eds.), *Les musulmans dans la société française* (Muslims in French society) (Paris: Presses de Sciences Po, "Références," 1988), 37; Georges Lavau, *À quoi sert le Parti communiste français?* (What good is the French Communist Party?) (Paris: Fayard, 1981).

this perspective, their identification is no longer with the Da'wa Salafiyya but with Islam, which supposedly authorizes defenders like Osama bin Laden, as echoed by the example that follows. The projected frame properly speaking is no longer true Islam but individuals defying Western imperialism all over the world.

We are once more in Cairo, in the Ma'adi quarter's Carrefour shopping center. We spent an afternoon in this symbol of globalization, frequented by the middle class that has benefited from the policy of economic liberalization since the 1980s. After immigrating, French Salafis manifestly maintain the typically French or Western structure of consumption, so we were sure we would find some in this hypermarket. And in fact we routinely came across Salafis from all backgrounds and countries. We met Omar and Ilyas, both in their thirties and from Lyon, accompanied by ten-year-old Mohamed, Omar's son. Ilyas is a convert from a family originally from Spain; Omar is a child of the Algerian immigration. The two practicants have been in Egypt for a year and a half and say that they came to "perfect their religion." We surmise from the presence of his son that Omar is in Cairo on a *hijra* of origin, the length of his stay buttressing the guess. Ilyas says that arrived in the country at the same time. We conducted the interview on June 28, 2009, in the shopping center's food court:

AUTHOR: And so you're done with France? You have no plans to go back? For you the *hijra* is it, you've done it, there's no going back?
[*The two Salafis look at each and smile.*]
OMAR: Ah, no, we've made our choice, we are fine here in Egypt. We're here to study, to learn, to perfect our religion. France, that's . . . There's such a big difference now. . . . We're not going. . . . Honestly, there's a big difference between France and Egypt. On many levels.
AUTHOR: Such as?
OMAR: Such as? [*Thinks a moment*] For instance, soon Muslims won't even be allowed to wear the veil. Looking at it, at this moment, you would say this is it: everybody lets go of Islam, that's it, it's gone. I would really like to know what the problem is.
AUTHOR: You're talking about the niqab, for example?
OMAR: Yeah, the niqab, but not just the niqab. There are lots of things. You think, for example, that the *kouffar*, when they talk about the niqab they are only talking about the niqab. Beyond the veil, there's prayer and the rituals. And that's a fact.

AUTHOR: What do you say to people who say it doesn't matter in Islam, you can wear the veil or not in the case of the women, they remain Muslim if they don't put on the veil?

OMAR: I answer you by telling you to return to the Sunna. Let me ask you a question: Does the Koran say you have to pray?

AUTHOR: Hmm. Yes, yes, prayer, that's in the Koran, yes, that's found in it, yes.

OMAR: [*In a professorial tone*] So then what do you do? If you want to pray, what do you do?

AUTHOR: You mean, if you're Muslim, how do you do it? I have a feeling you're going to tell me.

OMAR: You refer to the Sunna, you'll look up in the Sunna if they tell you to do something in the *kitab Allah* [book of God, i.e., the Koran]. And, bah, as to the veil, it's the same thing. What does the book tell you about the niqab? Eh bah, afterwards, you'll see by the example of the Prophet how it was done back then. There you have it. Does the Prophet tell people to wear the niqab? The answer is yes. There is the niqab in his tradition.

AUTHOR: So, for you, this is the ultimate secret as far as you are concerned?

OMAR: I guarantee you that the Muslims won't get anywhere if they don't return to the Book and the Prophet. You see very well what kind of state they're in. Don't be fooled, it's the end of the world. We'll soon get to the end. Look at the wars, the politics, all that. We're coming to the end.

AUTHOR: For example? What makes you think that?

OMAR: Bah, look around you. You see it, in Palestine, Gaza, in the Muslim countries. You don't think there's a meaning to all that? We are in the end times there.

AUTHOR: And for example, Palestine, the Gaza, what does that tell you?

OMAR: It tells me that . . . Well, the Jews, we know them, and you know they mean to harm Islam. We know, but all right. . . . Hamas, frankly, you can't say it followed the Book and the advice of the scholars. It's well known that Palestine, where there are *kouffar* now . . . Just as with the niqab, they must get back to the Sunna. We know that Palestine has to be left behind, it's a country now in the hands of the *kouffar*. Like Sheikh Albani said, the Palestinians must quit their country. Just like the sheikh said, *rahimahou Allah* [May God hold him in His Holy Mercy], as Sheikh Albani indicated, the Palestinians must leave the country. They must have confidence in Allah and quit the country. If not, did you see what Hamas did? They started a war, they massacred, you saw that? You could say they handed the, the, the . . . Like they say in the Maghreb, they handed white soap [a pretext] to the Israelis. There, that's the result of an *'aquida batila* [false dogma], and like the scholars of the Sunna put it, "al-'aquida al-batila hiya al-fassed fil-ard" [An erroneous belief or dogma is corruption on earth].

AUTHOR: And so, for you, Hamas, for example, is a movement that did not apply Islam?

OMAR: Not just Hamas, the Muslim Brotherhood. And the Muslim Brotherhood is a corrupted *'aquida* [dogma], that's what got them to where they are today. They did the opposite of what should have been done.

AUTHOR: And so, what is this *'aquida* by the Muslim Brotherhood?

OMAR: The Muslim Brotherhood, they have an *'aquida takfiriyya* [excommunication dogma]. They put the *takfir* on the rulers. They tell them they are finished... that they left Islam. However, that's very serious. There are also *takfiri* in France. They say weird things. When you hear them, you just want to...

AUTHOR: For example, what do they say? What do they say that's strange?

OMAR: For example, you see, they say what to do with the *kouffar* in France, that it's *bilad al-kufr* [a country of unbelief], you can loot them, you can... It's a war, and so you can steal from them, you can even sell them drugs, some say, it's halal for them. You can also take the women, it's the spoils of war, as they say, just like that, it lets them have more women than is permitted in Islam.

AUTHOR: And you, Ilyas, what do you think about all that?

ILYAS: Ah, me, I tell you, it doesn't concern me. I live according to the Prophet's example. Those political doings, I mean... The Prophet, they offered him power, but he said no. He did the *hijra*. And yet... [*Wide-eyed*] He could have had anything, but he chose the religion.

AUTHOR: One question: tell me, things went well with your family when you told them about becoming a Muslim?

ILYAS: [*Pained look*] Ah, no, it was... difficult.

AUTHOR: Meaning what? That is, if you want to talk about it.

ILYAS: How to describe it? My parents didn't at all, at all accept it. They told me... well, I won't... But it was hot. [*Brief silence*] My grandmother, even she said to me, "But why did you do that? You're not an Arab!" So there it is, all right, but all right, *al-hamdoulillah*.

. . .

AUTHOR: Omar, what do you say to people who say that Muslims are targeted these days? That it's not their fault what's happening to them, because people have it in for them regardless? There's some kind of overall conspiracy?

OMAR: But of course. It's clear, no need for debate about that. Listen, for example, me, I understand things, I see things, I tell myself, "It's not normal, it can't possibly be." If Muslims think they are going to succeed outside the *kitab* and the Sunna, they're mistaken. Modern life, as they call it, it's not... We know that, well, there are people who have it in for Islam.

AUTHOR: Would you mind being a bit more specific?

OMAR: For instance, I don't believe the theories about September 11. I'm sure they're trying to make us believe things that are completely... If you don't know that there is, like you say, a conspiracy... Yes, there's a conspiracy. Do you know the Illuminati,[15] the Freemasons, all that? And bah, let me tell you there are things that happen....

AUTHOR: For example, you don't believe the American thesis about September 11?

OMAR: Listen, I'm going to tell you something. I love bin Laden because of what he says about the rulers, when he puts the *takfir* and all that on them. But there are some things that are questionable. First of all, bin Laden denied he did it. He never said it was him. Moreover, I saw on TV that he wears a gold ring. Everyone knows that gold is forbidden in Islam for men. Also, they showed him eating with his left hand, but, I'm sorry to say, you just don't eat with your left according to the Sunna. There has never been a Muslim who, so to speak, knows his religion and wore a gold ring and ate with his left: I'm sorry, but that's odd.... After, I can tell you, I don't agree with bin Laden, and, I tell you, me... For me, I tell you... He left, he turned back to the *hukam* [rulers], so I don't care for him.

AUTHOR: So you believe in the theory of a September 11 conspiracy?

OMAR: If you don't believe me, type "Loose change French" into Google.[16] It's a documentary that explains all about September 11. You'll see, it explains a lot of things.

....

---

[15] Latin for "the illuminated." The name of a secret society whose project is to dominate the world by infiltrating governments and organizing revolutions.

[16] Here Omar makes references to a documentary series made by Dylan Avery whose main thesis is that the attacks of September 11, 2001, were not carried out by Islamic terrorists but by members of the U.S. government.

AUTHOR: So, you don't trust the Western leaders, regardless of who? In France, for example, you don't see any difference between Sarkozy and Chirac?

OMAR: None. There is no difference. I'm even going to tell you this: for me, Sarkozy is much worse. I heard him say once he wanted to change the Koran. He said that some things in the Koran needed to be changed. People indeed believe in progress, that is, by detaching themselves from religion, but, bah, let me tell you, it's false. Muslims today haven't understood that. It's in religion that they'll find their solution.

AUTHOR: Sarkozy said the Koran needed changing? You sure about that?

OMAR: [*A short laugh*] You don't believe me. And bah, you know he even put out some verse that caused him problems. I'm telling you, he said there are some verses that needed changing. And I'm going to tell you another thing. Do you know the book *The Signs of the End Times?*[17]

AUTHOR: Yes, I know it, sure.

OMAR: He even gave the pages. He said page 241 needed changing, 242, and 243. It caused him a problem. You realize, now, they are going to make us change Islam.

Toward a Politicized Puritanism for Some Salafis: Premises for a Mutation?

Despite disclaimers by a number of practicants, the Salafist field must not be thought of as a fixed space where the sole logic prevailing is that of a pure and simple application of norms established by the movement's clerics. While the majority of the faithful internalize the principle of political nonintervention, certain evolutions in the relations between Islam and French society lead others to reevaluate this principle. We thus find among the contemporary pious with a university degree a greater propensity for "existing politically,"[18] making it seem as if the intellectual capital as well as the mastery of social and political militancy's codes influence the perception of a doctrine that is less conservative and more subject to certain reconstructions than might be apparent.

---

[17] Yusuf Al-Wabil, *Les signes de la fin des temps* (The signs of the end times) (Paris: Al-Hadith, 2006).
[18] Salafis making the move to organized militancy thus are appropriating Abdelmalek Sayad's thesis that "to exist is to exist politically." See Abdelmalek Sayad, "Exister, c'est exister politiquement" (To exist is to exist politically), *Presses et immigrés en France* (Press and immigrants in France), nos. 135–136, 13–21 (December 1985).

The struggle against Islamophobia, for example, may be seen as a reinforcing factor in this Salafism of protests, illustrating the premises of a more classic politicization and militancy. Incapable of allowing itself to forgo a strategy of speaking out on this problematic of concern to a large number of Muslims in France, it illustrates the influence of context on the actors. The affair of the Muhammad cartoons in 2006[19] is a choice example of this new state of mind characterizing a segment, minimal but growing, of the practicants. Sometimes spread across generations, some believers are linked by an approach that is more militant than their preaching and driven to expand beyond strictly religious and private circles.

Nordine is a family man of Algerian extraction. He comes from a family of scholars; for instance, during the 1990s his brother knew Ali Belhadj (former leader of the Algerian Islamic Front for Salvation), who tried to save the *'aquida batila* [false dogma]. In his fifties, Nordine is a professor of management sciences in a business school. Awarded a doctorate in mass market retailing in the 1990s, he holds noticeably different views from those of the young practicants. While he is versed in the references and writings of the movement's major clerics, he does not dress like them; moreover he chooses to vote. Sometime after the affair of the caricatures exploded, he and Abdelwahid got the idea of writing a book to present a view of the Prophet's image opposed to that being conveyed by the media.[20] The collaboration between the two believers yielded the book *The True Face of the Prophet Muhammad: Beyond the Caricatures*; tens of thousands of copies were distributed free of charge.

Abdelwahid put his business and management skills in the service of the production, distribution, and promotion of this book. Based on texts about the Prophet sourced from Western literature (Victor Hugo, Bernard Shaw, Voltaire, Tolstoy, Goethe, etc.), the book even led to some conversions to Islam, according to Abdelwahid, a source of pride for him. Given away in large quantities at Islamic conferences, in bookstores, and at diverse other venues, this book, beyond its social impact, illustrates a "going upscale." Far

---

[19] An intellectual and diplomatic crisis stirred up in 2006 by the publication of drawings in the Danish magazine *Jyllands Posten* showing the Prophet Muhammad in situations that offended Muslims worldwide (for example, wearing a bomb as a turban). An international debate then ensued on how far freedom of expression can go, the defenders of the right to satire opposing those who saw in the caricatures an amalgamation of Muslims and terrorists.

[20] Kepel, *Beyond Terror and Martyrdom*, Cambridge, MA: Harvard University Press, 2010; Olivier Roy, "Caricatures: Géopolitique de l'indignation" (The caricatures: Geopolitics of indignation), *Le Monde*, February 8, 2006.

from adhering to the ethic of retreat adopted by the majority of practicants, *The True Face of the Prophet Muhammad* gives material form to the posture of speaking out that would henceforth characterize some of the practicants. Reactive instead of proactive as their position may be regarding transforming a society judged to be nefarious, Nordine and Abdelwahid can be seen as examples of the potential a dynamic assimilation of Salafist meaning holds. Because they own intellectual and social capital and are tuned in to an environment seen as dangerous to Islam, they embody a new Salafism, aligning itself with an agenda that is increasingly evident in France, characterized in particular by a growing desire to forestall animosity from the rest of society.

Abdelwahid is a good example of this new believer profile, seeking to translate the orthodox pious reference into the classic militant domain. His trajectory—he comes from a neotraditionalist family and has a college degree—makes him someone who is repulsed by life in France but who nevertheless engages in a defense of Muslim interests there. He subscribes to the conspiracy theory that September 11 was arranged by the U.S. Government and does not hide it. On a professional level, he trusts only entrepreneurship and business, seeking to imitate the Pious Ancients. He is condescending toward women who do not wear the hijab; in Algeria we watched him tell a woman with uncovered head, "God condemns the woman who goes out without her hijab." On the other hand, the prohibition on voting poses a problem for him. Indeed, after hearing Sheikh Ferkous's view of voting, he gave the following response, calibrated by the fact that he was disagreeing with a person of the religious stature of an *'alim*: "He did not convince me." It is true that, back in Paris, Abdelwahid did not hesitate to take part in any demonstration involving the image of Islam. We observed him joining dozens of people in front of the German embassy demonstrating on behalf of the collective Against Islamophobia in France[21] several days after a young Egyptian mother who was studying in Germany was murdered for wearing a veil. Intent on defending her right and that of her coreligionists to wear the veil, the pregnant Marwa el-Sherbini was in a Dresden courtroom when she was knifed eighteen times, while her three-year-old son watched. Abdelwahid did not shrink from taking action; standing up for the "martyr of the veil" and hoping to sensitize people to the growing Islamophobia in Europe, he made T-shirts and distributed badges in memory of the young mother. In his Al-Mouslim bookstore, polemical works are stacked beside commentaries

---

[21] www.islamophobie.net.

by Sunni clerics. One can also find books there on how to mount a legal defense when discriminated against because of a religious affiliation.

We came to know Abdelwahid during the release in 2008 by the CCIF in Paris (Group against Islamophobia in France, most visible organization against anti-Islam and anti-Muslims hatred in France) of its first report on Islamophobia. Only his *qamis* actually conformed to the Sunna, which clashed with the suits, ties, and sweaters worn by cadres of a more militant Islam. His attachment to a politically active approach by the Da'wa Salafiyya reveals a believer whose morality is at the core of the various tensions characterizing the Salafist sphere. He does not consider himself to be French and seeks to get back to Algeria, where a restaurant awaits him whose operation is supposed to provide him and his wife with a living. He is turned off by violent activism and appeals by some Muslims to overthrow the powers that he views as legitimate. Moreover he has developed an intensive entrepreneurial ethic, as attested to by his creation of the Halaldom retail business brand for marketing sheep sacrificed according to the Islamic home rite. He plans to profit from his firm's brand by contracting with one of the biggest Algerian delicatessens in France, a specialist in Oriental baked goods, in order to sell through his website products that a part of the Maghrebian population in France is very partial to. Besides that, his bookstore puts into practice his religious effort, allowing him to preach to people passing by on Jean-Pierre Timbaud Street. He says he does not like the *kouffar*, including the political officeholders he accuses of conspiring against Islam and Muslims, but he has empathy for some who challenge the "imperialist" order. The following vignette is illustrative. As a matter of fact, we were struck by remarks Abdelwahid had made on our sojourn in Algiers during Ramadan in 2009. We were watching a TV report on the visit to Algeria that day by the president of Venezuela, Hugo Chavez. The flagbearer of Bolivarism had come to discuss oil prices and production levels with his counterpart, Abdelaziz Bouteflika, to help stabilize the global market for black gold. The report prompted an enthusiastic, spontaneous reaction from the young entrepreneur, who pointed his finger at the South American statesman and exclaimed:

ABDELWAHID: Oh la la, I dig that guy! He's a star, all right! I like the guy. A fine guy!
AUTHOR: Who are you talking about? Chavez?

ABDELWAHID: Him, yes. A resister, someone who says no to the Americans, who doesn't roll over, who says "You can't roll me over." I really like the guy. He tells them "No!"

This is a rather surprising admiration, especially keeping in mind the principles of rejecting that which is not Islamic and detesting what God disapproves of, principles Salafis regularly proclaim. Regardless, the fact that a Catholic, leftist, anticapitalist head of state appeared on Algerian TV was enough to genuinely thrill the young orthodox entrepreneur. Abdelwahid's political and moral perspectives are joined by tendencies that we would have a fair amount of difficulty finding in other social groups. The hatred of the imperialist Western domination of the world, the appetite for the market economy, business and individual freedom associated with a distaste for the harm done by liberalism, the refusal to take part in a political project clearly out of fear of stirring up sedition, all the while recognizing the necessity of fighting in defense of Islam, are elements at the confluence of differing socializations that shaped a person like Abdelwahid. The scene we just described can therefore be interpreted on a microsociological level as a moment of reemergence of the peripheral and marginal socialization that Abdelwahid had known before his conversion to the Minhaj Salafi.

A Cultural Heritage of Antagonism as a Factor in Rupture
Identity Formation

The second prism for breaking down the predisposition to rupture formalized in sacred terms by the Salafist way attaches to the weight of familial socialization, one of whose consequences is distrusting society. Socialized affectively in an extraterritorial framework, Salafis conceive of the familial hearth as an extension of the family's country and of the cultural codes imported from the *bled* (country of origin); such a climate fosters an antagonistic religious socialization. The reappropriation of religious principles is in large part determined by the preexistence in the family of a difficult relationship with France; thus the assimilation of one ethic over another results from the road to be traveled between the native milieu and a new religious community preaching hierarchy and differentialism. While it is not the only factor authorizing the emergence of the "emmigré" (immured immigrant) who perceives himself as a stranger in the receiving society, primary socialization plays an important role in predisposing him to embrace the Salafist morality. The same observation applies to the post-Christian Salafis belonging to native French families who also are not sustained by a strong sentiment of belonging to the nation even before they embrace orthodoxy. The emmigré in this sense echoes the "marginal man," "torn between two worlds and with a conscience that is simultaneously revived and murdered by his condition [and] susceptible to creativity given his critical position toward a milieu which he confronts first of all as unfamiliar and which then is always in a position that potentially can be relativized. Never imprisoned in just one manner of interpreting situations, he enjoys a margin of supplementary maneuver, a distance."[22]

The Maghrebians: Inertia More than a Return to the Religious

Aside from the fact that from a demographic point of view the Maghrebian community is the prime face of the Muslim presence in France, the initially North African character of Salafist Islam in France is also explained by the attraction of a religiosity harking back to a positive image of Arabness. The dearth of individuals from the Turkish immigration, which totals between 200,000 and 250,000 individuals in France, tends to nuance the thesis of a sociocultural universality of this identity. Among different communities that, even if not proportional, are observable, the ethnic composition of Salafi communities reveals that the Maghrebians are most susceptible to the orthodox discourse. Due to this socialization, the individual rediscovers the spiritual charms of the Orient and, more specifically, of Saudi Arabia, the country that is at the epicenter of the movement on a global scale. Parental education has maintained the practicant in a logic of identification with the country of origin. However, in entering upon this career, the Salafi amplifies his empathy for the *bled* by including henceforth the entirety of the Arab or Muslim world in the list of societies he approves of in the name of his religious values. The *hijra* best illustrates this, since the choice of destination is between the country the family emigrated from and a country with even greater symbolic value thanks to the supposed respect for Islamic injunctions and its economic success (Malaysia, the Emirates, etc., not to mention Saudi Arabia). Salafist socialization can be understood as much as an assimilation

---

[22] Le Breton, *L'interactionnisme symbolique*, 31; E. V. Stonequist, *The Marginal Man* (New York: Charles Scribner's Sons, 1937).

of the identity of one part of the parents, starting with formal religious membership and the "myth of the lost paradise," that is, the country of origin, as a reaction against this religious socialization that is more ethnic than scientific. Certainly Islam is transmitted, but without the modus vivendi that normally accompanies the passing on of this religious heritage. Opposed to this Islam of "us," the Minhaj Salafi is much more an Islam of "me," the individual becoming conscious of himself and his responsibility for the need to revive an abandoned model of society. For the Maghrebian practicants, adherence to true precepts includes allegiance to the extraterritorial vision of the parents and the reaction against the incompleteness of their religious design for their offspring. As such, perceiving yourself as the equivalent of a born-again Muslim is highly debatable.

The rediscovery of a purified Islam is, in effect, perceived as the true point of departure for the Salafist career, theoretically symbolizing the true act of birth of the religious engagement. However, it can be explained only by the phenomenon of an inertia that predisposes the practicant to such a metamorphosis. Indeed, we observe among Salafis of Maghrebian ancestry a completely relative estrangement from the Islamic reference valued before their conversion, despite a discourse that praises the divine grace inherent in having been guided toward the Salafiyya. The pre-Salafi trajectory is in reality a synonym for integration of the religious norm, even if the behaviors and social practices were not always aligned with Islamic morality. Even though the identification with Islam is only derived from the Salaf reference, the religious life under parental auspices in a certain sense being neutralized by it, the Salafi has never cut himself off from the Muslim faith. The puritan offer thus touches individuals profoundly associated with a parental conscience that the migratory experience and settling on foreign soil have disadjusted. This notion of disadjustment is key for understanding the memory of the Salafi coming from a Maghrebian environment. On a religious level, he has not inherited any structuring practice that might have gone hand in hand with this essentially nominal Islamic socialization. Finding himself disadjusted will contribute to an individuation of the religious identity that situates itself both in continuity and in rupture relative to the primary Islamic socialization.[23]

---

[23] William Thomas, *On Social Organization and Social Personality* (Chicago: University of Chicago Press, 1966), 61.

The logic prevailing in the case of Salafist socialization, secondary to the primary familial stage, is one of passing beyond the inherited religious norm, all the while claiming prolongation of the Muslim affiliation stemming from parental education. Emancipating themselves by a certain kind of continuity, the Maghrebian Salafis end up satisfying their parents after a period of conflict and their peers as well as the scholars by dynamically perpetuating the heritage whose bearers they are. Above all, they enrich their heritage through a more rigorous and drastic approach to the religion. The sociocultural innovation that the Minhaj Salafi represents in fact can be understood as a differentialist response by some social actors situating themselves in a representational framework and religious matrix that are reinforced. Being Salafi means going beyond, in the name of denser Islamic references, a familial socialization that willingly accepts settling in France for socioeconomic reasons but is recalcitrant in fully identifying psychologically with this society.

Judging from this, Salafism must be seen as the perpetuation of an immigrant identity that crosses the assimilation of modernity's socioeconomic and cultural codes with the rejection of political and symbolic integration that prior familial socialization rendered irreconcilable with belonging to Islam. The parental instance constituting as much a model as a challenge, Salafist socialization among practicants from a Maghrebian background is a form of reaction *and* continuity. The phenomenon of inertia represented by inscribing his social being in a religious *and* communitarian perspective embodies the belief that Islam, as a sociological fact, cannot take root in France. This intransigent Islam simultaneously crystallizes both the victory and the defeat of religious socialization initiated by the parents discovering in religious affiliation a symbol of their national and cultural origin. Even if some of their offspring again take up a religious identity in an absolutist and antagonistic mode, doing so promotes a denationalized Islamic practice. Having noted the disconnection between "cultural parentage" and "puritan genealogy,"[24] it perceives the refusal to embrace the substance of the parental faith as a key moment while partaking of a real sociocultural inertia. This uncoupling is what is interpreted as a rebirth in the shadow of Islamic purity, when it fact it is a question of an identity strategy allowing a symbolic "rising above" a modernity that is in fact assimilated while continuing to take advantage of it in practical terms.

---

[24] Olivier Roy, *La Sainte Ignorance: Le temps de la religion sans culture* (Holy ignorance: The time of religion without culture) (Paris: Seuil, 2008).

The familial memory determined a relationship of mistrust with society, justified especially by the impossibility of thinking of the Muslim condition in an endogenous manner, but it did so without offering a religious modus operandi. One of the most striking examples of this phenomenon is undoubtedly the relation to religious ostentation, which differs in singular fashion between children and parents. Where the first-generation immigrants were set on not making waves and contented themselves with a low-key demonstration of their religious affiliation, the Salafist ethic considers their presence on non-Muslim soil an unacceptable reason for downplaying demonstrations of Islamic affiliation. In this regard, it is possible to see the mark of a higher respect among earlier generations for the receiving society or a wish not to attract the symbolic reproaches of the natives. This is different from the younger generation's disdain for the opinion of their fellows and for integration with a despised society, which nonetheless remains a pole they identify with.

This facilitates an understanding of why Turkish Islam paradoxically is more impervious to Salafist discourse. Taking this route must be analyzed as the product not of a return to Islam but of a dual dynamic: the inertia of the religious and then being clamped in a symbolic and sociological vise that is both French and globalized at the same time.

The weight of family history, and most especially of its migratory dimension, is palpable in the discourse of Salafis who have taken the step to *hijra*, for example. This rupture, represented as a liberation from the ungodly, can be seen as the best illustration of the symbolic weakness of the tie between Salafis and France. Hassan is forty years old. In his own words, he is "an Algerian who live[d] in France." Today he has given up on this country and rejoices because of it. For some years now Hassan has been able to enjoy his house in Algiers, in the Qoba district, near the mosque where Sheikh Ferkous officiates. We met Hassan by its exit; a friend of Abdelwahid introduced us. Not in the least intimidated by us, he began to describe the route he took from Villeneuve-la-Garenne to the Algerian capital. His journey is all the more interesting because it is emblematic of one by a person who never liked living in France. Hassan does not have a single empathetic word for France, even after having spent most of his life there. He speaks of his *hijra* as if it were a liberation and a successful conclusion. His son, all of ten years old, is close to him—seemingly very close, by the way Hassan holds him by the shoulder. Hassan juggles his interview with a few seconds of play with the boy, who, like his father, is dressed in Sunna style. Their complicity is such that when Hassan responds to our queries, he looks at his child, as if addressing him is of higher priority, ostensibly in the hope that the little boy will pursue the road he himself has traveled to provide his child the opportunity to live on Islamic soil.

In France Hassan was a tile layer, plying his trade in many houses owned by the French. That experience contributed to feeding an attitude toward them that oscillates between condescension and distaste. While he responded to our questions only by swearing by God and warning against any person who would argue for *iqamat fi bilad al-kufr* (living in the country of unbelief), two moments during our interview stayed with us. The first dealt with his vision of Algeria as his own country. Justifying his return by the religious necessity of living in a Muslim country, he cites the rhythm of life prevailing in France as the reason for having settled here and rejecting the uprooting that some Muslims have accepted:

HASSAN: But, tell me, when do we benefit from our country? When can we finally live in the house that we earned with the sweat of our brow? The people over there, I know how they think. They keep a house in their country, but they never benefit from it. Maybe . . . ten days, fifteen days, a month, a month and a half per year . . . I don't know what they are thinking. They say, "Yes, yes, let's retire, *inch'allah*." But when they finally get to retire, they're still over there, they can't leave. They take as their pretext the children, the routine; they are used to life in France. I don't get it. Here is their country [*points to the ground to indicate Algeria*]. When are they finally going to enjoy their home, their country?

AUTHOR: And so, for you, living in Algeria is fundamental because that's the place you must live? The fact that you have a house here, for example, that doesn't keep you from having one in France and enjoying both?

HASSAN: Let me tell you. I don't think of France as my country. I'll tell you a story. You know I have a Moroccan family. A part of my family is Moroccan. Well, let's say they are cousins. They mostly have girls, most of them are girls. You know what they did? They decided they had to buy a house in France because, well, that's where they lived, and so it was normal. You have to favor a house in France. As a result, you know what happened? They never bought a house in Morocco. And then they practically never again went to Morocco. Do you find that to be normal? They lost their country, their roots. Okay, they had their house, but they lived with the French. We, we live with Muslims. So the bottom line is, what did it get them?

The return journey occasions a sociological scene revelatory of the state of mind of numerous Salafis, starting with those with Algerian ancestry, which, as previously noted, constitute the principal community. We were riding in the car with Abdelwahid on the way back to downtown Algiers and asked him if he would mind making a detour past the French consulate, adjoining the embassy, the complex housing all French diplomatic institutions that spreads over a vast area (about thirty-nine acres) in the heart of the capital's Embassy Row. After taking longer than anticipated to find the consulate entrance, we finally were able to conclude our business. On the return trip, we again had to pass the administrative citadel, with its armed guards, who are actually a unit of French expatriate policemen in Algiers. At the sight of them, Abdelwahid exclaimed indignantly, "But that's not possible! Just look at it! You saw it! It's out of the question! It's finished, the era of colonialism! French Algeria is finished! But just have a look, their embassy takes up half the city. Look at the other embassies around it, over there, they're not like that. They think they can do anything, as if the country still belongs to them! It's not normal! It's intolerable! Who do they think they are?" When we answered that Algeria has more ties to France than any other country, making the imposing character of France's diplomatic and consular area in the city reasonable, he replied even more brusquely, "No! It's over, the Algerian war!" In a veritable syndrome of origins or paradise lost, Abdelwahid conveys the Salafi's complete identification with the country of his birth. Blending into the Algerian sociocultural landscape, Abdelwahid's journey to the cradle of his origins corresponds to a relegitimization of his own self. The Salafi, by his visceral attachment to the country of Algeria, refutes the thesis of a "double illegitimacy" of the children of the Maghrebian immigration.[25]

Surprised by the fervor of his outburst on seeing how deeply France is planted in the Algerian body, we learn a few days later that the young entrepreneur is a nephew of the first martyr of the national war of liberation. Indeed, while we accompanied him to exchange some currency near the harbor where young Algerians make money on the black market, we passed in front of an athletic field in downtown Algiers. This is where Abdelwahid told us the following: "You see this field, it's the Boualem Rahal Field. The first martyr casualty during the Battle of Algiers [in 1957] was my uncle. Every

---

[25] Abdelmalek Sayad, *L'immigration ou les paradoxes de l'altérité: 2. Les enfants illégitimes* (Immigration or the paradoxes of otherness: 2. The illegitimate children) (Paris: Raisons d'agir, "Cours et travaux" [Reasons to act, "Courses and works"], 2006).

year, on the anniversary of his death, the TV runs a documentary about him." The emotion in the young Salafi's voice was audible.[26] This love of his country reemerged the day he took us to the airport for our return to France. He took us to a souvenir shop in the airport, telling us he wanted to give us a present. Even though we politely begged off, the Salafi suddenly exclaimed, "Ah, of course! I know, you like books. I know just the thing for you." He went to the shelves full of books about Algeria and brought us one by Chems Eddine Chitour, *Algeria: The Past Revisited*,[27] which he was eager for us to have as a souvenir of our visit to his country.

The Turks, or the All-Included Religious Socialization: A Turnkey Islam

The near-absence in the Salafist communities of individuals from Turkish origins is an interesting indicator of the logics underpinning entry into this career. Addressing itself to all of humanity, this religiosity finds an echo foremost in individuals with memories of the Maghreb. But the extreme rarity of Salafis born to Turkish families is nevertheless striking. Practically nonexistent in France, the Turkish dimension of Salafism allows us to analyze in depth the success of this doctrine in other communities, Maghrebian ones above all. Based on our observations, a weak presence of believers from this origin is also a hallmark of the Tablighi movement; we noticed that the Tablighian religiosity, just like its Salafist competition, was distinctly more popular among Maghrebians, sub-Saharans, and converts. If such a balance sheet tends to confirm the idea that exclusive Islam is above all an affair of decultured people, it also reinforces the hypothesis that, despite the strictly religious differences, the Minhaj Salafi is a sociological continuation of the re-Islamization initiated by the Jama'at Tabligh.

In effect, it is a certain level of destructuring and deculturing that seems to explain differing predispositions between, for example, young Maghrebians

---

[26] On a conversational tangent about Algeria's political history with Abdelwahid one day, he shared a lesson on the importance of his country in the nonaligned movement following independence. He also discussed the importance of President Houari Boumediene, who made his mark with a voluntarist policy of getting out from under the East-West split to the benefit of defending his country's Arab identity. Here are Abdelwahid's words about the former Algerian head of state, spoken proudly: "He was the first ever to speak Arabic from the UN podium. The people were ecstatic about Algeria."

[27] Chems Eddine Chitour, *Algérie: Le passé revisité. Une brève histoire de l'Algérie* (Algeria: The past revisited. A short history of Algeria) (Algiers: Casbah Editions, 2004).

and young Turks when it comes to embracing the Salafist morality. By "destructuration" we understand that settling in France was accompanied by a rupture, partial or total, between the generations, which also affected religious representation. It notably engendered a reappropriation of the religious norm by the autochthonous generations on a basis that has little to do with the cultural tissue of the country of emigration. As such, the children's Islamic identity is integrated in a logic of differentiation relative to their parents' and is determined in the first place by the importing of religious conceptions from the country of origin. The profile of the emmigré thus assimilates the idea of not being of this country yet still not embracing the parental religious vision in its entirety.

The transmission of the religious norm is configured differently among the Turks. There we see a greater permeability to the influence of the state, for instance in the way worship is organized. It deploys by means of Turkish government-related structures such as DITIB (Türk-Islam Birliği de Diyanet Işleri, Turko-Islamic Union for Religious Affairs)[28] or the Milli Görüs (National Vision),[29] a transnational entity whose thinking is close to that of the Muslim Brotherhood but that primarily addresses itself to Turkish émigré communities in Europe. And here we are not even evoking other currents, like Süleymanci[30] or the movements close to thinkers like Fethullah Gülen.[31] More structured and more audible than Maghrebian consular Islam, with its proportionately fewer immigrant individuals in France, Turkish Islam appears as a more limited identity. The schools and mosques operated within this community framework are more youth oriented, for example. The religious socialization that results leads to a stronger identification with Turkey, which offers an explanation of the distance felt from the Da'wa Salafiyya, a religiosity perceived as being more Arab or Saudi.

---

[28] This is the main new consular organ. It operates most Turkish mosques in France and so constitutes the key religious and communitarian regulatory authority in France's Turkish Islamic landscape.

[29] Today it counts approximately 500,000 members in Europe. It is a re-Islamization movement created in 1971 in Braunschweig, Germany, stimulated by the Islamic leader Necmettin Erbakan (died February 2011), a cadre of the Refah Partisi (Party of Prosperity) and Turkish prime minister between 1996 and 1997. He also headed up the Saadet Parti (Happiness Party). He was one of the mentors of Reccep Tayyib Erdogan, current prime minister of Turkey, and one of the leaders in Adalet ve Kalkinma Partisi (Party of Justice and Development), in power since 2002 in Turkey.

[30] Sunni brotherhood founded by Sheikh Süleyman Hilmi Tunahan in the 1950s. See Samim Akgönül, "Islam turc, islams de Turquie: Acteurs et réseaux en Europe" (Turkish Islam, Islams of Turkey), *Politique étrangère*, no. 1 (2005): 35–47.

[31] Turkish imam, writer, and thinker (born in 1938) who influenced a great brotherhood movement that spread beyond Turkey. He is known for his role in interfaith dialogue.

Another, more fundamental vector of impermeability to Salafism is the compartmentalization of numerous families of Turkish origin, most of them from rural backgrounds. It should be noted that neither Tablighi nor Salafist preaching has ever really made inroads in the mosques operated by a Turkish community. This being an Islam in a sense partitioned off within the French Islamic terrain, the religious socialization engenders distance between itself and any form of concurrent Islamic acculturation. Religion, culture, and national or communitarian affiliation being perceived as consubstantial, to import a different Islamic referent would resonate like splitting from a clearly defined united group.

This second factor of deculturation is thus relatively weaker among Muslims of Turkish ancestry then among the Maghrebians. Adopting the Salafist norm results in real distancing from the parental cultural heritage. The act of embracing this career, theoretically refractory with regard to nationalist feelings, can occur only with individuals predisposed by their environment to think of religious practice independently of this communitarian vise grip. In this respect, the ability of some young Muslims of Maghrebian ancestry to embrace an Islam that is a-national in theory translates above all as a sociocultural porosity that is greater in the North African than the Turkish milieu. The religious strategies of young Maghrebians, such as quietist Salafism, can be understood only as being in the spirit of the greater sociological openness of Maghrebian families compared to their Turkish counterparts. Even though without question the worldviews are influenced by the "ghetto effect," the adoption of Salafist morals must be grasped while keeping in mind a complementary dynamic. This concerns the permeability of many children of the Maghrebian immigration to social practices generally interpreted as signs of opening, despite the facility with which they paradoxically think of themselves as representing a counterworld. This is the case, for example, with socioethnic exogamy, which is higher among the Maghrebians than in Turkish circles, or the mastery and usage of the French language, which is much less prevalent among the latter.[32] In this regard, the Salafist career is the indicator of a sociological opening that coexists with psychological partitioning and produces a phenomenon of religious exclusion.

---

[32] Trajectoires et origines, "Enquête sur la diversité des populations en France" (Trajectories and origins, Inquiry into the diverse populations of France), document de travail [working document] no. 168, October 2010, http://teo.site.ined.fr/.

The Converts, or the Melting-Pot Socialization

The sociological uniformity that is representative of the overwhelming proportion of individuals who have embraced Islam, even those not born into Muslim circles, illustrates another Minhaj Sahih trait. From the perspective of converts, the composition of these communities is once again very close to that of communities linked to the Tabligh. While not the main subgroup within the Salafi ensemble, the visibility of converts in both movements must be acknowledged. Although, in a sense, those embracing the Salafist principles consider themselves converts, even if they never abandoned the faith of their Muslim parents, we apply the term "convert" in this section to the individual born outside a milieu in which Islam is claimed as the constitutive faith.

This figure is without doubt one of the most important in the landscape of beliefs in contemporary Western societies. If the Salafi prides himself on an individualistic conception of the religious, the convert chooses disethnicization. A modern man of faith in our age, he reflects the serious developments of the religious field in a country like France. Two dynamics must be highlighted. The first concerns the sociological secularization of French society. It authorizes the individual's distancing with respect to the entirety of the religious discourse on the way to choosing what best suits his aspirations. Structured in the manner of a true marketplace of beliefs, in the individualist societies that tend to reinforce the effect of anomie tied to certain heritages, such as the immigrant legacy or territorial and symbolic apartness, the contemporary religious landscape permits the individuation of religiosity. In the case of Salafism, the project envisages the uniformization of belief and practice; adhering to this conception nevertheless occurs on an individual basis. The second dynamic operates in the decline of the regulatory power of the authorities of traditional religious socialization that are, for example, the family, the mosque, and to a lesser degree the structures connecting to consular Islam. The Turkish resistance to Salafism is explained in addition by the cultural solidity of immigrant families as well as by the proportionately higher and more effective density of structures of public regulation. This framework explains the porosity of one offer of Islam presenting itself as authentic, antisystem, and antirelativist; this is why the permeability of many converts is higher. Whether in cases of Tablighi or Salafi socialization, the receptivity to this type of discourse is due to the absence of intermediaries between the offer and the need for meaning.

The converts, who at a minimum constitute a quarter of all practicants, represent the ultimate state of modern religiosity.[33] Two kinds of explanation make it possible to identify the reasons why their numbers are so high in the Salafist movement. The first is of a sociological order and relates to the life the converts led before their first contact with the Islamic norm. The conversion of some of the individuals to this religion, for many resulting from immigration, cannot be understood without keeping in mind the existence of a melting-pot socialization that has young Muslims rub shoulders with non-Muslims in the districts where Islam is a social given. Despite what practicants say when they insist on a strong feeling of being the elect, there are marked similarities between youth in the suburbs in regard to identity strategies. Even before they decided to consciously embrace the Muslim credo, our interviewees evinced a real empathy for the fact of Islam. Mingling with the "brothers in the same boat" or "brothers in the hood," for many legacy Muslims the non-Muslims are distinguished by an unconscious religious socialization. This is the case with Adnan, who, even though he downplayed the influence of "mingling"[34] with Muslim friends during adolescence, hardly manages to hide the fact that Islam occupied an important place in his environment as a commonplace, legitimate source of identity. The link of brotherhood, in this sense, preexists the conversion, even if the Salafist morality establishes a symbolic demarcation between the initiated and those who are not. This emblematic closeness and group solidarity, if not class, within which the feeling of being relegated and dominated is structural, facilitates the integration of a more social than spiritual religious identity. Identifying with children of immigrants whom the system discriminates against, the convert is distinguished first by a predisposition for Islamizing his existence. Muslim by "absorption,"[35] whose prior life rendered him Muslimophile through solidarity and defiance in the face of an abhorrent symbolic order that rides roughshod over the inhabitants of the suburbs, the convert has access to the offer of Salafist meaning just like his ghetto brothers.

---

[33] Danièle Hervieu-Léger, *Le pèlerin et le converti: La religion en mouvement* (The pilgrim and the convert: Religion in motion) (Paris: Flammarion, "Champs," 2001).
[34] François de Singly, *Libres ensemble: L'individualisme dans la vie commune* (Together apart: Individualism in communal life) (Paris: Armand Colin, 2005).
[35] As for Jean-François Mayer, he brings up the case of "conversion by osmosis" in certain quarters of French and Swiss cities as a result of the structuring proximity between Muslims and non-Muslims where the former are in the majority. https://www.mayer.im/suisse-des-conversions-a-lislam-par-osmose/.

The second explanation touches on the nature of the links between practicants. If they are conceived as the pyramid type, the internal sociality of the movement sees itself as profoundly egalitarian, the sole source of hierarchy that is acceptable being linked to mastery of the '*ilm* (holy science). To the extent that the sole criterion of differentiation is religious culture, it is this personal investment that becomes the key to recognition within the Salafist field. In this scheme, in addition to the prestige connected with the fact of having passed more stages than those born Muslim, they line up with their peers, for example the Maghrebians. Salafism is a form of Islamic expression that in theory is not very sensitive to the influence of a culture based on the episteme of the Sunna; thus the differentiation criteria are neutralized, since the only reading filter attaches to the opinion of the '*oulama*. If the scientific capital is assimilated, then the practicant sees his prestige increase, be he Arab, black, or convert. This egalitarian dimension of Salafist preaching contrasts singularly with what can be observed in other Islamic socializations. For example, it works differently in an organization like PSM (Presence and Spirituality of Muslims), which gets its inspiration from that historic Moroccan opponent of Hassan II, the theoretician Sheikh Abdessalam Yassine, who died in 2012 after founding the antimonarchist Islamist movement Justice and Charity (al-'adl wal-ihssane). Attracting primarily Moroccan Muslims and converts with a Moroccan background, though fewer than the Minhaj Salafi, the preaching is strongly hierarchized. Here too the Tabligh and the Salafiyya are comparable in that the convert is less differentiated in them than in other preachings. By staying in a Muslim country for a religious apprenticeship, by immersing himself in a country of faith framed as a salutary migration, or by studying the authorized sources, the convert can claim a certain degree of precedence and act as a religious reference by climbing the ladder of orthodox apprenticeship.

The Life Cycle of Quietist Salafism: The Generational Effect

While the Salafist codes mostly affect postadolescents and young adults, it is useful to examine their age structure in order to highlight a dynamic vision of this identification. The path taken by these practicants involves a radicality differential in the approach to Islam that depends on the duration of this career. This is how their trajectory reveals an evolution in referencing the Salafist norm. Similar to the changes of perception that characterize the religiosity of many Tablighis[36] in the course of their religious commitment, Salafis also pass through several phases. To the extent that the stages inherent in their socialization are realized, with the salutary abandonment (*hijra*) ranking first among them, we observe a certain deradicalization both in discourse and in social practices. Four periods can be identified.

The first of these is linked to the figure of the "anti-me." This moment of Salafist memory is certainly not directly integrated with the orthodox journey, but it is crucial for understanding the practicant's psychology. The anti-me is what the pious contemporary was before conversion and what he should never have been. It is the result of deviant and soiled socialization induced by immersion in a society that is in all respects execrable. Synonymous with the erstwhile subjugation by the norms of the contemporary era, the Salafi rejects this self, especially because it symbolizes the moment in his life when he was "feminized" by being dominated by modern society. The Salafi in general refuses to talk about this period of his life, preferring to present himself as "born again" in Islam. We noticed the extreme difficulty our conversation partners had in divulging the content of their existence before their Salafization, even though we know their previous course proved decisive for their adopting Salafist morals.

The second phase begins at the moment of election. The pariah becomes the elect, the lost individual is saved by entering into the group of victors. If the practicant regards this moment as the first stage of his religious career, it is all the more an essential phase because it marks a moral reorientation. During adolescence, postadolescence, or young adulthood (under thirty years of age), the conversion to Salafism is plainly the expression of a quest for coherence but also the product of interactions between the individual and an environment in which Islam occupies an important place. What matters is that the religion represents a potential for eventual rupture and opposition. The stage of election is thus decisive in the anomic individual's course as he is carried toward a radical understanding of the sacred. The discovery of the orthodox canons corresponds to a period of psychological wonderment, when the practicant becomes progressively sensitive to the enveloping perfume of

---

[36] This part about Salafism, and specifically its dilution in a life cycle that, ultimately, encourages moderation of the demand for breaking with the rest of society, owes a great deal to the analysis by a specialist in the Tablighi movement in France, Moussa Khedimellah, a researcher at the École des hautes études en sciences sociales (School for Advanced Studies in the Social Sciences). Even if we identify stages in the Salafist career and explanatory logics distinct from Tablighi sociality, we owe much to his epistemological intuition.

the truth as the proofs of his religious superiority accrue to him. It is also a period of opening up to other people. The elect is happy with his fate, and the wonder that he feels ebbs dynamically with the project of setting others on the same path. The state of election lasts through the pyramidal socialization and begins to decline in step with the immunizing sociality beginning to replace the preceding stage. The time when Salafists interact with other Muslims according to an aristocratic logic is short compared with the period that follows. Still, it lingers for as long as there is hope for a conversion of coreligionists to his way of seeing outweighing the menace of perversion that stalks intrinsic purity. As long as the proselytizing effort induced through a unity of marginal extraversion prevails over the risk incurred of sullying himself, the pyramidal socialization is perpetuated.

In the opposite case, a phase of positive retrogression occurs. This is the longest and most radical stage. After the period of zeal, the practicant falls back on himself, deepening and bettering his condition. This third anthropological moment coincides with the phenomenon that most merits the term "rupture." It certainly is the moment that contributes the most to the view of Salafism in France as a sectarian and asocial religion. The check on the offensive posture leads Da'wa Salafiyya adherents to a more defensive positioning. The pious contemporary generally devotes several years of his career to this period. This withdrawal for deepening his Salafity in a country and era hostile to true believers coincides with the years of youth, when the Salafi situates himself betwixt and between. Usually single and still living at home, often performing insecure socioprofessional functions, emblematic of an incomplete integration into the labor market, the practicant during these years also retreats to the peer group. The involution that depicts the sociality of this phase is one of retreat to a religious path that badly accommodates alterity and bases itself on the ethic of resistance against contemporary developments. While Salafis are aware of the criticism that is leveled at them in this regard, with some inhabitants of the suburbs humorously turning the *Salaf* into the *talaf* (lost/disoriented ones), they respond that this drift is nothing more than the application pure and simple of Islamic injunctions. This period of retrogression, experienced as beneficial, fixes the young practicant in a posture of salutary renunciation and specialized existence. The fertile retrogression is long and drawn out to the extent that it translates into several years of limitations on interacting with those who are dissimilar, although the time is actually not spent totally cut off from the environment. These years of closing off express, *ceteris paribus*, the propensity to identify with a political group viewed as radical, whether of the right or the left, just as the university years do for students at the age of intellectual awakening. The involution phenomenon is reinforced if the practicant makes the leap to physical migration to the Muslim country of rebirth. With certain exceptions, the *hijra* is mostly an affair of young singles or young couples, triggered in that case by the birth of the first child and the wish not to make the same mistakes with their offspring that the first-generation immigrants made. Marriage, life as a couple, and starting a family are reasons for pursuing a positive retrogression, which is reinforced in a nonhostile country. Feeding on each other, migration and starting a family combine to effect a change of degree but also a change in the nature of the rupture.

However, these two factors must also be interpreted as dual to the extent that they echo a ritual passage important in the Salafist career: they have effects that are going to reorient the course of the rupture. Positive retrogression and what it implies about healthy reclusion last only a short while. While Salafis tend to see in marriage the foundation of a pious family and see in the departure to a majority-Muslim society a successful outcome, these positionings can also initiate a relativization of radicality. Getting married or emigrating can redefine the drastic relationship that characterizes the preceding phase. While still being as uncompromising in relation to the religion's ritual and dogmatic dimension, the Salafi no longer systematically seeks confrontation with his congeners. When telling him about legal decisions or the deviant behaviors of certain sects claiming Islam as their own, we can hear him say, *Allah ihdihoum* (May God guide them).

Another important factor in diluting the rupture's drastic aspect in certain cases is the *hijra* itself. Conceived as an experience from which the individual expects a revelation about himself, settlement in the believing country, permanently or not, leads a great many practicants to lower some of their ideals relating to Muslim countries. A social practice that permits gauging the tenor of the break, the *hijra* also offers the possibility of measuring the developments in their religious socialization. The fact of having sojourned in a Muslim country leads many promoters of the Salafiyya to envisage a return to France under the impact of an incomplete or defective integration in the receiving country.

5
Imaginary Socialization

Imaginary socialization refers to the gap between the perception of an identity that makes no concessions and the leeway for interpretation permitted by authorized clerics. It relates more generally to the part of reciprocal construction between the subject and the object. The manner in which the former constructs, and is constructed by, the latter is the source of a vision of the world and the different positions that derive from it. Imaginary socialization echoes the polysemy of religious concepts but also the different ways of apprehending the social space, with a single one perduring in this socialization in order to render coherent the acts and positions taken by the practicants. In other words, the believer finds on this path what he looks for.[1] Consequently this imaginary socialization allows hatching a "utopian mentality,"[2] which will frame the process of reifying the space and time on which this construction is based.[3]

A New Age of Orientalism?

The first domain in which an imaginary vision of religion and of the world unfolds is geography. Those in the Salafist viaticum promote a look at the territories that make them the physical support for a symbolic dichotomy whose foundation is the respect or lack of it for Islamic morality. Everyone defines himself according to his religious essence. This Weltanschauung determines the hierarchical relationship with and immunization against anything that is not Islamic and on which, among other consequences, is based

---

[1] Patrick Legros, Frédéric Monneyron, Jean-Bruno Renard, and Patrick Tacussel, *Sociologie de l'imaginaire* (Sociology of the imaginary) (Paris: Armand Colin, "Cursusm," 2006), 2.
[2] Ibid., 61; Karl Mannheim, *Idéologie et Utopie* (Ideology and utopia) (Paris: Marcel Rivière, 1929), 127.
[3] The utopian construction may just as easily refer to "the Golden Age" or "the Land of Plenty." See Mircea Eliade, *La nostalgie des origins* (The nostalgy of origins) (Paris: Gallimard, 1991); Alexandre Cioranescu, "Utopie: Cocagne et âge d'or" (Utopia: Land of Plenty and Golden Age), *Diogène*, no. 75 (1971): 86–123.

Salafism Goes Global. Mohamed-Ali Adraoui, Oxford University Press (2020). © Oxford University Press.
DOI: 10.1093/oso/9780190062460.001.0001

the duty of salutary migration. The territory is therefore perceived through the prism of religious imagination, which splits the world between those who identify with Islam and those who assign no importance to it.

This division has the principal effect of producing a view of the Muslim world imprinted by an Orientalist dimension. This is possible only because the practicants view the world of the exterior as socialized actors in a context that is first European or Western. For this part, we adopt Edward Saïd's definition of "Orientalism," which entails a conception of this artistic and intellectual tradition that permits grasping and criticizing its epistemological and moral postulates.[4]

As an intellectual and imaginary construction, the Orient is an object of reification in that it is in outline, content, and specificity the receptacle of a Western regard that thinks of itself as superior and seeks to confine itself within precise anthropological rules. One of the principal consequences of this construction is of a political nature, because this essentialist and particularist vision of the Orient lets the Westerner compare himself favorably with the Oriental. Thus a relationship of superiority is legitimized and comes to justify the European domination of the colonial era.

The Salafis have an Orientalist view of the Muslim world because they develop a discourse about the Orient, an entity to which they above all give a religious consistency. The theme of the "Orient refuge" encapsulates their relationship with this world of Islam as supposedly grounded in an ethical perspective diametrically opposed to what prevails in the West. The religious reference makes of this part of the world a veritable symbolic place of asylum. To cite an example, Saudi Arabia is represented as the most telling illustration of perpetuating the time of the Pious Ancients. A pole of religious stability remaining distant from the intellectual and political evolutions that have touched the rest of the world,[5] this country is lionized because it symbolizes a constancy lasting centuries. The archaism and anachronistic character that some people paint it with, beginning with certain modernist Muslims, cannot be understood as anything but a critique actually aimed at pristine Islam.

However, the study of Orientalist socialization highlights certain peculiarities of this view, reifying as much the world of the Muslim Orient as the

---

[4] Edward Saïd, *L'Orientalisme: L'Orient créé par l'Occident* (Orientalism: The Orient created by the West) (Paris: Seuil, 2005), 15.

[5] Eric Hobsbawm, *L'Âge des extrêmes: Histoire du court vingtième siècle, 1914–1991* (The age of extremes: History of the short twentieth century) (Brussels: André Versaille Éditeur, 2008), 155.

Muslim Oriental. It nevertheless needs to be said that this Orientalism turns most of its historical postulates on their head. The Salafist conception of the Orient is therefore distinct from the tradition born in Europe, which saw a mirror flattering the self when looking at this part of the world.

The Orientalism of the French Salafis: To Begin with, a Western View of the Orient

Presenting the world of Islam like a unidimensional entity corresponds to an attempt at reification of these societies through a grid of culturalist reading. The Oriental is a Muslim. However, the relation to the Orient is not so much linked to a sensory or potent vision as it is to a scientific examination. Its principal attraction is the fact that it shelters the scholars, human vectors for transmission of sacred knowledge without which the human being cannot access the Truth. A land of science, the Muslim Orient first of all distinguishes itself by representations linked to the 'oulama. These are in effect the most powerful symbols of the singularity of this world. Because they call forth grace on the rest of society by preaching an authentic teaching, they incarnate the spinal column of the Islamic civilization. The Oriental is no longer a body, an impassioned character, or even a human being inclined by nature to a magical reading of the world, but a person who rationalizes his relationship to religion and thus to the world by the scientific intervention of the authorized clerics. By refusing to consider the Muslim religion, it is the Westerner who is revealed as the passionate being. Unified in the Salafist perception, the world of Islam is foremost that of the scholars who are meant to rule over it, making it the form of social organization most antinomic to the West. Rootedness in history being its greatest advantage, the Muslim world thus separates itself from the Western sphere. The various divisions that arise from this furnish the substrate for the Salafist imagination. Cut off forever from the West, the Orient becomes the receptacle for a purely Occidental vision. Reducing the Oriental identity to the Islamic identity, the social rules that predominate in it are perceived as emanations from scholarly opinions. Consequently, more than being a *Homo islamicus*, the Oriental is seen as a being fortunate to live under legal aspects judged to be more favorable in the land of Islam than in the West. He is thus understood as *Homo legalis* to the degree that he escapes from a context that looks down on all religious references. As for the Islamized, super-Islamized, or "Koranized" Saudi country, it is valued because all that happens in it is interpreted as emanating from the basic social compact that connects the political power and the religious magistery.

To fully grasp this, it pays to look at this country's image projected by the Salafist web and, more precisely, the fact that it jumbles together clerics and institutions. The video *The Nation of Tawhid, Like It or Not*[6] had more than a thousand hits. It must be understood on at least two levels. It is first of all clearly a defensive message made by a pious contemporary under the pseudonym of *frioum*. It expresses itself through images and stances tending to exceptionalize the Saudi Kingdom *de facto* and *de visu* as the state and social model for Muslims. The nineteen-minute video is essentially a defense of the Saudi state as Islam's protector, namely of the *tawhid*, and it is thus an element in the religious debate and competition sought by the practicants. We underline the second part of the title, *Like It or Not*, which seems to thumb its nose at Muslims who vilify the Saudi state. In making it the incarnation of the defense of divine unicity, the quietist Salafis reify this country, thus confirming a unidimensional—because specifically Islamist—vision of the Orient and of Saudi Arabia especially.

Another interesting thing about this video is how it captures part of the Salafist imagination by projecting the symbols that carry along Saudi society and, beyond it, the Orient. We may note in this regard that the images correspond generally to those conveyed by numerous Western media in reporting on the societies of the Middle East. The video opens with these words written in white against a purple background, after which rapidly scrolls the ritual formula "In the name of God the merciful in essence and excellence"(written in phonetic French):

> We hear Saudi Arabia criticized a great deal and it seems to me wise to tell you one thing....
>
> It is a strange fact.... Have you already asked yourself to what this stupefying consensus is due...?

The following frames contain extracts of speeches, television broadcasts, and classes taught by imams or selected clips of believers engaging in acts that Salafism disapproves of. For instance, during a phone interview on the news program of the Shiite Sahar TV network, you can hear the journalist

---

[6] https://www.dailymotion.com/video/x8mv6u.

Thierry Meyssan evoke the intent of the Saudi state to destroy Hamas during the Israeli offensive in the Gaza Strip. Also, in a clip with an echoing soundtrack played against a galactic background, we hear a Muslim belonging, according to the video's author, to the Ahbaches (Islamic branch related to Abdullah al-Harari who passed away in 2008) and declaiming that it is time to finish off the Salafis and the sect they represent. Then there is a Shiite imam, calling the Wahhabis a monstrous people, evildoers who must be killed. The journalist Mohamed Sifaoui during the "trial of the cartoons" in 2006 in a Paris court is also presented as an enemy of Saudi Arabia. He answers a journalist while holding up a Saudi flag and accusing that country of also making "an amalgam of Islam with violence because the profession of Muslim faith there is sustained by the sword." Tariq Ramadan is paraded in a clip of his debate with Abdelwahab Meddeb on the *Ce soir ou jamais* program, broadcast under the headline "Islam: Is It in Need of Being Cured?," in which he exposes his opinion "of the country of holy places." Finally, there is President Nicolas Sarkozy, the only non-Muslim appearing in this video, described as the "CEO of the fifth world power [who] has to duck," who is inveighed against while images march across the screen of him delivering a speech in Riyad during his visit to Saudi Arabia in January 2008, in which he speaks of "[his] dear friends of Saudi Arabia" and his refusal to see "imposed a sole model of civilization." At the end of the Sarkozy clip the video segues into a second half. Now comes the moment when the filmmaker slips in the following comment, sounding like a quip aimed at the ensemble of the figures in the first part displaying their hostility or their self-interested allegiance to Saudi Arabia. We note, in passing, that the language echoes a suburban argot as well as an elevated language when things need to be spelled out. Beyond that, we also note the recourse to a metaphorical construction, reflected in talking about the *tawhid* as if it is an essence that envelops all things, starting with the Saudi environment, where the defense of this principle has been erected into a cardinal institution:

> Less relaxed than usual this Sarko... What's he feeling? Well, if it isn't... the presence of the *tawhid*.
> Still not convinced of that which pushes toward so much hate, that of so many people gathered together.
> An odd consensus nevertheless? Isn't it? Listen, over there is where it's happening.

The video moves on to a call to prayer in the background. Next is a brightly lit scene where a crowd of people are lined up listening to an imam recite verses from the Koran. In these verses, the imam droning out the Koran promises moral victory and divine approval to all those among the believers who have shown patience, righteousness, a spirit of justice, and honesty. The next image is of the Saud family attending this recital. King Abdullah is clearly recognizable, as are many of the princes. One Koranic verse follows another; you can hear an exhortation to patience and wisdom in the face of adversity that the preceding images are meant to depict. Also noteworthy is the mention of a pivotal verse in the quietist Salafi doctrine, number 59 (and the following ones) of the sura *The Women*, which here seems purposely aimed at the subjects of the Saudi monarch:

> O faithful ones! Obey Allah and obey the Messenger and those among you who hold command. Then if you quarrel about anything, send it to Allah and the Messenger, send it to Allah and the Messenger, if you believe in Allah and in the Last Day. That would be much better and a better interpretation.

The rest of the video consists of a dialogue between images in other televised reports and responses mostly written in white on the freeze-framed images. This is how the filmmaker responds to the various points raised in the reporting and debates inserted into the video. What emerges is that Saudi Arabia is not a hypocrite country but one of the *tawhid*. As proof, non-Muslims are prohibited from entering into the sacred precincts of the holy cities of Mecca and Medina. Stolen images of the ʿ*alim* Sheikh Ibn Baz delivering a sermon to Muslims on the subject of how they neglect their duty of dying in defense of the religion fade into images of King Faisal (ruled 1964–1975) in discussion with a cleric of his time, one Ibn Houmeyd, a former member of institutions responsible for legal opinions at the highest level of the state. These last images symbolize practically all on their own the image the Saud Kingdom projects to the French Salafis: that of a bicephalous pairing of the scholars of Islam and the holder of legitimate political power, on the understanding that the former legitimize the latter.

Another sequence revolves around a prince paying a visit to Sheikh Ibn ʿOtheimine during his lifetime and seating himself close to him in a room in his modest house. Once again the filmmaker slips in a remark addressing the viewer: "There he is, the prince, seated on the ground. . . . How much time do you spend on the ground? Two, three minutes?" Then, while the now-deceased cleric accompanies the prince, you see him kiss the ʿalim, which, once again, moves the maker of the video to ask ironically, "See who is kissing whom on the forehead? The scholar . . . or the governor?" More glimpses follow of other ʿoulama on good terms with princes and Saudi kings.

The questions put by the filmmaker always make reference to the same attacks launched against the House of Saud and, by proxy, against the "nation of the *tawhid*": "These are the people who honor the scholars and not the Egyptian singers that you call apostates?" "Power and religion as one, hand in hand. . . . We, too, have our strong signs." The images of Sheikh Ibn ʿOtheimine's "last journey" after his death are still more revealing of the vision of the Orient prized by practicants. The crowd accompanying the cleric's mortal remains conveys the image of a people unified in suffering at having lost a great "servant of the *tawhid*." The exclusively masculine crowd represents, after a fashion, the deserved crowning of a life of authentic preaching: "Where did he die? How many prayed for him? How many still weep today? . . . But how many eat of his flesh?[7] And you, how many will pray for you?"

Images of the sacred cube of the Ka'ba surrounded by a crowd of believers accompanying the deceased sheikh on his last journey reify an Orientalist vision of this country, understood solely through the prism of religion. The crowd's behavior, its movements, even more the political dynamics existing at the top of the state have no way to escape being filtered through a purely Islamic analysis. The scholar is the guarantor of order and the explicit circumstances prevailing in the country. Inserted in a passive vision of history, by virtue of which Muslim Orientals do nothing but reproduce gestures and the sayings of the first Muslims, the Salafist representations find in the Saudi example the paragon of authenticity what they are looking for. The video continues in this logic, repelling each attack launched against "its country of the heart" by putting in evidence a report, a Koranic verse, or a video clip aiming to shine a light on the "Saudi reality" as of a country viscerally attached to Islam's precepts and defender of the integrity and dignity of the faithful throughout the world.

---

[7] The reference to the hadiths here is explicit, warning believers against the bad speech uttered against the scholars and emphasizing the fact that eating their flesh is metaphorically equivalent to speaking ill of them. http://www.3ilmchar3i.net/article-26962002.html.

This Orientalism leads to assumed pro-Saudi positions and organizes a symbolic allegiance to a favored state because it is supposedly under the influence of clerics who are unyielding in promoting the dogma. The French Salafi, in solidarity with this country, can be viewed as the guardian of the Saudi throne in the name of a reterritorialization of the religious identity that sees in this society the most excellent country for a purified practice of Islam. This Saudiism induced by the love of scholars equally touches the political power heading the country, just as it can be confirmed with the defense of King Abdullah basking in the aura of the ʿulama. By its moral ascendancy the Saudi state thus is able to control the representations and the feelings of allegiance of most of the practicants the world over. Despite a discourse notably preaching denationalization while the Salafi belongs to an impious society, the imaginary socialization in fact engenders a return of the feeling of belonging to the Orient. Improvising himself as the guardian of legitimacy of Arabia, the French Salafi is the loyal "defender of the throne of Saud."[8] In addition to rediscovering the Arab heritage, the Salafist career is equally synonymous with a certain pro-Saudi nationalism. The symbolic centrality of Arabia thus makes space for a true feeling of allegiance that—as shown in this video—can engender a militantism geared to defending that country.[9]

An Orientalism of the Interior, or How to Reify the Orient When You Are from It

The Salafi Orientalist view is also distinguished by the fact that it is a Western look at the world of Islam cast by actors who, for the most part, come from families native to this reconstructed Oriental space. The Salafist vision is not only a Western Orientalism, allowing one to build a knowledge of the Muslim world from the outside and turn it into a homogeneous society, but also an Orientalism by the Oriental for those who never stopped thinking of themselves as Arabs. This view of the Orient, endogenous because of its provenance from believers who resisted the discredit cast on the Muslim

---

[8] Rémy Leveau, *Le Fellah marocain, défenseur du trône* (The Moroccan fellah, defender of the throne) (Paris: Presses de Sciences Po, "Références," 1985).

[9] Jean-François Mayer coins the term "theopolitics" to describe the religious dynamics that structure new forms of solidarity with entities all or part of which attach to a religious resource. See Jean-François Mayer, "Facteurs religieux et relations internationales: Une approche théopolitique" (Religious factors and international relations: A theopolitical approach), *Religioscope, Études et analyse*, no. 8 (August 2005), http://www.religion.info/pdf/2005_08_theopol.pdf.

world in Western countries, thus manifests itself as a paradox. The positive vision of the Orient proceeds from a form of reification that finds its justification in part in socialization within European society, even while the Salafi refuses to think of himself as belonging to this society. His Orientalism is typically Western in the way it represents the world of Islam as a world apart but also specifically Oriental and thus in a sense endogenous by insisting on constantly valorizing this part of the world. Echoing the necessity of setting up a model of society as an entity of refuge, Salafist Orientalism interprets itself as stemming from a phenomenon of inertia caused by a parental education that insists on nostalgia for the native country.

Salafist socialization, if it opens into a sort of pro-Saudi nationalism, leads the practicants to perpetuate the "paradise lost" syndrome characterizing the psychology of some parents who migrated to France and conceive of a permanent return home as too difficult. The love of Arabia, that country showing a genuine rigor in applying Islam's norms, is motivated by strictly religious reasons. When it comes to the Maghrebian countries, it is more emotional, since it involves personal and familial history as well as a vision of the Maghrebian man as generous, warm, and simple, in contrast to the European man. The *bled* is valorized as a society that remained apart from modernity's bad aspects. While housing construction or increasing access to information technologies are hailed as signs of economic progress, Morocco, Algeria, and Tunisia are regarded as havens of tradition that contrast with the frenzy of Western societies. The fact that the Orient is experienced as an allegory for a world that has not fallen into modernity's torments, where even poor people have not forgotten the essence of existence, namely by remembering God, must be seen as reconnecting with a deep self whose roots are sunk south of the Mediterranean.

Reverse Orientalism: An Orient Better than the West

The imagined nature of the Oriental makes him superior to the Westerner; therefore Islam serves as a value scale for comparing the two societies. This view of the world of Islam valorizes the countries that make it up, starting with Saudi Arabia. The image conveyed by the country of Holy Places is an illustration of the fact that a Muslim society that applies its precepts transparently is not to be compared with the societies of the West. Perceived as the country of scholars, Arabia is valorized for being continually irrigated by the preaching work of the 'ulama. We see it in the images of order and justice mirrored by the Saudi reference. Orientalized by a Salafist view that Islamizes the Saudi reality, this country becomes a model for the world. Embodying all the West does not want to be, Saudi Arabia illustrates both temperance and strictures. By initiating a globalized preaching whose aim is to socialize all Muslims in a purified framework, this country is undeniably a vector of rupture in numerous cases. However, it is also a country that puts on a show as an agent of moderation on a political level, since it has the same clerics calling for a sociocultural rupture while condemning useless dissent, disorder, and confusion within a society.

If it is a matter of not recognizing any morality in the values that undergird the current social contract in France, there is no question at all of entering into a logic of confrontation or, in a different register, of negotiation. Withdrawal and militant apoliticism alone are justified behaviors. Saudi Arabia's role thus is ambiguous, because by the intervention of the scholars it is truly a project of sociological rupture that is fostered globally in parallel with a de facto legitimization of all sociopolitical orders. A practice like the *hijra* must consequently be understood as a way of overcoming this tension almost in a dialectical fashion. Saudi Arabia's place in the epicenter of the mobilizations and demobilizations of the practicants hence finds itself reinforced. Reflecting an image opposed to the Muslim Orient, the West is the negative counterpart of the Saudi model of society. The Janus-faced aspect of Saudi Arabia, itself echoing the bicephaly of power in that country, plays a role in the impossibility of evoking Salafist Islam in unambiguous terms.

This double dimension of preaching forms the basis of the reverse Orientalism that French Salafis adopt when they pay attention to the Muslim world, especially Saudi Arabia. The images they associate with it in this respect are explicit, as illustrated by the words of Samir. Thirtyish, with a neotraditionalist profile, the son of a Tunisian merchant, Samir distinguishes himself by having a critical view of other Salafis. According to him, a number of his fellows are too inclined to think of themselves as "unique" Muslims. While disapproving of the "deviationism" of other tendencies, he exhibits a certain disdain for his peers who, barely converted, make a point of rejecting other believers. The principles of Salafism may be paradigmatic for him, but that does not justify vanity. On the contrary, in the manner of the 'ulama he admires, many of whom live in "the country of the two sanctuaries," his religiosity first of all commands a spirit of responsibility. One day he hopes to settle in this country so that he can be inundated by the "sacred science" behind which the "scholars" are the moving force.

AUTHOR: How would you define your practice of religion?
SAMIR: ... Let's just say I try to follow my religion ... in a non-Muslim country
AUTHOR: Which means? Can you elaborate?
SAMIR: Well, without being paranoid, you can easily see ... The Muslims, they are treated like ... Anyway, right, and you'll tell me that's nothing new. When I became interested in Islam, I read a book. A book of history-geography, published in 1962, as I recall. It talked about Muslims, but you know what it said?
AUTHOR: What was it?
SAMIR: They called them "the Mahometans," "the Mahometan sect." See, okay, there, when you don't even call people by their right name ... Fine, like I told you, without being paranoid, you can easily see that it doesn't reflect today. The Muslims, this is my impression, they pose a lot of problems for some people in this country. Okay.
AUTHOR: You just said that you became interested in Islam. What does that mean, that before it wasn't the case?
SAMIR: No ... well. [*Brief moment of reflection.*] Well, I come from a Tunisian background, my father, my mother, my family, all Muslims. Well, all right, one day I started to ask myself questions, I chose my own path, in a sense. I read books, I found it interesting. I put a lot into it, I studied sects, all that. In Islam, there are sects. Now, I didn't get everything. This division, I didn't get it ... when the Prophet preached to a single community.
AUTHOR: That, then, is how you discovered the Salafis?
SAMIR: The. . . ? You mean the *ahl sunna wa jam'a* [the people of the Sunna and the consensus]? Me, no, I don't describe myself as such. I'm Muslim, that's all. I don't like labels. I'm French, a Muslim by confession. Good, sure, if you talk to me about Shiites, I'll tell you I'm Sunni. What is Sunnism? It's what the Prophet says. I do what he says, I accept it.
AUTHOR: So, as far as you're concerned, you apply Islam, full stop?
SAMIR: Yes, that's it, when I see something, I do it. You notice I wear the beard, I'm dressed a certain way. I see there's a certain something in Islam. I do it.
AUTHOR: For example, talking about the beard: you saw it in Islam, and so you did it?
SAMIR: Yes. There are seventeen hadiths that talk about the beard. So there it is, I have no excuse. I wear the beard they wear in the Sunna. We know that

certain beards and mustaches, for example, are not Sunna. One day the Prophet received the ambassadors of Chosroès [emperor of the Sassanid Persians during the era of Muslim revelation], who wore mustaches that were long and covered part of their faces. They had mustaches à la Frédéric Thiriez [president of the Professional Soccer League, who wears a handlebar mustache]. He criticized these people. He turned away from them in disgust. The ambassadors told him, "But our emperor commands it." And the Prophet said, "As for me, my God commanded me." There you have it, to answer your question, they talk about a *look*. Me, in my *look*, I take after the Prophet.

AUTHOR: And when you were talking about sects in Islam, you wanted to talk about who?

SAMIR: Lots of groups. The *ikhwan*, for example. The Muslim Brotherhood, who engage in politics. Their aim is to engage in politics, to politicize Islam, while Islam is all. For if there's a confrontation, conflict follows. In Islam there's no party, no *hizbiyya* [partisan spirit].

AUTHOR: So, for you, politics is too little for you?

SAMIR: Listen ... In fact, I know politics. In the 1980s, I don't know if you recall, the March of the Beurs,[10] all that. Hey, I knew that, I remember the marches, the demonstrations. Good, I didn't vote during my youth, and I'll tell you it's not for lack of a card. Anyway. I remember that time: Mitterrand (French President from 1981 to 1995), the Socialist Party. Today I know that all of it didn't do a thing. The rose, as they used to say back then ... The people who trusted in the 1980s, what did it get them? There was a slogan at the time: "Mitterrand took the rose, he kept the petals and left us the thorns." [*Laughs.*] The Beurs, as they said at the time, let themselves be had. Supposedly they were going to change to Giscard (French President from 1974 to 1981), he did nothing for the suburbs.... The politics of hope of the left at the time went nowhere. Most of the brothers who were part of the time are in *din* [religion] today. Why? Because it was a human utopia, not a divine one.

AUTHOR: You mean to say that you were militant as a youth in this type of association? How old were you at the time?

SAMIR: No, well ... I was young, but during my youth, I was in this delirium. After, there were the Muslim associations, all that. All right, so that's where you had the UOIF, for instance. It did no good in the end.

---

[10] [Henry Randolph's note: Young Frenchmen or -women of North African origin.]

AUTHOR: But there are Beurs who quote unquote succeeded. Some are in Sarkozy's government.

SAMIR: Who do you want to talk about? Rama Yade (former Minister under Sarkozy's presidency), Fadela Amara (another Minister under Sarkozy's presidency)? Yeah, it's clear, they made it. [*Ironic chuckle.*] Rama Yade, she gave up Islam. Fadela Amara, she, she got going, you can at least say that about her. [*Another ironic laugh.*] ... But if that's not being Sarko's puppet, what is?

AUTHOR: Did you vote in 2007?

SAMIR: No, I don't vote. But, honestly, you want to know? If I had to vote, I'd vote for Sarko.

AUTHOR: Oh, really! Why?

SAMIR: Because the other one, she has a thing I'd never accept.

AUTHOR: Ségolène Royal?

SAMIR: Yes, gay marriage. I'd never accept that.

...

AUTHOR: And, in your view, who defends the true Islam?

SAMIR: There are scholars, there's science. We know all that's needed is [to] return to the scholarly texts. I know what they often say. They say that some young people apply what they hear, they dress like I do, they have the beard, but their behaviors, let's say ...

AUTHOR: Who do you mean by that?

SAMIR: Just now we talked about the Sunna. Me, I'm Sunna. There are the Salafis. Some of them you could compare to cholera. They have a sickness. They didn't purify their souls before doing all they do. But, well, that's how it is. At first they are interested in the symbols: to call themselves Salafis. Just because you recite Verlaine, Baudelaire, doesn't make you a poet. You can study Ahmad [Ibn Hanbal], Ibn Taymiyya, Ibn Qayyim [a student of Ibn Taymiyya and the other great name in Sunni Islam], Ibn Kathir [exegete of the Koran, famous in the Sunni tradition], but they weren't disparaged. That's why they are still current.

AUTHOR: And which scholars do you identify with?

SAMIR: Frankly, well . . . I say that the scholars, you find them in great numbers in Saudi Arabia already. Well, it's the country . . . the country which ... where ... Right. We know that Saudi Arabia distributes cassettes for learning how to do the hajj [pilgrimage]. All right, after that, what can you say? They have scholars there, the *masheikh* [another plural of "sheikh"] who teach Islam correctly. You know where you're headed.

There's one book, one Koran. Everything that's added on is not my religion. There are movements that are heading for disaster trying to introduce things that are not in Islam.

AUTHOR: Which ones, for example?

SAMIR: Bah, you know well that I'm talking about the *ikhwan* for one. Hamas is driving into the wall, the *ikhwan* are heading for disaster, the *khawarij* [reference to the jihadists] are also. From the start, they have not been in Islam.

AUTHOR: What do you reproach Hamas for, for example?

SAMIR: Let's say, all right, with them you're far removed from religion. If you look at the Palestinians, well, you see that they are carried away by politics. There's one thing that always struck me about the Palestinians and that's their keffiyeh. I'm sorry, but it has become a curse, this keffiyeh. When I read magazines or newspapers, I often see mannequins now wearing the keffiyeh. In the fashion magazines, I see keffiyehs now! It's even become a symbol of resistance among the anarchists. It's a politicized sign today.

AUTHOR: So, for you, it's the Islam practiced in Arabia which is the most . . . ? The truest, the most authentic?

SAMIR: Like I told you. It's a country that practices the Da'wa. It translates Korans, it prints Korans. Under King Faisal, Arabia has built mosques. There has been a historical continuity all along. A king, it's a sheik with a thousand times the power, in a sense. If he decides to do the Da'wa, then the country turns into a center of the Da'wa.

AUTHOR: So, for you, the truth, then, is found over there?

SAMIR: The truth is known. The unfortunate thing is ignorance. All right, I won't hide my dream from you, it's to live in Saudi Arabia. It's the dream of all who follow the Sunna. I went there on the hajj. I touched the dream with my finger for three weeks.

AUTHOR: So Arabia is the dream for you?

SAMIR: It's the country of scholars. That's where they are, the scholars of the Sunna.

AUTHOR: And what do you answer to those who say that over there the scholars obey the people in the royal family? The political power is still in the hands of the monarchy.

SAMIR: Let's imagine it's a pear cut in half. Or an orange, if you like. In this country, there is an eternal pact. The scholars and the king march hand in hand. Not like in other Muslim countries, like Morocco, for example.

In Morocco, it's a picture of modernity. In Arabia, you can't. It's a pact between the two that dates back to . . .

AUTHOR: And what do you say to those who say Arabia isn't what it pretends to be? That there's a great difference between the country and the image it wants to project?

SAMIR: They attack Saudi Arabia, but I understand why. It is Islam's base. The Prophet warned against a time when Islam would be persecuted and Islam would find its home like the serpent returns to its burrow. This is Medina. Me, I don't reject anyone, but they reject the whole world. The Prophet, in a hadith, he said that the entire world will go to Paradise except those who turn it down. By that he wanted to say that you have to follow the Koran and the Sunna. We know therefore that religion is finished and that there is a sole path to follow. This road we know is the one they follow in Saudi Arabia.

Constructing a West as a Negative Mirror of the Orient, or Salafi Occidentalism

For Edward Saïd, the main consequence of the Orientalist tradition in the political domain has been to justify the domination of the Oriental countries by the Western states, starting with the Europeans launching a colonial enterprise. The Salafist view runs counter to that conception: in a reverse move, the Western world, essentialized in turn, becomes the negative of the Muslim Orient. Burdened by all the defects that can plague a civilization when it does not recognize Islam as the foundation of its values and its laws, the West finds itself reduced by virtue of the same reflex by which numerous men of letters, artists, and politicians for centuries conceived of the figure of the Oriental. This reversal of representations is at the heart of a veritable Occidentalism. Because they are all attached to values that deprecate Islam, this collection of supposedly homogeneous or even identical societies is the favorite target of the practicant's duty of rejection. The West becomes the negative mirror of the Islamic countries. Shriveled spiritually and built on sand, the Western way of life is decadent, removed from the "divine utopia" Samir describes. The essence of the West reflects madness; it is a society that lives too fast, which makes even more important the need to structure the Muslim personality around representations that offer refuge and the certitude of revering an eternal dogma. The Westerner has nothing to teach the

Muslim, the technological superiority of some countries reflecting divine benefaction and not the model of a virtuous society. Having everything but the essential, the *tawhid*, Westerners are left with nothing. Their feeling of superiority is a mirage; they think they can influence the world in a positive manner but wind up corrupting it and distancing it even further from the straight and narrow.

The Invention of Tradition: Reifying Saudi Politico-religious Power

The Salafist Sphere's Harmonious Character as Construction

On closer inspection of its genesis in the contemporary era, the heterogeneity of the Salafist sphere is real. It highlights the gap existing between some clerics and numerous practicants on the issue of mobilization even of Salafism. Comparable to a religious enterprise started by individuals setting themselves up as producers of an unsurpassable norm, Salafist preaching is far from being a homogeneous whole. The field can be understood as a construction that proceeds from the imaginary aspect of Salafist socialization. Some preachers, even though regarded as spokesmen for the movement, themselves remain neutral if not unwilling to promote a Salafist identity, overdetermined though it is in France. This symbolic deficit affects numerous young Muslims in French society.

Salafist socialization rests on an internalized presupposition that is taken for granted: the fact that the Salafist realm is a preexisting given, based on the predicative work performed by scholars clearly identified and deriving their legitimacy from the lineage that links them to the Pious Ancients. The principal manifestation of this in the current era is most famously furnished by Sheikh Al-Albani, for whom claiming an Islamic identity would not seem to suffice: it also has to be accompanied by religious worship in the Salafist, i.e., orthodox mode, without which purity is lost. Sheikh Al-Albani is doubtless the main figure of the past few decades in the Salafist sphere. Held to be the reviver par excellence of Islam in the contemporary age, it is he who has worked the most to focus the Muslim identity on the Salafist model, all the rest representing nothing but deviance and impurity. This is how Salafism little by little broke through the surface, benefiting from Saudi punching power. Finding an attentive ear among the *'ulama* of the official establishment,

Sheikh Al-Albani's preaching coupled with Saudi Arabia's historical specialization in large part explains the reemergence of a Salafist domain during the twentieth century. Additionally, it is by reason of the founding pact between scholars and politicians that the institutional structures that today are so dependent on Saudi political power support a kind of homology between the political constraints weighing on the kingdom and the religious discourse emanating from official bodies.

The imaginary character of identification with the Salafist ethos here is due to the imprecise and largely artificial dimension of the Salafist sphere. More precisely, while many clerics, with Sheikh Al-Albani in the lead, have made the necessity of reproducing the original norm the heart of their teaching, others, including some of the most revered names, have not put Salafism forward as a first element in their preaching. This is where we encounter this domain's specificity, which is due to the fact that the ordering principle is invoked much more loudly by the practicants than by the movement's cadres. More heterogeneous than it appears, the position taken by many scholars is that constant promotion of the Salafist identity has to be relativized. This lets us grasp the symbolic value and the quest for prestige that characterize the identity strategy consisting of subjecting all of the Islamic sphere to the Salafist tension. The act of mobilizing capital that is lived as both exclusive and objective has to be interpreted as the fruit of a psychological and symbolic quest for differentiation aiming to give birth to a countersphere with a hegemonic calling. The fact that many clerics contribute to de-Salafizing not the preaching but the language of differentiation, even though they are important figures within it, illustrates the socialization's imaginary character.

The willingness of many clerics to adopt a less divisive language constitutes a form of delegitimization of the breakaway project prized by many of the practicants. Certainly the content of the teaching coming from individuals like Sheikh Fawzan, the great Saudi establishment figure, does not diverge with respect to the exigencies of dogma; nonetheless Sheikh Fawzan is known to have nuanced the necessity of posturing as Salafi in the community of the faithful. The cleric, less attached to this term than numerous French practicants who see in it the very reason for their existence, embodies in this regard the evolving and reflexive aspect of this habitus. One of his talks on the necessity or lack thereof of calling yourself Salafi is explicit on this issue. Warning against the pride and vanity that could lead to seeking the etiquette rather than the morality inherent in Salafism, he calls on believers to deepen the value of things behind the statutes, the names, and other denominations.

The following passage transcribes a question-and-answer audio recording session that touches on the act of constantly referring to oneself as Salafi or Athari (He who follows the trail):[11]

> Question: Some people put *assalafi* or *al athari* after their names. Should this be considered a form of boasting [*Tazkiyatou-n-nafs*]? Where does it say so in the law?
> Answer: What is called for is for the individual to follow the truth. What is called for is for the individual to seek the truth, to require the truth, and to act according to it. As for the act of calling yourself *assalafi* or *al athari* or something else, nothing says that is required. *Allah subhānahu wa ta'ālā* [God the glorious and the exalted] knows better.... Hence the act of calling yourself Salafi, Athari, and other names, this has no origin. We ourselves look at reality: we do not look at the word, the name, or the pretensions. It may be that he calls himself Salafi and he is not Salafi, Athari and he is not Athari, or it may happen he is Salafi and Athari without saying "I am Athari or Salafi." Therefore we look at the realities, not the names, nor the pretensions. And the Muslim must be humble before Allah *subhānahu wa ta'ālā*.... You owe it to yourself to search for the truth and act in conformity with it. Reform the intention, and Allah will know the realities, glory be to him.

Service to authentic Islam and the Saudi social contract: the two organizing tensions of the Salafi clerics and the invention of a new Tradition.[12]

The Turning Point of the Gulf War: Explosion of the Salafist Sphere and Debut of a Defensive Salafism
Religious proselytism, backed by an economic powerhouse multiplied by the soaring price of oil starting in the 1970s, structures a true Saudi soft power[13] that is legitimist and conservative on the domestic front, dynamic and image-conscious toward the outside. That Saudi Arabia is assured a choice place within the space of Islamic meaning is thus at the heart of the politico-religious contract. The double developmental movement, economic and

---

[11] https://www.youtube.com/watch?v=8Ba3DDiiIcE.
[12] Eric Hobsbawm and Terence Ranger (eds.), *L'invention de la tradition* (The invention of tradition) (Paris: Amsterdam, 2006).
[13] Joseph Nye, *Bound to Lead: The Changing Nature of American Power* (New York: Basic Books, 1991).

religious, allows the puritan religion, identified with the Islam practiced in Saudi society, to feed its prestige within the Muslim world. The bicephalous Saudi regime nevertheless does not hesitate to deploy the most authentic religious rhetoric to disqualify its political and ideological adversaries, domestically as well as abroad,[14] the puritan project acting every time to legitimize Saudi positions.

This "blessed time," during which the strategic and religious bet looked like it would pay off, coincided with a religious conception that can be seen as dynamic and extensive. By this we mean that, although the Islamic principles defended were those of Salafism, the leaders relying on the religious authority did not engage in the logic of blame that characterizes the country's scholarly production particularly since the 1991 Gulf War. The Saudi strategy at the time consisted more of a quest for expanding the country's audience. Under this heading, these are the elements of similarity and politico-religious synergy that dominate, as illustrated by the hand extended by Faisal to the Muslim Brotherhood persecuted by the Nasserite government from 1954 on, or the financing of movements based on Salafist rhetoric for violently defending specific "Muslim causes."[15] Saudi state doctrine is satisfied with conspicuous emulation within the space of Islamic meaning, this Salafism of accommodation moreover accepting the political intersections between Saudi power and other movements of re-Islamization, despite strictly religious quarrels.

This syncretic moment within Sunni Islam, guided by the consolidation of Saudi leadership, because of political evolutions leaves room for a return to the ultra-legitimist Salafist discourse marked by defiance toward competing offers of Islam. This is why the religious authority integrates more of the constraints linked to the explosion of the Salafi sphere, which touched the Saudi power notably under the effect of the bin Laden factor. In this regard, one event marks a decisive turning point in the official Saudi positioning that materialized as the severe opposing scission in the Salafi realm between revolutionaries and legitimists. This tension, taking shape starting with the Gulf crisis, is another illustration of the organic

---

[14] In 1986 the Saudi monarch's religious preeminence is reaffirmed when he added to his title of sovereign that of guardian of the holy places of Islam (*khadim al-haramayn al-charifayn*) as part of the rivalry with Khomeini's Iran, which every year sent activist pilgrims to erode the monarchy's symbolic authority over Islam's most holy places.

[15] Kepel, *Jihad*; Olivier Roy, *Généalogie de l'islamisme* (Genealogy of Islamism) (Paris: Hachette, "Pluriel," 2002); Gilles Dorronsoro, *La révolution afghane des communistes aux tālebān* (The Afghan revolution from the Communists to the Taliban) (Paris: Karthala, 2000).

link between political power and religious authority at the summit of the Saudi state. The greater solidarity between the two pillars of the state engenders a radical change of discourse concerning the "false Salafis" who committed the error of turning against the leaders regarded as the legitimate governing power in the state. The "Islamist consensus,"[16] which had been the source of the central position conceded to Saudi Arabia, from that point on was undermined by the action of delegitimization pursued by the "revolutionary" Salafis, who also presented themselves as the defenders of authentic Islam. Opposed by the palace scholars (al-'ulama al-balat), who distanced themselves from the "corrupted Salafis" particularly with regard to taking up arms to combat attacks on the divine sovereignty on earth, these antiestablishment Salafis felt the full wrath of the preaching initiated by yesterday's 'ulama who today vilify the "*khawarij* of the present times" as truly the "lost of contemporary times." Perceived by the protesting Salafis as "blind scholars" who abandon the theoretical core of preaching, even the Islamization of the power and the law,[17] the official clerics support Saudi political power by virtue of their anti-anarchist conception of the dogma.

The presence of Western troops in the country of sacred places of Islam is why "the conquerors of Afghanistan" went after the monarchy, in order to bring to light its duplicity and hypocrisy. The defense of Islam going forward must be entrusted to this avant-garde more cognizant of the hatred of Islam than the establishment's scholars. The objective is to discredit the bicephalous Saudi powers that be.

Toward a Salafism of the State?

Saudi Arabia is the source of a change of scale in how to think about and transmit the Tradition. The practicants in France find themselves in the original position of being intransigent outsiders, in conflict with any element

---

[16] This expression describes the political and religious configuration that assured Saudi Arabia a central place for several decades, until the crisis precipitated by the invasion of Kuwait by Saddam Hussein on August 2, 1990. The Islamist consensus referred to a Saudi hegemony accepted as beneficial for a majority of Muslims within the space of global Islamic meaning. At the end of this explosion, the "sprinkled Saudi sprinkler" (Kepel, *Jihad*, 330) found itself in need of reactivating as never before the historic alliance with the body of the 'ulama by conferring more prerogatives in return for legitimization of the kingdom's policy, including what there was in the way of an alliance with the American power. See James Piscatori, *Islamic Fundamentalism and the Gulf Crisis* (Chicago: American Academy of Arts and Sciences, Fundamentalism Project, 1991).

[17] This is the reason why the revolutionaries pejoratively call the legitimist clerics "scholars of the menses" ('ulama al-haïd), to indicate that the object of their teaching leaves out the essential, i.e., the Islamic morality of the exercise of political power.

that does not correspond to their ideal, in parallel with an institutionalization and growing bureaucratization of the religious references at the summit of the Saudi state. The passage from a Salafism of accommodation to a defensive Salafism poised to become a Salafism of state opens a large gap in the perception of the practicants intent on serving an orthodoxy that more and more bears the seal of the Saudi state. Drawing on the most authentic Sunni tradition, in other words, the corpus of the school that is most attached to scripturalism (the Hanbalite school) complementing the apostolate of Sheikh Abdelwahab and of his heritage, "the sultan's scholars" unquestionably make an impact on the conceptions of initiates in France. For an Islam antagonistic to modernity, the production of the norm linked to the Sauds suffices to deradicalize morals even more. An organizational and political consequence of defensive Salafism, this state religion contains a kind of controlled puritanism.

Awareness of the circular transaction[18] is raised by the scholars who, within a specifically "Hanbalowahabite" framework, accept a secularization inside this fundamentalism to negotiate in addition other margins of freedom and thus end up eventually in a cooperative re-Islamization of society. Proceeding from a rational vision of the links between religion and politics that must eventually engender a religious enterprise with a bigger hold over society, this Salafism of the state is an updating of the foundational contract between scholar and politician on Saudi soil. As such, the permanent institutionalization of the body of the *'ulama* is the last stage in constituting a clergy linked organically to the Saudi monarchy. In exchanging a religious legitimization for expanded social control, the clerics, assuming the function of a crutch for the regime, participate in an original mutation of the Tradition. Religiosity rendered capable of being historicized, the Minhaj Salafi in its inclinations is explained in large part by the nature and objectives of the organizing interaction between religious men and political men at the summit of the state.

Today the evolutions characterizing the politico-religious domain in Saudi Arabia have brought about a reworking of the religious institution around specific reforms, most notably because of the legitimacy crisis that the monarchy had to confront after the Gulf War. Nabil Mouline, for example, shows that while the official establishment figures mainly come from the region around Najd, among others the "co-founding *'alim*" of the Saud

---

[18] Mouline, *Les clercs de l'islam*, 126.

family state (Muhammad Ibn Abelwahab), geographical origins becoming a factor in religious reproduction, the rupture today has all the traits of a real process of clergification of the ʿulama.[19] This indicates, for example, the dynamic of globalization of the religious degree program, which explains why, along with striving for the title of sheikh for obtaining the religious diploma (al-ijaza),[20] some in other domains seek the title of duktur (doctor, holder of a doctorate). This clergification also concerns the careerism of the scholars under whose terms those who ascend to the Council of Senior Scholars become high functionaries or ministers. But beyond the religious competencies and academic success in this cursus honorum, the principal vector for promotion and integration within the highest instances of the religious authority is political quietism.[21]

It is therefore in a number of political positions promoted by Arabia that we can identify the evolutionary potential of the French Salafis, be it in the sense of moderation or of radicalization. The Saudi power today is undeniably a factor in deradicalization, in particular since the strengthening of Saudi hegemony over the globalized quietist Salafi landscape that started with the Gulf crisis. This phenomenon is corroborated by the revolts in the Arab world since the winter of 2010, which led to the fall of the presidencies of Ben Ali in Tunisia and Mubarak in Egypt. We can see it in the statement issued on the occasion of demonstrations touching Saudi Arabia in March 2011, which provoked not only a religious call to order critical of these events but also a summons to the battlements to defend the regime as an organic supporter of Islam:[22]

> As-Salāmu ʿalaykoum wa rahmatoullahi wa barakatouh. Bismillāhi r-Rahmāni r-Rahīm. Praise be to Allah, the Ruler of the Universe! May the Salvation and the Prayers of Allah be on the master of the first and last generations, our master and our Prophet Muhammad, as well as on his family, his Companions, and all those who follow in their way and who hold fast to their tradition until the Last Judgment! This is a fatwa from the Council

---

[19] Ibid., 223–258.
[20] Each of the Islamic sciences corresponds to a precise ijaza: exegesis of the Koran, knowledge of the hadiths, jurisprudence, etc.
[21] Mouline, Les clercs de l'islam, 256.
[22] "The Council of Senior Scholars calls for maintaining unity and stresses the prohibition on demonstrations": https://www.islamsounnah.com/les-manifestations-sont-interdites-par-les-grands-savants-de-lislam/, my emphasis.

of Senior Scholars of Saudi Arabia exhorting Muslims to maintain the union and the prohibition on demonstrations. I ask Allah *Soubhaanahou wa ta3aala* [sic] [Glory to Him in the Highest] to make this *fatwa* beneficial for Muslims throughout the world and especially the Muslim countries touched by these *fitan* [turpitudes, great corruptions] because it is necessary to obey the scholars when they counsel us....

The Council of Senior Scholars implores Allah (the Exalted) to accord to all Muslims the help, the stability and the regrouping of the governing and governed around the Truth. *The Council praises Allah for having accorded the Kingdom of Saudi Arabia the favor of joining its word and unifying its ranks around the Book of Allah (the Exalted) and the Tradition of the Prophet (Salla Allah 'Alaihi Wa Sallam) in the shadow of a wise governance legitimized by a legal allegiance,* may Allah grant it affirmation and permanence and may Allah perfect for us this act of generosity and make it last forever....

Allah (the Exalted) has allowed the people of this country to unite with their governors around the guide of the Book and the Tradition, without straying or dispersing their word according to currents coming from elsewhere, or parties with antagonistic principles....

The Kingdom has succeeded in conserving this Islamic identity. Thus, despite the progress and development the country has experienced and the recourse to legal means of this earth it does not permit nor will it ever permit—by the Strength of Allah and his Power—currents of ideas proceeding from the West or East to sap this identity or to disperse this group.... By the grace of fulfilling this mission, the Kingdom possesses this special status in the world of Islam. Thus, it is the *Qibla* (the direction a Muslim should be faced to whenever comes to time for prayers, foxed as the direction of Mecca) of the Muslims, the country of the two holy Mosques, and it is the country to which Muslims from all regions of the world are coming on the great pilgrimage during the season of the *Hadj* and for the small pilgrimage (*'mra*) of a year's duration.

Conscious of this act of generosity, which consists of the unification of the word around the guide of the Book and the Sunna, in the shade of a wise governance, the Council of Senior Scholars invites everyone to expend every effort to reaffirm unity and consolidate solidarity. Also, the Council warns against any cause that can lead to the opposite of this. To this effect, the Council insists on the necessity of installing the dialogue, the harmony, and cooperation around the good and devotion to avoiding the bad and transgression; and, on the contrary, to fear all cause of transgression, injustice and smothering of the Truth....

Thus, seeing that the Kingdom of Saudi Arabia is the guardian of the Book, of the Sunna, of the allegiance to and the prescription for preserving the Group and submission, reform and counsel in this country may not use as means demonstrations and other measures and proceedings that foster stagnation and fracture the Group. It is of these that this country's 'oulemas, the old ones as well as the recents among them, have offered proof of their illicitness and warned against them....

Let the prayer and salvation be on our Prophet Mohammed, his family and all his Companions.

> The Council of Senior Scholars in the Kingdom of Saudi Arabia

6
Postmodern Socialization

Fundamentally, the socialization in Da'wa Salafiyya is less about an attempt to cut oneself off from the world than about a religious and puritan way of acting as though one were living in the "time of the tribes." United by spiritual and moral affinities that let them consider themselves "separate," Salafis embody the superiority of the affinity paradigm in a society with which they negotiate a contractual relationship. There is no recognition of the religious engagement that legitimizes the modern era and its social, political, or cultural avatars, such as the nation, secularism, citizenship, democracy, individualism, and liberalism, or, especially, the "polytheism of values."[1] It is no surprise that the practicant feels ill at ease with them. He finds in his fundamentalist configuration all he needs for leading his life, being focused on his coreligionists and not on the state or the nation. Life in a group cemented by a transcendental order can be analyzed as the religious version of the "new times of the tribes"[2] characteristic of the decline of individualism in favor of a collective structured around a true "neotribalism."[3]

Salafi Socialization, or the Time of Religious Tribes: Atomization and Forming a New Organic Link of an Aesthetic Nature

The fragmentation and evolutions of traditional socialization structures (family, faith, party, etc.) that enabled the atomization of the individual and the redefinition of collective projects measured solely by personal preference explain the transformation of society into constellations. Each of them relates symbolically to an ensemble of actors choosing to unite as a function

---

[1] Julien Freund, "Le polythéisme chez Max Weber" (Max Weber on polytheism), *Archives des sciences sociales des religions* vol. 61, no. 1 January–March 1986): 52.
[2] Michel Maffesoli, *Le temps des tribus: Le déclin de l'individu dans les sociétés de masse* (The time of the tribes: The decline of the individual in mass societies) (Paris: Méridiens Klinksieck, 1988).
[3] Xiberras, *Les théories de l'exclusion*, 180.

Salafism Goes Global. Mohamed-Ali Adraoui, Oxford University Press (2020). © Oxford University Press.
DOI: 10.1093/oso/9780190062460.001.0001

of an affective and aesthetic ordering. The constellation is a form of social morphology, meaning it is a method for some number of players to tap into and unite around a given set of values. Modernity has structured a certain number of morphologies basically linked to the passage from a society of organic solidarity to a mechanistic society, the process of individuation having superseded the traditional forms of social ties (school, family, church, etc.). More or less organized unions, political parties, or ideological movements that used to manage the socialization framework in modern times have declined under the impact of this hyperindividualism. Identity thus gives way to identification. The constellation hence represents the ensemble of persons linked by an affinity,[4] a project unfolding outside the political framework and founded on a common adherence to an experience that Michel Maffesoli terms "aesthetic."[5]

The postmodern type of social link is explained by the capacity to unite around a moral and aesthetic experience; in other words, it is marked by a basic emotional and organizing connection to one or several values in which alone "the tribe" recognizes itself. From the Salafist point of view, if their claims are not shared, the fault lies in the other since they have incontrovertible proofs of the authentic nature of their practice. This sentiment of plenitude of sacred references held in common suffices unto itself; if their sociality is limited, it is not their responsibility. For them, the aesthetic paradigm defined as "the act of sharing experience . . . a collective experience likely to foster common values,"[6] dovetails with the beauty inspired by the knowledge and mastery of the Truth. Every expression of Salafism reflects a geometric shape or scenography of beauty. Every gesture is magnified because it draws its meaning and its origin from the resemblance to the "betters" that were the first Muslims. Marrying the contours of an imagination constituted of purity and truth, an act that to the external observer may seem anodyne, for the Salafi unites two eras in a single way of apprehending the world. The aesthetic paradigm mirrored in this socialization is the vehicle for what almost is an artistic contemplation of existence inasmuch as every gesture relates to the sacred. The disintegration that some see in the practicants' way of life is for them a perpetual reinvention of authenticity more than ever founded on the connection existing among individuals united by the project of reviving the

---

[4] Ibid., 183.
[5] Ibid., 182.
[6] Michel Maffesoli, *Au creux des apparences* (Hollow appearances) (Paris: La Table Ronde, 2007).

Tradition. This organic solidarity of an aesthetic nature[7] no longer finds its foundation in the cultural or familial tradition inherited particularly through socialization in a milieu in which Islam is more of an identity reference than a normative, total, and exclusive path. The exercise of worship as well as the Salafist conferences are, to illustrate the point, occasions for the practicants to espouse the contours of an aesthetic that, while not ecstatic, at least is likely to accord a greater role to the sentient experience.

Examples of this postmodern type of socialization are to be observed particularly during science conferences in the mosques when an ʿalim promulgates to the initiates the Islamic way of life of the first faithful or of their principal inheritors, the ʿulama. The scene we illustrate next symbolizes the nature of the connection between practicants and clerics built on the believers' identification with the purified dogma.

One Saturday morning in 2008 in a Montreuil mosque, the lesson deals with the exegesis of part of a book titled *Riyad as-Salihin* (*Garden of Virtues*) by Imam Nawawi. When the lesson ends and before the call to prayer of the Dohr (noon prayer and second of the five daily ritual prayers starting after the sun reaches its zenith), brother Abdeljalil, as is his habit, answers questions passed to him on small pieces of paper. Diverse subjects concern both the rules of worship and problems touching the lives of the faithful. One question is on the status of dreams according to the scholars of the Sunna: whether a dream can be premonitory and if it can portend good or bad news, whether, as some Muslims suggest, specific dream images can, for example, predict events. Brother Abdeljalil's counsel is taken seriously because everyone knows that it comes straight from his readings, from his encounters with more senior ʿulamas, including those from his sojourns in Saudi Arabia, and he has a reputation for never twisting the legal opinions of scholars. The orthodox answer by the young *talib al-ʿilm* (student of religious science) is not so much our concern here as is the reactions of the audience members when he expounds the view most prevalent among the ʿulama of the Sunna. Here is the substance of his response: Dreams do have meaning in Islam.[8] The texts show this clearly. The scholars explain that some elements (animals and certain people appearing in the dream) may announce news, which is shown, as it were, by the example of the Prophet Youssef (Joseph)

---

[7] Xiberras, *Les théories de l'exclusion*, 182.
[8] "L'interprétation des rêves selon le Coran" (The interpretation of dreams according to the Koran), http://www.cherchonslehaqq.com/2017/02/hadiths-concernant-les-reves.html.

in the Holy Book, who had a gift for explicating his contemporaries' dreams to them.

Aside from the response itself, the ensuing scene was one of the most striking we had a chance to witness during several years' empirical observation of Salafism in France. Abdeljalil, after giving the academic response to the question, asked his peers seated around him in the mosque if they would like to hear a few true stories involving the great scholars that the question about dreams brought to his mind. The reaction of all the pious contemporaries present on the occasion in the prayer hall is striking and by itself nearly suffices to illustrate the aesthetic nature of Salafist sociality:

> Would you like me to tell you a story about Sheikh Ibn Baz? [*Enthusiastic response.*] One day when he was giving a course in a mosque, a woman came to ask him to explain one of her dreams. The sheikh agreed and asked her what the dream was about. The woman then told him that she dreamed of a person who did the *tawaf*[9] around the Ka'ba.[10] She also told him that this person was naked as he was circumambulating the Ka'ba, but at the same time that person was bathed in a light that hid his nakedness. The woman then asked Sheikh Ibn Baz to explain her dream and what it meant that this person walking around the Ka'ba by himself was bathed in light. [*An amused smile creases his face as if he anticipates the audience's astonishment.*] Do you know what the sheikh answered? [*Negative response.*] He told her that it meant that the person she saw in her dream was a person of the Sunna, a person who was precisely on the right path and had God's blessing, hence the light. And you know what the woman then said? Sheikh, the person in my dream—he was you. At that, the sheik started to cry.

The reaction by the believers present in the mosque was immediate, and, as if on cue, they shouted in unison, *Ma Cha Allah* (God wanted it so)! *Soubhan Allah* (Glory to God)! They were wide-eyed and you could see on their faces a real emotion, which segued into several seconds of silence during which heads were lowered as if to reflect on the beauty of the faith, most especially when raised to such a level of authenticity. Several had tears in their eyes. Sheikh Ibn Baz's experience produced this aesthetic, responsive rapport

---

[9] This term refers to the circumambulation of the Ka'ba, "sacred cube," the structure in the center of the Sanctuary in Mecca that the faithful walk around in one direction.

[10] The name of the "sacred cube." This edifice contains the "black stone" revered by Muslims, which every pilgrim has to try to get as close to as possible during the pilgrimage.

wherein the nature of the grace with which God touches His favored servants establishes the social tie between the practicants. Unquestionably, what is fundamental is the application of norms contained in the Minhaj Salafi, but it is just as much this faculty for letting yourself be touched by, and knowing yourself to be an inheritor of, the virtuous ancestors as well as allegiance to the origin times. The light here shines from orthodoxy to structure a morality that in turn determines an aesthetic rapport with the world, life, and religion. The aim is not a work of art properly speaking but rather an image of purity and truth. It is to this that the young preacher's discourse alludes as he continues in the same vein:

> Another time, a woman also came to see Sheikh Albani to have him explain her dream. The sheikh agreed, and so the woman started to tell her dream. She told him of having seen someone walking up a hill, this person walking in a roundabout way, by stepping all the while into larger footsteps and in this fashion kept on climbing. Now, she asked him what this meant. You know what he told her? He told her that this person who walked by stepping into footsteps that were already there in front of him and that were larger signified that the person was on the path of the Prophet *sallatu salam* [May prayer and salvation be upon him], that this person was on the right path and in the way of the Sunna. The woman who had asked him the question then told him, "Sheikh, the person I saw in my dream—it was you." With that, Sheikh Albani broke out in tears and could not stop. He asked his students to leave him alone. So it surely touched him.

The reaction by the Salafis in the mosque was even more remarkable. Words of admiration, astonishment, and praise rendered unto God were even more explicit. Their faces imprinted with emotion, the pious listeners communed in the feeling of beatitude conveyed by the young imam's recital. Bodies were touched the same as souls and consciences, at the price of a socialization at once organic and aesthetic to which each believer subsumes himself in a sentient collective. The mosque becomes the place where this type of experience is possible even though other scenes relating to the individual reading of certain works or visiting internet sites promoting this same type of teaching can also provide similarly blissful moments. In this collective osmosis, the link between practicants is reinforced as they deepen a career constructed in the main on the importance of sensitivity and the capacity to identify with a religious message which, beyond presenting itself as rational-legalistic, knows how to have an aesthetic mode serve as a vehicle for morality.

The interpreting of dreams would not be the only question arousing reactions of this kind among the faithful in the Montreuil mosque. Some weeks later we had a chance to watch practically the same scene, testimony to the constancy of this aesthetic paradigm. The question-and-answer session once again centered on evoking the character of Sheikh Ibn Baz and more particularly the wisdom he displayed when confronting specific problems. In passing, it is interesting that the story that follows was not tied to a question put by someone in the assembly. Instead Abdeljalil agreed to address certain criticisms concerning the manner of conducting the *dars*. So it was that once all questions had been answered, and before the prayer, the young imam offered to tell a story involving one of the grand names of the viaticum that those attending his courses are very fond of. In response the faithful once again touched their chest or face while invoking Allah and giving him thanks:

> Since I know that you like to learn about the lives of the great scholars, today I'm going to tell you what happened to Sheikh Ibn Baz, the way in which he meted out penalties and how he understood the religion when some would do well to follow his example. One day, a young man came late at night to burglarize his house. He did not know it was the house of Sheikh Ibn Baz. So he entered, and he was going to steal whatever there was to be stolen. So he entered. But he was caught in the act, and when they brought him before Sheikh Ibn Baz for punishment [involving the *houdoud*, legal punishments reserved for specific crimes], the sheikh told them, "No, listen, leave me alone with him." He therefore stayed with him and asked him why he had done it. The youth, an African, in fact, he came from some country in Africa... well, I'm not going to tell you which country, no... because otherwise I'm going to upset some people like the last time. [*Laughter. He is referring to a previous course when he told stories involving people from certain African countries whose actions were objectionable under Islam.*] Anyway, while the others were telling him to deal harshly with the young African, he said no. He asked the youth why he had done it, and the fellow told him it was because he was poor and that he had lived in Saudi Arabia for a long time but that his family lived in Africa and needed money. The sheikh, what do you think he did? He asked for one of his students who was in that country, because, well, the sheikh had students in all the countries

of the world. So he asked one of his students who lived in that country to go check it out. He gave him the address and so on. To make a long story short, what the young man had told him turned out to be true. The family, all that. So then what did Sheikh do? He took the young man under his wing as his student. He was charged nothing, and so he harmlessly went through this hardship. And you know what? Several years after the sheikh's passing, the young man in question continued to attend the mosque of Sheikh Ibn Baz [in Riyad], and every time he came in, he would faint. He would tremble and then faint. When they asked him why he fainted every time like that when he entered the mosque, he said, "I remember Sheikh Ibn Baz and that day. All that he did for me."

Thriving on the Crisis of Islamism: The Minhaj Salafi as a Post-Islamist Mode

Islamism versus Minhaj Salafi: Militant Ethic of World Transformation against the Neofundamentalist Post-Islamism of Withdrawal

The study of principles, discourse, and politics that Islamist thinkers have claimed since the birth of the first movement presenting Islam as the source for its social and political program makes it possible to distinguish a certain number of constants. These reflect on the vague desire to convert a system of Islamic norms into a militant project designed, for one, to reintroduce the religious reference as source of a sociocultural identity being lived as anomie and, for another, to emerge on a secular level from a situation of historic decline and lagging behind. This dual agenda constitutes a first attempt at an analysis of the movement known as Islamism. It is useful for grasping the logics inherent in the establishment of a project of re-Islamization having sought, on numerous occasions, to move into the political realm in order to act on the rest of society, especially by driving legal reforms inspired by an orthodox reading of Islam.

This consideration pushes us, on first glance, to a conclusion about the theoretical and practical compatibility of the project carried out by the Muslim Brotherhood and of the Salafist preaching we have studied so far. Considered as the movement that fathered the re-Islamizing of Muslim societies by promoting a militant ethic, the genesis of the Muslim Brotherhood represents a fundamental rupture in the history of theorizations in the name of Islam. Propelled by the Brotherhood movement,[11] a Muslim country in the contemporary age experiences a mass militant project focused on the need to remake this religion into the moral, legal, and identity core of the system of social regulation. As such, the fundamental slogan of the thinking and action of the Muslim Brotherhood, "Islam is the solution" (*al-islam houwa al-hal*), with its religious foundation and the sociocultural practice that it induces, is perfectly comprehensible to the practicants of Da'wa Salafiyya.

Moreover the act of postulating Islam as a system of norms to be rolled out in every segment of human and social life is shared by Salafist doctrine. Even the totalizing character of this religion, which is supposed to subsume all the problems of existence, hence its appellation *choumouliyat al-islam* (all-encompassing Islam), is identical at base to the vision that both the Brotherhood thinkers and quietist clerics lay claim to. This should not come as a surprise, given the degree to which the two groups recognize the necessity of returning to Islam's first centuries in order to recover the purity of a religion decimated by the prevarications and deviancy of believers caught in the trap of history. Nevertheless, beyond these similarities, the two conceptions do differ substantially.

Certainly the fundamentalist vision that the Muslim Brotherhood inherited attaches to the same canonical references that are, for example, the great founding imams of the jurisprudential schools. But it also draws on the more rationalist preaching by clerics with a different conception of the Salafiyya. Having been sensitized to the works and reflections of the Salafi reform thinkers Jamal al-Din Al-Afghani[12] and Muhammad

---

[11] The Society of the Muslim Brothers (Jama'at al-Ikhwan al-Mouslimin) came into being in 1928 (although the exact date was probably in 1927) thanks to a teacher named Hassan Al-Banna, the inheritor of the religious reformers of the second half of the nineteenth century. The movement's founder and principal figure until his assassination in 1949, the year the *ikhwan* became the primary political movement in Egypt and spread to other countries in the region, he is known for his work on synthesizing Islamic fundamentalism and political modernity that would serve to define Islamism. Al-Banna established a seminal break in Muslim societies, which were henceforth characterized by an identity and political option that placed Islam in the center of a social transformation project. See Olivier Carré and Michel Seurat, *Les Frères musulmans* (The Muslim Brothers) (1928–1982), Paris, L'Harmattan, 2002, 24 (the movement's organization chart clearly mirrors that of the Communist parties); Amr Elshobaki, *Les Frères musulmans des origines à nos jours* (The Muslim Brotherhood from its origins to today), Paris, Karthala, 2009; Richard P. Mitchell, *The Society of the Muslim Brothers* (Oxford: Oxford University Press, 1993); Brynjar Lya, *The Society of the Muslim Brothers in Egypt: The Rise of an Islamic Mass Movement, 1928–1942* (Ithaca, NY: Ithaca Press, 2006).

[12] Jamal al-Din Al-Afghani (1838–1897) is the principal figure in the reformist and rationalist movement that spread through the Muslim world beginning in the second half of the twentieth century. See Lire Niki Keddie, *Sayyid Jamal ad-Din al-Afghani: A Political Biography* (Berkeley, University of California Press, 1972).

Abdou,[13] and reading articles by Rashid Rida[14] in *Al-Manar* (The Beacon) magazine, Hassan al-Banna embodies at once a moment of continuity and of rupture in relation to this project of improving Muslim morality, centered on a strategy of returning to the sources. Beyond his militant vision of Islam's credo, from his earliest youth, particularly under the influence of his father, he consumed the teachings of thinkers advocating a return to the foundations of Islam who sought to go beyond some of the traditional sources of Sunni Muslim thought, such as the output of imams during the early centuries. The reformist Salafism (al-Salafiyya al-Islahiyyah) of Afghani and Abdou certainly does insist on the necessary rediscovery of Koranic teaching by surpassing the schools of Sunni interpretation (*al-madahib*) in particular, but it also postulates the compatibility of the Revelation and transcendence on the one hand and of reason and immanence on the other. Renowned *'ulamas* like Abou Hanifa, Malik, Chafi'i, and Ibn Hanbal fostered a first-rate moral and legal teaching; still, it did not manage to become paradigmatic in the eyes of the fathers of reformism in the second half of the nineteenth century. In this respect, and with the aim of guiding Muslim societies toward showing a greater fidelity to their religious heritage, it is important to reconnect with the intellectual ferment of Islam's early days, when the doors were open to the interpretation of sacred references (*abouab al-ijtihad*). Islam's vocation essentially being that of the bearer of the values of emancipation, liberation, and spiritual and material progress, it is the manner of converting the moral and legal injunctions contained in the sources that needs to be questioned, and not the faith itself. This way of regarding Islam's potential as intrinsically progressive and salvational certainly constitutes the principal sticking point in comparing the reformist and Brotherhood preaching (despite the evident differences) with that of the Minhaj Salafi practicants, for whom human reason cannot be the principal foundation of scriptural interpretation.

In contrast to those who theorized the imperative of a return to understanding the Islam of the Pious Ancients during a time when the Muslim world saw its sovereignty pass under European domination (Great Britain,

---

[13] Muhammad Abdou (1848–1905) was the student and companion of Jamal al-Din Al-Afghani and can be considered on the conceptual level the true theorist of Salafi-inspired Muslim reformism. See Antony Black, *The History of Islamic Political Thought* (New York: Routledge, 2001); Montgomery W. Watt, *Islamic Philosophy and Theology* (Edinburgh: Edinburgh University Press, 1985).

[14] Muhammad Rashid Rida (1865–1935) was a Syrian Lebanese student of Muhammad Abdou; he founded *Al-Manar* magazine, which helped sensitize numerous Muslims (especially among the elites) to the reformist ideas of the late nineteenth century. The Muslim Brothers, starting in 1935 also published a magazine bearing the name *Al-Manar*, even though the ideas it developed were substantially different.

France, Russia, and the Netherlands), the men of the Da'wa Salafiyya opt for a more puritan perspective. From the very start, the secularity they slot into takes less account of sociopolitical contingencies with which the community of believers has to come to terms, above all the domination by some nineteenth-century foreign power or other. If the fact of rediscovering the authentic and liberating virtues of Islam is interpreted as a natural factor of expansion and progress, Salafist religiosity is not animated principally by a secular intent. Quite the opposite; this religious matrix seeks orthodoxy for orthodoxy's sake without depicting the act of reconnecting with the spirit and letter of Islam primarily as a crisis exit strategy. This socialization corresponds to the assimilation of norms outside a true theorizing of history, since the latter is conceived of as a succession of cycles during which the Islamic structures must continually reproduce themselves. The reformist ethic is significantly different, in that the religious values, while certainly central, may in theory accommodate themselves to intellectual or cultural references that do not contradict the injunctions of the Muslim religion. The Islamism born in 1920s Egyptian society, marked by a façade of independence from British power and a distancing from an early Islam seen as problematic, picks up a number of Salafist presuppositions; however, a fundamental distinction separates the two forms of preaching. Although the mythic dimension is valued in Salafist religiosity by virtue of a role as a recall to order, it does not have an assumed secular finality. The only acceptable action model is soliciting counsel from the authorized scholars and the application of the norm thus laid down to regulating the legitimacy of behaviors.

Applying some Weberian categories, this viaticum corresponds to value-rational action where Islamism rather more echoes an action lodged in finality. If we consider as central the relationship to history and the advent of a re-Islamization project by mobilizing a mass political party, the Brotherhood's aim is properly modern since it intends to put forward a grand mobilizing narrative. Articulated around a rhetoric emphasizing the return to the sources as an identity *and* mobilization strategy, the narrative of Islam must allow society, distorted by the double effect of the colonial presence and the loss of religious values, to recover the secular means of sovereignty. From there, the Brotherhood project offers the possibility of reviving a religiously based identity matrix; it also aims to turn that matrix into the source of social connection *and* of jurisdiction This makes it a move of a secular nature since it relies on the tools of political militancy, starting with setting up a mass activist movement (and a predicative one in the case of the

Muslim Brothers) organized on the model of numerous European parties. The act of reconnecting with the past or what some may perceive as "outmoded," "obscurantist," or "archaic," is the most paradoxical illustration of the movement's modernity.[15]

Islamism is about a rational action in finality, since the act of recentering the religious norm in social regulation by promoting a militant ethic lets believers shake off the lethargy into which modernity has plunged them. As such, if the problematic of the Islamic state (*al-dawla al-islamiyya*) is not a key concern in early Muslim Brotherhood history, its members preferring to give a push to Egypt's re-Islamization from below through education and welfare activities, it is easier to understand why it has become essential with the passing years. Moreover, while some heterodox young *ikhwan* in the 1960s and 1970s, influenced by the excommunicating ideas of Sayyid Qutb,[16] are going to cause an important rupture by disputing the Islamic character of Gamal Abdel Nasser's and later Anwar Sadat's Egyptian state, Brotherhood-style Islamism from the beginning distinguished itself above all by reserving the right to question the Islamity of the society on a qualitative but not a dogmatic level. At no time did al-Banna gainsay the Egyptian society's Islamic character.

Islamism is therefore difficult to separate from its global militant dimension, in which it advocates for the introduction of the Islamic reference in every area of social space in order to cure Muslim societies of their inability to deal with modernity but, for all that, without breaking with an identity matrix furnished by the religion. It is easier to understand why Salafist socialization diverges on this point, because where militantism presupposes the legitimacy of questioning society and the state, Salafism promotes a purely religious fundamentalism, delegitimizing involvement in the political arena.[17]

---

[15] Olivier Roy, "Quel archaïsme?" (What archaism?), *Autrement*, no. 95 (December 1987): 208.

[16] The reference here is to the founding work of Sayyid Qutb, *Maʿalim fi-Tarik* (translated as *Signes de piste, Jalons sur la route,* or *Signaux sur le chemin* [all three: Road signs], an injunction bequeathed by the Islamist intellectual to the avant-garde to come), in which he illustrates a more radical vision of the Brotherhood militancy. The Brotherhood theorizes, in fact, the tipping of the Muslim countries from "pagan ignorance" (*al-jahiliyya*) on whose rubble the Prophet Muhammad had to build the first Muslim society. Qutb established an equivalence between the pre-Islamic era and the contemporary age, which, in his view, justifies, if only symbolically, speaking of "the impious power" (*houkm al-jahili al-kafi*) and of the "tyrant" (*taghout*).

[17] Olivier Roy, "Le passage à l'Ouest de l'islamisme: Rupture et continuité" (The passage of Islam to the West: Rupture and continuity), foreword, in Amghar, *Islamismes d'Occident*, 7.

Faced with this militant ethic and imbued with a clear finality, namely the Islamization of social, judicial, and institutional structures, quietist Salafism surely comes closer to being a value-rational action. The militant ethic corresponds to a rational form of action by which the agent seeks to attain an objective. The political goal of Islamism resides in the advent of a state structure aligned with norms drawn from the religious corpus; it thus echoes a modern manner of thinking about politics, to the extent that the modern tools of militantism must be put in the service of the birth of an Islamic society and state. For its part, the Salafist conception can be understood as a value-rational action, to the extent that the socioreligious practice, notably inspired by the opinions of authorized clerics, is apprehended outside a true reflection on the consequences. The fact, for example, of not taking into account the context in which the interaction between a practicant and his environment is formed obeys such a logic. Wanting to wear the full veil is normal because normed, since it is the authentic value that trumps all others. It is a question of a unique wish to revive a system of principles following from an identification with a blessed age as opposed to a time of moral decadence. It seeks nothing more or less than materializing the belief in its system of values by its action.[18] Islamism emanates from a thought of finality since the sought-after goal is to act on society and on the course of its history, whereas the Salafist religiosity offers a relationship liberated from history. The career that relates to this is not inclined to forcibly transform society by a politically dynamic ethic. The initiates certainly do emphasize a predicative posture but one that, most of the time, does not shrink from converting itself into a salutary withdrawal. In this they embody a self-sufficient fundamentalism since their project does not integrate the necessity of acting on society other than through puritan education. The great Islamist narrative of transforming the state thus scarcely resonates with them. In characterizing the aspirations of a youth full of defiance when it comes to politics and the enterprises of world transformation controlled by the state and that is desirous of cutting itself off from the world for the sake of individual well-being while all along arranging spaces for negotiation with it, this socialization is well within the ambit of a postmodern dimension of life in society.

On the political level, one of the fundamental presuppositions of Islamist militancy is the conviction that the believer has the right to

---

[18] Max Weber, "The Nature of Social Action," in W. G. Runciman, *Weber: Selections in Translation* (Cambridge, UK: Cambridge University Press, 1978).

question the adherence of society and state to Islam and, more precisely, the degree of their fidelity to the sacred injunctions. This clear difference between the Salafi and the Islamist[19] can be understood with the help of analytical categories highlighted by Hirschmann. In terms of social (de) mobilizations, Islamism must be understood as a strategy of religiously motivated speaking out by the introduction of the reference of Islamic transcendence and the sacred within a repertoire tied to the politics of power. The lexicon of political militancy (power, elections, dissent, alliance, parties, chief of state, legislation, etc.) then finds its source and legitimacy in the importation of a religious and fundamentalist vision into the political arena. The Islamist movements, be they the Muslim Brotherhood or other organized groups cast in this mold in whole or in part, distinguish themselves by a vocal strategy whose objective is to set the society back on the path to Islam. It is nevertheless proper to specify that the means implemented for nearly a century by Islamist projects often knew how to forge compromises insofar as they came to work with a power situated outside the sphere of militant and political Islam with the aim of establishing a dynamic of Islamization of morals and of the legislative framework. In this regard, the questioning of the political power, as the basis of the Islamist initiative, can dissolve into a strategy of cooperation with or even of loyalty toward the political power, to the extent that the Islamist cadres construct, deconstruct, or reconstruct a militant project sometimes by relying on integration of one part of their agenda with an institutional, constitutional, and legislative plan of action elaborated by the powers that be.

With the Da'wa Salafiyya, the logic is different—both by degree and by nature. The sole religiously legitimate political positioning, at the risk of inflating the ranks of the "people of deviance," echoes the strategies of loyalty and leaving. For reasons linked to a Hobbesian vision of the social contract, Islamic references are interpreted as inimical to sedition, a conception that, in a certain sense, partakes of a secular fundamentalism since politics does not conform to the same prescriptive catechism as the common run of believers. The cleric, for his part, is at once a key political

---

[19] The first *ikhwan* distinguished themselves by introducing a new qualifier to describe themselves to their coreligionists caught in an Islamity that was cultural, traditional, and, in fine, incomplete. They started to present themselves as *islamawiyoun* (plural of *islamawi*, which can be translated as "aware or lucid Muslim") having integrated the intellectual, political, legal, and moral implications of a full and total adherence to the principles of the religion.

actor and the arbiter of the process of legitimizing power, in that he invites the people to obedience and loyalty all the while he is endowed with the prerogative of sanctioning or influencing the political authority by giving it sound advice. This being the case, the only acceptable posture in Islamic lands is a consensual loyalty connecting the holder of power and the population composed of believers, which in this way draws nearer to salvation. The ʿalim, whose duty is to vouchsafe respect for the religious injunctions here on earth and to guide the Muslim nation to divine approval, ensures the demobilization of society vis-à-vis the prince's daily reforms and actions in a direction that, in theory, is always oriented toward loyalty to the scriptural sources. This is why, from this perspective, the population is not a legitimate political actor unless the cleric decides otherwise subsequent to a moral judgment casting aspersions on the political. In fact the people may not become involved in an initiative guided by any motive but loyalty. This loyalty is distinct from the historical and critical cooperation of some Islamists with power, something that is impossible for the quietist practicants. In a non-Muslim context, secularizing fundamentalism has to keep its distance from the political arena to protect itself against the torments of a decadent morality. Put another way, the strategy of leaving is, under this scenario, the only one that even corresponds to the exigencies of the Salafist career. The political arena tolerates only two types of players. One is the politician, legitimized by the other type, the ʿulama, the theoretical pillars of the system. This is why the dimension of Islamism that is not just militant but almost Hegelian and that emerged fairly early in Muslim Brotherhood activity is foreign to the Salafis' legitimist matrix, which is also structurally resistant to morphing into Islamism. Even if the religious sphere is supposed to rule the entire social space, the political arena is the only one that is treated as an exception, because the norm that prevails in it is more minimalist than anything else. In other terms, if the agenda of the clerics aims to push the common run of believers toward ever more conformity with the spirit and the letter of the religion, the politicians are appraised through another analytical grid by virtue of which their sovereign function of protecting against sedition and their religious mission of defending Islam minimize the judgment of the ʿulama, making them less demanding. The sanctuarization of the political arena prevents the emergence of generalizable militant structures that potentially could challenge the monopoly of the scholar and the prince in the political arena.

The Quietist and Legitimist Salafi Viaticum: An Islamism for Leaving Islamism?

We define post-Islamism as the result of the postmodernization process of the Islamic ethos.[20] Faced with the impossibility of evoking a *Homo islamicus*, by definition a resistor against the evolutions that typify the march of contemporaneous societies, post-Islamism has at minimum a dual dimension. The first concerns the fact that the individual is his own measure. While religious discourses are important, he is the one to decide what is good for him, even if this personal mediation translates into a delegation of sovereignty and the assimilation of a message negating individual specificity. The second is tied to a form of disconnection between the fate of the world and self-realization. The two destinies henceforth are lived and understood differently and are capable of entering into contradiction. It is here that "hyperindividualism" describes better than "individualism" the passage to a postmodern relationship with the world: if the former is compatible with cooperative logics by which a person can accept wanting to change the course of history, the latter cuts the individual off from this type of consideration. He certainly becomes his own vector of interpretation of the meaning of existence, but he is from now on autistic to the tensions and dynamics that structure a history of humanity. The relationship to the world certainly is heteronomic since it interposes an explicative screen of the world that is not endogenous; even so, the practicant does not seek to accelerate the course of history. If the concept of post-Islamism can reflect different meanings, all of which at least present the same definition of the concept as "inherited historical framework of Islamism, after the latter's failure principally concerning Islamization of the political arena and of the State,"[21] allowing "the "privatization of re-Islamization,"[22] it refers above all, in our view, to the inrush of the referential of postmodernity into the system of Islamic meaning.

On a microsociological level, the profiles and hence the motivations put forward by the players may differ, but, viewed from the macropolitical angle, the reinforcement of these norms will not be understood without keeping in

---

[20] The title of this section is influenced by Marcel Gauchet, *Un monde désenchanté?* (A world disillusioned?) (Paris: Les Éditions de l'Atelier, 2005), 143–144.

[21] Amel Boubekeur, "L'islamisme comme tradition: Fatigue militante et désengagement islamiste en Occident," in Amghar, *Islamismes d'Occident*, 133–134n6. See equally Olivier Roy and Patrick Haenni, "Le postislamisme" (Post-Islamism), in *Revue des mondes musulmans et de la Méditerranée*, nos. 85–86 (Aix-en-Provence: Edisud, 1999); Asef Bayat, "What Is Postislamism?," *ISIM Newsletter*, no 16 (Fall 2005).

[22] Roy, *L'islam mondialisé*, 53.

mind the upheavals that have affected the Islamic meaning space over several decades. Although now more than ever it fights the Islamic groups taking it on themselves to challenge the state in a militant mode by mobilizing the most modern political categories, official Saudi Islam contributed to the grand Islamist narrative before today distancing itself from it. Favoring legitimist, quietist, and postmodern strategies of re-Islamization, the Saudi state, however, for several decades made orthodoxy, with the most famous scholars in part acting as intermediaries, a factor in the legitimization of an Islam on occasion even more dissident and more violent. Justifying a specific type of "state Islamism," or Islamism as a foreign policy tool, the 'ulama have been a force, despite the apparent paradox that attaches to the impossibility of going militant on the internal level without upsetting the people's allegiance, acting for "the expansion of Islamism" just as today they mean to work for its "decline."[23] It is this bundle of politico-religious considerations that permit us to evoke the Minhaj Salafi as the Islamism for exiting Islamism.

From a Socialist Conception of the Economy to a Liberal Ethic: The Islam of the Pious Winners

In the economic and social domain, the Islamist rational action in finality must coincide with a larger social justice, the Islamic collectivity having to watch over material conditions guaranteeing the moral dignity of the believers. Such a principle legitimizes the Islamist movement's grander hold over the judicial and institutional apparatus, with the goal of re-Islamizing the structures of society and of providing more socioeconomic equity. Islamism therefore stresses a veritable Islamic socialism. Moving the need to gather the fruit of the *zakat*[24] to the center of the prerogatives of the Muslim Brotherhood in order to reestablish solidarity among Muslims, the Islamist project incorporated an indisputable social aim from the start. The thoughts of al-Banna, followed by those of Qutb,[25] comprise large elements that bear on the socioeconomic problem, both men assigning it a fundamental place in raising a more Islamic, hence more just society. The mobilizing project, which is, in the eyes of the first Islamists, the consequence of their revivalist

---

[23] Kepel, *Jihad*.
[24] "Obligatory purifying alms." Representing the fourth pillar of Islam, it equals 2.5% of revenues and capital accumulated during the year and is to be distributed to needy believers.
[25] In 1949 Qutb he published *La justice sociale en islam* (*al-'adala al-ijtima'iyya fi-islam* [Social justice in Islam]). See Carré and Seurat, *The Muslim Brotherhood*, 84–88 (the paragraph is headed "Le socialisme de l'islam" [The socialism of Islam]).

ethic, must erect the principle of social justice at the heart of the Islamic society that they intend to (re)construct.

This dual dimension characterizes the welfare and social morality of the Muslim Brotherhood, as well as of numerous other movements of militant re-Islamization in the Muslim world. Salafist socialization differs significantly from such an approach in that the individual reference, organizing the wish for its own success, is at the core of assimilating this system of values. The scriptural sources and religious principles are summoned up to justify personal achievement in a way that will pull others into accepting Islamic dogma. The pious predecessor is presented as an active devotee, a virtuous, worldly man who knows equally the imperatives of worship and morality as well as the importance of building wealth and material success. It is God pushing his creatures to take charge of themselves and adopt a dynamic posture here on earth. The triumph of liberalism on an economic plane thus influences a materialist ethic laid claim to by many Muslims, Salafis foremost among them. The Islamist Muslim, once marked by cooperative and solidarist values, progressively ceded the ground to a Muslim whose desire for success and social ascent is far from being the exception today. Such a phenomenon has all the more impact because, in the French context, the new moral perspective opened by entry into this career cut across the hope for self-realization and of social advancement in the economy by numerous individuals socialized in the suburbs and coming from immigrant communities. The model of the "pious winner,"[26] which pervades the Salafist communities just like other re-Islamization movements, is more sought after, to the detriment of the ethic of collective solidarity that characterizes early Islamism.

From Militant Movement to Status Group: Mass Ideology and Neotribal and Elitist Sociality

The switch from militant movement, organized around the politicization of the re-Islamization project, to status group, uniquely interested in a strict predication formulated in a puritan mode, represents a less common mode of leaving Islamism behind. If, in effect, other offers of Islam are familiar with this fatigue of organized engagement, the Salafis present an originality that they are practically the only ones to test. Detached from the desire to transform the public square by agitating in it, even if only through individual

---

[26] Patrick Haenni, *L'islam de marché: L'autre révolution conservatrice* (The Islam of the marketplace: The other conservative revolution) (Paris: Seuil, "La République des Idées," 2005).

influence, the practicants could be described as following a kind of *introvert* logic. By contrast, the ethic of the militants, be they inheritors of the Islamist matrix or simply those wanting to create a space for a minority Muslim sensibility, can be qualified as *extrovert*. Interested in all the spheres where their identity strategy permits, the militants are led to interact with many players and to deal with a number of situations that, at first view, are difficult to reconcile with the Muslim vision of the world. If, for example, we argue from an analysis of the relationship to a geographic space, it is not surprising to realize that the militant profile is as comfortable on a university campus in contesting an election to represent the student community, in the streets demonstrating during a time of crisis, or even in meetings with politicians before election day. Here the Salafist posture is different, more introverted: the home, the office, and the mosque are the cardinal places for exercising their puritan, exclusive ethic. Space and time offer as many dimensions in which the disinterested and self-sufficient relationship to the world finds itself ready to unfold. The sole point in common between these two re-Islamization projects in defending their respective conceptions relates to their intensive use of the internet. Yet even there, when the initiates evoke the dogma and diverging analyses of different *ulama* concerning Islamic jurisprudence, the militants favor campaigns of boycotting Israeli products, raising consciousness against Islamophobia or announcing conferences where preachers mingle without difficulty with seekers, fellow militants, and politicians.

The Islamist current laid bare the necessity of re-Islamizing especially the Muslim societies that had gone through a bitter colonial experience by importing the political modernity materialized in techniques and tools of mass politicization. The Salafis, grounding their revivalist project outside a sanctuarized political arena, therefore are nothing less than a status group in Weber's sense. For the religious sensibility, the political party is a heresy, having a partisan spirit it has to reflect speaking to the governing powers being abhorred elements. Beyond that, what matters most for the mode of organization prized by the competing actors of re-Islamization is their relationship to the world and to history.

It is thus that the Salafist socialization corresponds as easily to a fundamentalist project as to a mode of postmodern control over the relationship to society. The status group is, for example, optimal for experiencing the aesthetic paradigm that is central to a new form of organic solidarity. It is equally adapted to exercising a hyperindividualized way of life that seeks to negate the individual, which is the case upon entering into this career. In the mass militant Islamic movement, for which the Muslim Brotherhood furnished the historical matrix, or its past or present avatars in the Maghreb (Movement for the Islamic Society, Islamic Tendency Movement, Ennahada, etc.), in the Middle East (Hamas), in the Gulf (al-Islah in Yemen), in Pakistan (Jamaat- e-Islami),[27] or elsewhere in the Muslim world, the foundation of the prevailing social link is very different there. The return to Islam is envisioned from the angle of politicization and thus the strategy of speaking out. To the degree that the Salafist ambition is different, including both the envisaged means and the action framework, the political party cannot be an effective solution. The status group seeks prestige, which explains why the practicants are largely indifferent to politically linked initiatives.

From an Integrated *Hijra* to an Ethnic and Globalized *Hijra*

For the majority of practicants, the *hijra* is obligatory, following most notably a logic of immunization. By spiritual but above all physical distancing, they must reconnect with themselves, repair their being and their morality damaged by an extended sojourn in the land of unbelief. This corresponds to a vision of a purely personal career stripped of the militant dimension. This form of *hijra* differs fundamentally from the ethic of departure Egyptian Islamists hew to, advocating an integrated vision of *hijra* in the 1970s as preeminently political and antiestablishment. It distinguishes itself, in effect, from the version embraced by the radicalized activists that were both the inheritors of and at odds with the *ikhwan* after 1966, the year Qutb died. Some militants socialized in the Muslim Brotherhood, the young representatives of generations of demographic expansion, of endemic poverty, and of the Nasserite dictatorship, assimilated the thinker's work on breaking away and found in it the justification for an extreme radicalization toward a regime henceforth viewed as anathema. Perceived as the cause of the departure from Islam of the people who wrongly thought of themselves as Muslim, the Nasserite state, whose religious reference is usurped in the view of the Qutbists, became an object of ferocious hatred and a target for this generation of Muslim Brothers who would from now on preach struggle instead of spiritual and social reform. This is what led certain small groups, advocating in some cases the rediscovery of the value of jihad, defined as an armed sacred struggle against

---

[27] Seyyed Vali Reza Nasr, *Mawdudi and the Making of Islamic Revivalism* (Oxford: Oxford University Press, 1996).

the iniquitous and usurping entity,[28] to revolutionize Islamic militantism as it had been organized in Egypt since the late 1920s.

Others took the path of a spiritual and physical break from society, henceforth stamped with impiety. The objective in this case is the reconstitution of an authentic community without connection to the avatar of the Mecca-related pre-Islamic model that prevailed in Egyptian society of that era. Socialized in the Muslim Brotherhood, Shukri Mustafa (1942–1978), an agricultural engineer by training, will theorize the necessary schism between the true Muslims and those who compromised their faith by refusing to fight the Egyptian state. An active member of the *jama'at al-islamiyya* (Islamic groups) that again are going to take up and radicalize the Qutb epistemology, Mustafa will go so far as to apply this binary, cutting thought to the Brotherhood militants, whom he came to know in prison but who refused to embrace his view of the world. When the premises of a liberalization by the regime, announced as a relaxation of sanctions levied against the Muslim Brotherhood accused of having plotted against the state, came to light after Sadat's taking power in 1970, Mustafa decided to spearhead a realist preaching with his successors whom he united in an organization that a number of journalists began to call Takfir wal-Hijra (Excommunication and Exile or Anathema and Hegira).

---

[28] One version of this term can refer to armed combat with the aim of defending Islam and Muslims, provided the clerics decree it. A young electrical engineer would theorize the dormancy of jihad as organized violent action for the purpose of defying the adherents of a false Muslim power. Muhammad Abdessalam Faraj (1954–1982) popularized the idea that Muslims have neglected the religious yet axial obligation of armed jihad. An activist in one of the most important radicalized Islamist groups of the 1970s, Tanzim al Jihad (Organization of jihad), definitively founded in 1970, he wrote a seminal text on the contemporary Islamic revolutionary fighting doctrine, *Al-farida al-ghayiba* (The hidden imperative) in Gilles Kepel, Muslim Extremism in Egypt: The Prophet and Pharaoh (University of California Press, 2003, 242–273). In this text he refers to jihad as the sixth pillar of Islam that has been disregarded by the average believer. Faraj takes up the idea advanced by Qutb that jihad is an imperative for every Muslim (*fard al-'ayn*), not just some (*fard al-kifaya*). This is how the logic was hatched that led to the operation ending on October 6, 1981, in the assassination of the "impious president" Anwar Sadat and, more generally, to the development of an excommunicational and revolutionary thinking of which Al-Qaeda is without doubt the most famous inheritor. Faraj was executed in 1982, but certain of those close to him, among them Ayman Al-Zawahiri, continued his work, the latter, for example, becoming the principal media spokesman for Al-Qaeda after Osama bin Laden's death in May 2011. Among the Muslim Brotherhood cadres, some had a presentiment of the dangers that a certain reading of Qutb's work would incur. This was the case of the society's guide, Hassan Houdaybi, who in 1969, in order to fight the radicalization of the "Qutbists," would write the work that reaffirmed the primarily reformist role of the movement and the necessity of bringing the *ikhwan* out of the clandestine existence they had been cast into by Nasser. He would refute the possibility of excommunicating Muslims and reaffirm that Egyptian society could not be compared to Mecca before Muhammad's apostolate. The title of his book is explicit: *Dou'at la Qouda* (*Prédicateurs et non pas juges* [Preachers and not judges]).

Mustafa then declares the necessity of cutting oneself off from the godless world in order to lay the foundation for a community purified in its practices and view of the world, an avant-garde with responsibility for the re-Islamization of society, being duly cognizant of the weak state (*marhalat al-istid'af*) it was in during those years. This is why forsaking active militancy embedded in Egyptian society is abandoned in favor of socializing in an authentic context true believers dedicated to the next Islamic revolution. The *hijra* that Mustafa advocates will take several forms, depending on the context, but it will remain marked by the postulate that it tallies with a political analysis of the state of things; engaging in it should not present an obstacle when the time is ripe to a full and complete reintegration into the Egyptian political arena of violent action organized in the name of a rehabilitated jihad. The Society of Muslims (Jama'at al-Mouslimin), nicknamed by the Egyptian press of the time Anathema and Hegira, will become known for group discipline induced by the need to protect itself from a godless world and for constructing a countersociety with the mission of reproducing the way of life of the first Muslims.[29] Fleeing the urban environment for caves in nearby mountains and so keeping their distance from nonbelief on a physical level, the members of Takfir wal-Hijra express their leaving the society of their birth behind geographically in order to develop a social tie built solely on an exclusive allegiance to the principles of Islam. Certain of the group's men will be invited to migrate to countries importing unskilled labor and know-how, such as Saudi Arabia and Kuwait, to provide for the needs of congregation members who stayed at home. On returning to Egypt, they were authorized to marry one of the celibate women belonging to the group, as a way of sealing, with the most endogamous marriage possible, the purity acquired at such cost by abandoning the majority Egyptian society. According to the rules of the countersociety being gestated, the couples and families had to live in a community, in dwellings created with that in mind, in such a way as to lay the foundations of a solidarity and an Islamic identity confined to the members of this avant-garde. Mustafa will be executed in 1978 for his role in the assassination of Sheikh Dahabi, a religious dignitary at Al-Azhar University and former Sadat minister who was very hostile toward the Society of Muslims.

The *hijra*, as practiced by quietist practicants, and the Takfir wal-Hijra's ethic of withdrawal and temporal disengagement are poles apart. The salutary

---

[29] Kepel, *Le Prophète et le Pharaon*, 73–118.

emigration of that kind of group is eminently political because it is part of a broader strategic vision calling for a temporary disengagement from a society impossible to transform in the short term. Mustafa certainly exhorted his adepts to purify their faith and religious practice but also to keep in mind that it was not a question of abandoning the rest of Egyptian society irrevocably. The goal is surely to return, not to make a permanent physical break. Migration is a voluntary sacrifice, even if it is endowed with an indisputable regenerative virtue for the adherents of the religiosity taught within Takfir wal-Hijra. By contrast, the Salafis situate themselves in a logic of erasure, to the point that their presence on godless soil must be forgotten for the sake of a rebirth on Muslim soil. Apparently the finality of their departure is to be found in a purified vision of religious practice, so their *hijra* has its own dynamic. Once the diagnosis has been made that holds that every true believer must distance himself from the society of unbelief or risk perdition daily, it is not the object of a real interest.

It is therefore a question of a migration of disintegration, different from the Egyptian excommunicator group clinging to a vision of return and victory over the majoritarian part of Egyptian society still caught in the torments of unbelief. It is in no way limited like that of the small group influenced by Mustafa, which continues to dispense a teaching of rupture to his congeners while still assuming authority, both moral and political, over the rest of the community after the *hijra*. In Salafist socialization, while the clerics will give religious backing to the physical and moral rupture with French society, they impart no precise living instructions once one has arrived in the land of Islam. The practicant continues to seek interaction with the *'ulama*, but the content of his existence after settling in Muslim country is strictly up to him. In this the Salafist migration is individualistic, since independence is an appropriate condition for the career on the social, professional, and geographic levels. For the clerics, settling in the Maghreb is basically no different from settling in the Levant, even though the practicants almost without exception put Saudi society at the top of their wish list. Moreover the country left behind, in this case France, is not the object of regret, compared with the Meccaesque society with which the first Muslims intended to reconnect after a founding exile in Medina. The partisans of anathema and salutary isolation that gathered around Mustafa planned to return victoriously to the places they wanted to distance themselves from in order to build a countersociety that would permit thinking about an ultimate transformation of Egypt. The Salafis form not a vanguard but a morally self-sufficient elite whose calling is to shine and restore a religiosity supposedly deserted by strayed Muslims. They do not assume responsibility for changing the rules and values ruling the rest of society other than by preaching and the good example. In parallel with that, they are not prohibited from enjoying or benefiting from self-realization spaces such as commerce, entrepreneurship, or consumption. A progression can be detected in their ethic of the *hijra*, a linear relationship in the career, their condition as believer improving in step with the damage done by socialization in France fading and the growing identification with the country of emigration. The migration of the small Egyptian group is, by contrast, cyclical, since it is about returning to the point of departure after having reconnected with an authentic approach to Islam and having defined a coherent, organized political action plan given a chance of real success. The Salafis, in a postmodern relationship with time, space, and grand narratives, promote an individualist and initiatory vision of the saving migration. To the great departure attaches a political dimension announcing the refusal to remain subjected to an alienating norm, the grand journey here coming close to being an act of voting with their feet. Nevertheless a will to change the world remains foreign to the basic tenor of such a practice. The post-Islamic impact of the migrations is situated in the overtaking of the state, of militant action, and of the collective aspect of migration for the sake of an atomized conception that is initiatory and voluntarily blind to any phenomenon of assumed politicization.

From Protester-Revolutionary Theorist Back to Theorist-Pillar
A fourth exit path from Islamism pertains to the place and the role of the cleric; he will take it to either embark on an Islamist or a Salafist experience. The nature of the action taken by the *'alim* and his influence, beyond the representations that he conveys as a cardinal figure in Muslim society, differs in a fundamental way according to the socialization mode studied. The *'alim* in the quietist perception is an insider, a stakeholder in the political system. He dispenses sound advice to the prince in a manner that brings the project of fidelity to scriptural sources into daily life. Although he has to be differentiated from the purely secular wielder of power, he nevertheless remains a source of legitimacy as well as a veritable engineer of day-to-day religion, for he is the institution by which the Islamic logos is understood and put into practice. On the political sidelines, he is really a key player in the system of power.

Conversely, the Islamist experience leads to the conclusion that the cleric holds the position of outsider. The right to question the exercise of power, an epistemological foundation of Islamism, no longer belongs exclusively to the body of scholars lodged close to the summit of power; it becomes a private prerogative in certain cases, as we see in personages like Muhammad Abdessalam Faraj and Shukri Mustafa, who took it upon themselves to define a norm of rupture with the canons of Egypt's main religious institution, Al-Azhar University. Here it is first of all a matter of political logic, since it is the analysis of society's evolution that brings in its wake a revolutionary religious theorization or, at the very least, one that has broken with the interpretation that comforts the powers that be, as long as the latter show themselves to be sensitive to the words of the ʿulama.

However, there is another profile of the ʿalim that typified an important period of the Islamic experience in Egypt, to wit: an individual who is trained in traditional religious learning but who has been led, by political socialization, to move into the power arena as an antisystem player. Comparative study of the place and role of the cleric in the Salafist conception and in the Islamist current reveals a fundamental difference. It constitutes an important factor of the passage from a militant and activist vision of the Muslim identity to a posture stripped of any notion whatsoever of acting on the world, for the benefit of a recentering in the heart of the matter of religion, i.e., in its dogma. It is almost possible to analyze in management terms the remediation of the extroverted ethic of Islamism by a politically more introverted quietist Salafism. The shrinking audience for the grand Islamist narrative, especially because of the increasing atomization of society, has negatively influenced the credibility and capacity for mobilization of militant movements, making possible a return to an Islam that is foremost a spiritual and cultural tradition. A parallel can be perceived in the evolution, on an economic level, to a dynamic of recentering on the core business of an enterprise whose strategy of conglomerate diversification did not achieve the expected results. The Islamic movements can be compared to companies that tried investing in different sectors with the goal of marketing their brand and seizing promising growth opportunities, but at the risk of straying from their core business. As a result, once the failure was locked in, they reflected on the need to concentrate again on their core activity in which they are the undisputed leaders. The visibility of the Daʾwa Salafiyya may in part be analyzed using this key to understanding.

Under the influence of the cleric state, Saudi Arabia, the Islamic reference has touched nearly all the countries in the Muslim meaning space, where it was adopted in a puritan manner in order to promote that country's place as the center of the global religious scene. The defensive Salafism promoted most especially by the Saudi authorities starting with the Gulf crisis of 1990–1991 illustrates the influence of the country's political agenda, which we find in the increased legitimism taught by the clerics. It is thus that the ʿalim paradoxically finds a more central role in shoring up power but becoming more circumspect in exerting his political influence, because one of the primary objectives is the defense of the state that presents itself as the organ for diffusing this norm. Returning to preaching that adamantly protects the political arena to better focus himself on the private implications of the dogma, the ʿalim promotes his dimension as the pillar of sociopolitical stability. It can still be seen today in the internal debates in the religious arena concerning the Arab Spring, with the quietist clerics inveighing against sedition, especially when it comes to Saudi Arabia, that could lead to an eventual overthrow of the regime.

The pillar imagery lets us grasp the ethic of responsibility of the scholar who, more than ever, takes on the charge of buttressing the secular power at a moment when it is liable to waver. The Salafist scholar is therefore a vector for leaving and preventing Islamism, which constitutes a break relative to the central role played by the kingdom of the Sauds in Islamism's dynamic expansion starting in the 1960s consequent to the policies of King Faisal. A force for conservatism and appeals to the common people for endurance, the ʿalim limits as much as possible the inclination in some quarters for conflict and political change. If his historical function confers on him a dual position by which he operates as the interface between the people's aspirations and the constraints under which the secular power labors, he becomes, because of the political crises that characterize the Islamic meaning space, an insider organically tied to the fate of many regimes in charge of Muslim countries.

The contrast in this forced post-Islamism is all the more striking because the epistemology of the Islamist moment has to take into account the importance of the revolutionary or protesting ʿalim, who perceives himself as an outsider in the politico-religious field. In setting himself up as defender of the fate of believers neglected and tyrannized by the pernicious prince he incarnates an explicit break from the priority quest for stability of the cleric-pillar. Conservatism is discredited by the drive to reform or delegitimize the powers that be. If the Islamist ʿalim is not obligatorily a revolutionary figure, one of his fundamental action principles is the right to question the wielder of political authority on his manner of dispensing justice or converting religious values to the political, social, and judicial domains. Seeking to create an independent religious realm, whose mission is the re-Islamization of institutions that sometimes are anything but Islamic, when they are not constructed on other references, Islamism is more than ever a strategy of speaking out. In this movement's history, it has often taken on the aspect of purposely severe religious preaching against the installed regimes. Be it a question of flaming sermons or taking positions of blacklisting the powers that be, the *ulama* in this category often took these regimes to task, justifying such a campaign by the need to change an exercise of authority that strayed far from the Islamic vision.

The example of the *'alim* Sheikh Abdelhamid Kishk (1933–1996)[30] illustrates the scale of the religious and political difference between a cleric-pillar and a cleric-protester. In the Egypt of the 1970s–1980s, Sheikh Abdelhamid Kishk represented the scholar of opposition, his sermons against the state recorded on audio cassettes that enjoyed wide distribution throughout the Arab world. He was the megaphone for part of the population. From a modest family, blind from birth, known for his eloquence and straight talk, he became the imam of the 'Aïn al-Hayat (Spring of Life) mosque in Cairo. Close to the Muslim Brotherhood and refusing to condemn the thoughts of Qutb, he was imprisoned from 1966 to 1968 for having protested Nasser's suppression of the Brotherhood movement, then a second time during the Sadat presidency. Refusing compromise with power, he crystallized, especially in his lectures broadcast to the entire Arab-speaking world as *Madrassat Muhammad* (The lectures of Muhammad), a popular aspiration hostile to the repression, to the peace treaty with Israel, and to the endemic inequalities. For many believers, his death, which came on December 6, 1966, while he was prostrated in prayer, added to his renown. His sermons were full of everything the cleric-pillar warns against. The chaos and trouble from taking a position in the religious arena, motivated by a desire to challenge the political power, are directly imputed to the sermons of *ulama* abandoning the way of orthodoxy for deviationism.

In Gilles Kepel's landmark study on the sociology of Egyptian Islamism at the turn of the 1970s–1980s,[31] it is possible to peruse the content of a

---

[30] Ibid., 214–237.
[31] Ibid.

sermon by Sheikh Kishk delivered in his ʿAïn al-Hayat mosque on April 10, 1981. The opposition cleric begins his discourse by citing a story in the Brotherhood magazine *al-Daʾwa* (The Preaching) that related the practices of a group he termed a "sect" and that was vilified for having offered the ritual prayer facing toward Jerusalem and not Mecca. While such a warning would certainly also sit right with the ʿulama of the Salafist school, what follows in the sermon is fundamentally different from anything the cleric-pillars would call for. Arguing that, in his view, such sects could grow in Egyptian society only with an external "hand" helping, Sheikh Kishk goes after the political leaders who took power following the 1952 coup d'état led by the Free Officers with the involvement, in particular, of the future *raïs* Nasser. The imam does not shrink from hurling invective at "the men of the revolution," accusing them of having sought to stamp out Islam, for example, by replacing religious judges applying divine instructions with magistrates deriving their authority from the state and basing their rulings on human, hence "inept," legislation. The cleric-opposer extrapolates lessons to be drawn from what, in his view, constitutes a real infamy and takes as his witness the members of the assembly listening to him. At that point he asked them, in his stentorian voice, whether they are prepared to accept such a "crime" and to tolerate such a "denaturing" of the Islamic order.

While it is easy enough to imagine such a scene, one of many like it in the city of Cairo in the early 1980s, we need to compare this sermon with those we have generously excerpted. For ontological reasons linked to the precepts the Minhaj Salafi stands for, it is strictly impossible to take leaders to task and even less to proclaim some sort of intent on their part to destroy Islam. The ʿulama-pillars in a sense can be seen as a centripetal force while, the cleric-protestors or cleric-revolutionaries make up a centrifugal force by distancing believers from the obedience owed to the wielders of political power. Both in the substance of their preaching as well as its form, the Salafi practicants, in contrast to Sheikh Kishk, would not know how to buy into a logic of defiance in which God is called as a witness to the "treason of the clerics," since, for Salafists, politics is a black box that must remain closed to the average believer. In this light, Islamism can be analyzed as a factor for a certain degree of democratization of the word and engagement by people the opposition clerics stood up for. Post-Islamist socialization, given the reticence that it manifests when it comes to engaging in and militating under the influence of an ʿalim-protester, translates thus, in paradoxical fashion, as a retreat from the democratic spirit since the political field is ceded to the discretion of the scholar-politician duopoly.

The Rehabilitation of the Islamic State

The rehabilitation of the Islamic state can be seen as the consequence of the differing dynamics of exiting from Islamism shown up to this point. By choosing to abandon any kind of militant posture and all strategies of speaking out against the legitimacy or manner of conducting the affairs of state, Salafist socialization rebuilds a religious regime in which the political power occupies a privileged place. If the Islamist experience, especially starting in 1960s Egypt, coincided with a democratization of political prerogatives, post-Islamism, in its quietist Salafi version, corresponds to a resanctification of the state as long as it does not explicitly renounce the Muslim religion as its reference. For example, the Shari'a thematic, that is, the legal and moral system grouping the provisions of Islam, is gone into in an inclusive manner. Indeed the decisions and laws willed by the prince are presented as fitting legal emanations of the religious corpus approved by the 'ulama. The Islamity of the state is thus guaranteed by the clerical act of legitimization. In fact witnessed here is a veritable rehabilitation of the state as an entity that is central to the religious life, while Islamism, symbolized for example by an 'alim like Sheikh Kishk, is based on the principle that Islamic society may, through the outsider cleric, elevate itself to the level of the state and hold it to account. It is in any event this sort of postulate that has fed the very essence of the Islamist dynamic since, without questioning the state's Islamity, the strategy of irrigating anew the political field with a sacred reference formulated according to a fundamentalist vocabulary would never have seen the light of day. As such, Islamism, in this displaying a modern aspect, signifies an egalitarian access to the option of stating the religiously legitimate, and to warn believers, key to the success or failure of such an enterprise, in the name of Islam against certain practices by the power. When claiming to be acting for the sacred is no longer enough and proof must be presented of a true integration of the norm with state action, this qualitative break in apprehending the religious reference is therefore basic for the Islamist ethic.

The Salafist post-Islamism differs categorically from such a conception when it renders the passage from the religious to politics as actually impossible. The break here has to do with the act of replacing the state outside its secular sphere to keep it from being questioned by believers, which is left exclusively to intervention by the outsider or antisystem ʿulama. Thus the rehabilitation of the Islamic state goes hand in hand with the act of shielding it in the sphere of deliberation or opposition, as had been the case in the Islamist experience. Salafist postmodernity thus includes the willingness to let the allegiance of the faithful slumber in a consensual disinterest in the way civic affairs are managed. Being wary of politics contributes in unexpected ways to restoring politics to the center of systems supposedly built on the authentic norm. Partly rid of the Islamist menace thanks to the umbrella provided by the legitimist ʿulama, the state gains, in addition, freedom of action, since it is impervious to the challenging and interrogatory dynamics coming from all or part of the populace. It also regains a certain freedom of maneuver stemming from the fact of Salafist preaching's demobilizing character. Postmodernism explains the entry into this career, permitting an apoliticism on the microsociological level that goes hand in hand with a consolidation of the state on the macropolitical level. As a result, Salafist socialization has a more antirevolutionary influence than ever.

This rehabilitation in due form of the statist institution in the name of the religious reference that had nearly swept the prince and his regime away several decades ago was made possible by the advent of a postmodern relationship with the world. This dual dynamic of relegitimization and sanctuarization of the political arena is explained by the atomization of the individual and the triumph of postmaterialist values such as success, self-affirmation that overrides collective action, and the revenge of the individual on the great mobilizing narratives. With politics mattering little after all, the individual can attend to material as well as spiritual occupations, while showing solidarity with the Islamic state when called for by circumstances, as during the Arab revolts. The practicant, for whom excommunicating the sovereign or community of coreligionists is impossible, has no choice but to keep his distance from the political arena in which only two families of players have legitimacy. Having to consent to the existence of a kind of Islamic ceiling above which it is impossible to rise canonically without running the risk of anarchy in society, the believer sees himself expressly guided by the scholars to a stance of loyalty. As such, the Islamic state is indeed distanced from any public accusations, the option of asking for an accounting being relegated to the cabinet authorities and resulting solely from interaction between scholars and politicians. The post-Islamic Salafi is opposed, most notably under the impact of reflection by the clerics on the subject of militant Islam, to the modernity included in the Islamist ethic.

In this regard, Saudi Arabian jurisprudence is a perfect example, since the success of a large part of the precepts of the Da'wa Salafiyya is the direct consequence of the change in that country after becoming aware of the danger represented by those gone astray. The Arab Spring illustrates today like a textbook case the organic solidarity that is at the heart of the compact involving the 'ulama, politicians, and common believers. In the face of the tremors shaking a number of Arab countries, the Salafist social contract is once more put to a hard test by events. Most of the time, it is possible to observe within these French communities a fidelity to the principle of preservation and demobilization inherent in this career. Going against the current of the ferment roiling a number of movements and organizations structured around the Islamic reference, the supporters of this viaticum illustrate more than ever the impossibility of calling on God to witness against the custodians of political authority.

Conclusion

> The destruction of the past, or rather of the social mechanisms that attach the contemporaries to the previous generations, is one of the most characteristic and mysterious phenomena of the late 20th century. In this day and age, most young people grow up in a sort of permanent present, without any organic link to the public past of the age they live in. The historians, whose job it is to recall what others forget, therefore become more essential than ever as this second millennium closes. But, for this reason, they must be more than simple chroniclers, compilers or memory men, even though this, too, is one of their necessary functions.
> —Eric J. Hobsbawm, *L'Âge des extremes*

What is an ideal, and can it possess a functional dimension? Putting it another way, how does the religious socialization that we have been studying proceed from a social and political language, that is to say, from the forging of a new relationship with the world largely determined by former social lives, that would explain the identification with Salafism? This viaticum promotes a conception of the environment in sacred terms, to better live in it or, if necessary, reject it. The ideal in this instance looks like a rationale. Because it vehemently stresses what differentiates beings, it must first be analyzed as a source of lessons on the place and representations of certain actors living in France. It also represents a message about today, as attested to by the systematic extolling of the past in the form of reverence for a Golden Age.

Three elements need to be clarified in this respect. First, what are the factors capable of explaining a career of a religious nature among certain circles in France? We have seen that the distinctive traits of the actors opting to pledge allegiance to Salafist views distinguish a certain profile. Without deducing any kind of determinism, we noted throughout our work that this religiosity came to be grafted onto a type of prior relationship with the world, often linked to a familial history conflicted about the idea of belonging to France, to an earlier socialization in the suburban districts encouraging the emergence of counterworlds, and to a youth ripe for certain questionings that facilitate creativity in forming identity. In this environment, the Minhaj Salafi must be seen as a response to the multiple tensions characterizing these profiles. How to distance yourself from your family without permanently cutting ties? How to cultivate the wish to live elsewhere while justifying only rarely following through in actuality? How to cultivate a moral discourse on the state of society without lapsing into an authentically militant agenda? How to sustain a vision of the world assumed to be unidimensional when you have been imprinted by several previous socializations, some of which were far removed from religious imperatives? Viewing this career as a desocialization does not make sense, because that would amount to taking up the discourse of the interested principals and essentializing their approach while, seen from an epistemological perspective, preventing us from inquiring into their way of life except through the strict prism of the sacred. This religiosity is a social phenomenon that must be studied as such, beyond the current discourse of Islamizing to excess the behaviors and rhetoric of players presenting themselves as affiliated with this religious tradition. This language comes from a derived process, which is to say, from the importation of a reference reconstructed from sociological givens that are in reality endogenous, to rationalize a largely preexisting relationship to the world. If many see in such a journey the product of an ideological radicalization nourished by an obscure project of re-Islamization, centered on imams laboring in obscurity, our work has shed light on a more complex reality.

To conclude from this that the Salafist socialization is a rupture at very little cost is a gap that requires qualification. This viaticum without doubt harbors the potential for conflict, if only from a symbolic point of view. However, it seems to be characterized most of all by a wish to retreat or to escape. The practicants are not of this world. They oppose but do not take action. They contest but do not organize. They oppose vehemently but do not destroy. They call for awakening but not for responsible activism. Their message is one of morality, not strictly speaking political. Their positioning addresses key values of society in a discourse that is pronounced by actors comfortable in this moralizing and disengaged posture. They inspire but they do not lead. At the same time, their socialization combines easily with the rest of the sociocultural norms admitted as normal in a modern society, it being understood that we are not referring to values here that they judge to be immoral. They are the children of a society that they do not recognize and that, in their heart, they want to sap of legitimacy even while they benefit from the opportunities it offers, yet all the while complaining about the lack of social justice and equality (notably religious), as we were able to verify on numerous occasions during our interviews. Still, there is no need to see in this the preeminence of a utilitarian relationship with society, even if it is not entirely lacking, rather the rationalizing of a connection that the interested principals are good at redefining to their advantage. The practicants negotiate the nature of their relations with other people, institutions, and dominant values. They are the daily engineers of their existence and the meaning they give to their religious engagement. If, in the name of an intransigent morality, they criticize most of the principles the majority of their fellow citizens adhere to, there is no need to see in their contradictions a form of hypocrisy or cynicism. Instead this is the result of previous socializations, some of them conflictual, that interact to dispute or ratify certain social rules. The social deviance they own to is constructed day by day in a manner that systematically puts a religious frame on how they construe their place in the national community. The sacred then becomes the favored resource for transcending their problematic connection with the rest of society and confirming tendencies well beyond those observable in fundamentalist Muslim circles.

Still, quietist Salafism must above all be considered a posture mobilized for translating a relationship with the world made up of frustrations and impeded projects; it presupposes as well that the identity demand, a radical one here, is more significant than the supply, to put it in terms of economic analysis. Indeed if this system of meaning is more polysemous and dynamic than it appears to be, we are obliged to state that a number of elements that lead to identifying with it have to do purely with the French context. We proposed to study the factors capable of influencing the path of an individual toward a fundamentalist religious career. Salafist preaching incarnates better than any other the example of a globalized religious offer. As much due to the action of a true regulatory state, Saudi Arabia, as to a specific proselytism at the national level, the orthodox canons have managed to make inroads among a certain youth. Yet while this statement is irrefutable, focusing only on this dimension would amount to remaining silent about the basic tendency observable in numerous suburbs where the immigrant heritage in large part organizes the relationship of many young people to the world. Were we to focus on the existence of a "ghetto mentality" or a "peripheralized identity," one could not help but notice the existence of a sentiment of subjugation reinforcing the objective stigmatization vectors of unemployment, of urban segregation, or of a certain vindictive political and media discourse dating back some years.

We thus observe the persistence of a habitus of rejecting, contesting, and defying on the part of numerous classes of people that the new face of immigration and religious belief in France has come to enrich with new problematics and to color Islamically. In the past this has translated into a certain appetite for the discourse of the extreme left or of other more or less organized groups, all marked by wanting to throw off the domination of one part of society by another. Here is a factor that we think is essential for explaining the preeminence of the demand for radicalism by a religious offer that is more elusive than one might have postulated at first sight. This observation will benefit from being validated by remaining attentive to the emergence, in the near or distant future, of new identity offers, religious or not, in those areas where, in French society more than anywhere else, the symbolic mixes with the political. Accordingly, if quietist Salafism looks like a centrifugal force relative to the rest of the collectivity and when contrasted with a respectable—because centripetal—offer of Islam, reasoning without separating the identity level from the purely urban, political, and social dimensions allows a downward reevaluation of the religious reference. The act of not applying an exclusively pathological template of interpretation is all the more understandable when an individual is not so much the product of a desocialization that denatures him as the fruit of different circles of acculturation and previous socialization. In other words, while the idiom is sacred, the content is profane.

Beyond the idea that the Da'wa Salafiyya pertains in part to a socially determined career, one of the key findings of our work is that the fact of Islam follows the arc of time. This means that the representations and social practices that we observed inside these communities do not reflect any fundamental differences with the dominant values of our era despite the religious veneer. Islamism, despite the evident cultural and moral specifics linked to the Muslim sphere, coincided with the time of the great narratives, one of whose pillars was the belief in the possibility of transforming the world through engaged social and political activism. It is therefore no surprise that the Brotherhood experiment occurred in the early twentieth century, at a time when mass ideologies spread in the name of a fierce struggle for a monopoly over the course of history in European societies. We have seen that Islamism first of all must be understood as a rational action in finality, an enterprise aiming to serve the community of believers (*al-oumma*) supposedly suffering in history and, more particularly, under the domination of non-Muslim powers. The response to this had to be an organization seeking to promote a militant religious, activist ethic founded on the belief that Islam can justify forceful engagement and speaking up in the ensemble of arenas constituting society. The modern dimension is evident here since the engaged posture and militant mass tools interacted fully during the Islamist moment.

The era into which quietist Islam inserts itself is different. This religiosity, as resistant to speaking out in the political sphere as it is desirous of reforming the morals of human being by education and appeals to morality, develops no animosity toward numerous attitudes observable in the contemporary era. The crisis of the state and of institutions, just like the disintegration of the allegiance to the values of modernity as a result of hyperindividualism and affinity for the codes of market globalization, are that many points in common with numerous social groups feebly aware of ancient legitimization spaces of the social tie (political parties, unions, schools, etc.). It is the reason why the microsociety constitutes the most pertinent degree of organization and identification and the one most adapted to Salafist socialization, the umma for one offering a horizon, an ideal to reach for, especially through the *hijra*, whose relative character we have seen. Thus the quietist posture finds its raison d'être in a very specific era: that of postmodernity precisely marked by the preeminence of the aesthetic paradigm that is sufficient unto itself, the veritable moral finality of a way of life that asks nothing of society.

As children of their time, on which they act in turn through a socially compatible religiosity while opposing it daily on a symbolic level, the Salafis embody the gravity of postmodernity's codes and the decline of the logics that once used to underpin the state as well as a certain feeling of national cohesion. Their horizon is no longer the same, and the efforts of struggling between an attachment to their origins and the pull of another world, of whatever kind, however physical or virtual (cyber *hijra*), are examples of the difficulty of passing decisively from traditional structures of socialization to new instances of solidarity and identification. On a methodological level, our work demonstrates that the essentialist readings, for which categories like "Islam," "identity," "fundamentalism," "rupture," and "return of the religious" are the object of preliminary definitions, buttress thoughts of a uniquely sacralized perception that is largely insufficient for correctly describing the issues raised by Salafism.

This offer of meaning reflects, moreover, another face of Islam's history in France in how it takes shape relative to the rest of society (institutions, media, etc.) and to the globalized Islamic landscape (currents, countries, networks, etc.). Added to this are the tensions existing between different Muslim players in this country, making it part of a highly competitive Islamic offer on the national level. Adherence to Salafism then explains itself mainly by the evolutions that have touched this field for many years. By getting an attentive hearing among youth with little appetite for organized militancy and wanting to take part in market mechanisms without, however, buying into a logic of civic allegiance, this viaticum is markedly different from other producers of Islamic meaning. Be they traditionalists or militants—and therefore ready to engage with the non-Muslim other to assert their views—or exclusivists in following the example of the Da'wa Salafiyya but ascetics, the other players on the Islamic scene are not on the same wavelength as the practicants that we encountered. As we have highlighted, few systems of meaning and instances of resocialization combine so many traits that, at first glance, would seem to be incompatible: religious puritanism, mistrust of institutions and organized politics, withdrawal as a way of life, anti-imperialist and anti-Western postures, a strong appetite for human and market globalization, a distaste for disorder and sedition, empathy for Muslim religious regimes such as Saudi Arabia, and so forth. The ensemble of these traits cannot be understood without keeping in mind, beyond the structure of previous socializations, the relational dimension of the re-Islamization phenomenon at work in France for several decades. In

Salafism's case, there is a mismatch with the dominant morals of French society, which explains this authenticity premium to the detriment of an appropriation of the national social contract.

What, then, might be the perspectives of a puritan movement unwilling to get involved in official politics, hardly inclined to think in terms of sinking national roots, and constantly dreaming of somewhere else that is prized as much as French society is deprecated? After studying its principles, its sociology, its apparent paradoxes, and its evolutions, we see three possibilities for coming years take shape, it being understood that the Minhaj Salafi, more than any other offer of Islam, is structurally dependent on variations in the Islamic meaning space.

The first possibility would follow from the application of the Salafist agenda by the massive implementation of a complete, decisive migration cutting the practicants off from the society of their birth to continue their religious career on Islamic soil. From having a French Islamic face, the Da'wa Salafiyya would return to its historical geographic space, the Muslim world, thereby signifying its eternal incompatibility with pursuing an orthodox Islam in a non-Muslim-majority context. While not impossible, especially when keeping in mind the numerous references to the anti-Muslim hatred seemingly at work in France for many years and, more particularly, taking the form of legislation perceived as aimed at the religion, this option appears unlikely to us. The main reason for this is that the Salafis have problems getting acclimated to the receiving Muslim countries, never mind the security and administrative problems that tend to make establishing permanent residence there difficult. The *hijra* is foremost a horizon rather than a tangible project. It is certainly a strong initiatory rite, the practicants who have done it symbolically outranking the others, but it is still a reversible move that is not consequential, especially when it is of the Erasmus type. In this regard, it must be understood above all as a stage by virtue of which the believer changes his perception of himself and his religiosity. While he may continue to dream of the Muslim East, his sojourn is reformative of his career since he either opts to stay in the chosen country, especially if it is the one from which his family emigrated (ethnic *hijra*), or partially backtracks on his initial vague desire for making the break. Consequently, detaching is more difficult than might appear. Closeness with the family left behind in France and difficult integration in the new country are often cited as factors that permit relativizing the desire for permanent migration; however, that does not prevent seeing in this learning effect an orientation of Salafist socialization toward a better awareness of the complexity of existence and of life in society. Perhaps more at ease in French society than they would like to admit, the difficulty a majority of practicants have in taking the plunge pushes them into a new register of rationalizations of the type "If I had the same quality of life over there, I wouldn't hesitate for a second." Sometimes even the breach of the obligation to emigrate is clearly rationalized by deconstructing the necessity of it. A number of the pious contemporaries thus come to admit the possibility of staying in France as long as certain religious conditions are respected (presence of mosques, access to halal food, etc.). The *hijra* is therefore, without question, a physical movement, but it is ultimately a voyage into the self.

The second possibility could be a perpetuation of the hybrid that we observe today. Salafist socialization could continue to be characterized by mistrust of the surrounding society while defining itself, from an empirical standpoint, by a neither-nor corresponding to the impossibility of biting the bullet on the *hijra* coupled with a categorical refusal to invest in making Islam work in France and a fortiori to engage in a debate with national institutions. This has a higher degree of probability. The investment in the economic field then would constitute a pertinent indicator of sustained disinterest in integrating into society, paralleled by the impossibility of permanently burning the bridges to their origin environment. Obviously this does not apply to the profile of the most capitalistic Salafis, those who have managed their affairs so well that they no longer consider permanently settling in a Muslim country. For the others, the provisional becomes identity. Between partial and pendular migration and subjected to living in the banlieues among religious peers, neighbors, and family, life in France is still to be thought of as a source of damnation. But yet the great departure never occurs. In a certain way, this viaticum finds itself constrained here by having to come to terms with a difficulty born of its principles. The Salafist career conceives of itself objectively as an individual progression in which the believer travels a road marked out by appropriate teachings, puritan preachings, and elitist practices, with the *hijra* at the intersection of these three elements. This means that every day this journey must take the practicant closer to the realization of his ideal. Hence, not to emancipate himself from the unholy reality while continuing to eschew coming to terms pragmatically with it represents nothing more nor less than a problematic halt in his career. The Salafis, moreover, are aware of it, because they are the ones to take umbrage at the invective of some of their coreligionists mocking the fact that they talk of a saving migration without walking the walk. In their eyes, it is a test of their faith, and the efforts dedicated to coming out on top of such a situation illustrate their creativity and reflexive posture when it comes to their religion. This is why, as much as their fervor for their religion and its founding principles may remain unchanged, they experience the almost dialectical impossibility of surmounting their forced residence on French soil as a source of frustration. This posture is, for the moment, the one most commonly observed in the Salafist communities.

The third possibility resides in a modification of the agenda as the result of a change in doctrinal order. This preaching would become more aware of the endogenous challenges and would engage in a more active and organized undertaking of defining the Islamic agenda, in this way bringing the look of orthodoxy to bear on the evolution of French Muslims and of society in general. This is not impossible, although unlikely in the short term. It would require a minimum of three preconditions. The first depends on Saudi Arabia, the country at the epicenter of global Salafism. To a lesser extent, it is also a question of the less august ranks of this epistemic community in other countries. In effect, it would call for the margin of interpretation permitted in this system of meaning to be widened in the French context in a way that would legitimize the act of engaging in certain practices of a political nature, such as voting, organizing movements with a defined agenda, or, more generally, implementing a clearly militant vision of preaching, starting with action in the mosques or on the web. To date, we have not seen any such beginnings. There are certainly young imams susceptible to justifying a more activist conception of the viaticum, but they do not yet represent the Salafi mainstream. In discussions with practicants about an eventual trend to an assumed politicization, we could almost always validate empirically that they consistently preferred preachers who are firmly attached to invoking the religious injunction without losing themselves in this type of thinking. This strong tendency in the French arena is accentuated still more by the fear of adopting postures seen as the preserve of revolutionary Salafis or of militants. It is all the more pronounced because it creates the feeling of chasing an Islamic agenda that they did not buy into when they converted. We saw that the clerics in this movement know very well know how to take positions that could be generally qualified as political. The unit of account is certainly respect for the credo, but taking Muslim interests into account is fundamental, which makes it possible to imagine, at least on a theoretical plane, the possibility of an arbitrage in favor of an ethic that is more attuned to engagement in civic affairs. However, we have seen that the tensions that characterize the political and religious order at the top of the state—which, while not the exclusive actor, does count for a lot in organizing the global Salafist field—ought to presage, even if only in the short and medium term, a still more conservative positioning mainly driven by the desire to demilitantize Islam by dogmatically disqualifying this religion's potential for political speech. Despite this, the possibility exists.

It is nevertheless necessary for two other, more sociological conditions, to come together. One is that the movement in France suffers from a lack of individuals even capable, in the sense of mastery of the tools of activism and possession of academic and intellectual capital, of carrying the Salafist preaching to a more politicized state, at least in the short term. This has more to do with the composition of the Salafi communities, in which even the most highly educated do not stand out, almost without exception, by their willingness to nourish a more political conception of their religiosity. On the other hand, such a project, if there were to be one, would have to run counter to a much more essential sociological given. The Salafist career is, in fact, chosen by actors who want to stay away from civic affairs and are not disposed to join militant groups. Were they to change their ethos and move into a more engaged posture, one would have to ask if they could do so in collaboration with other Islamization platforms or in parallel with them. Still, one question remains: Should a number of practicants join in the public debate and in militant actions in a decisive manner, would they do it based on their vision, or would they be ready to form an intra-Islamic syncretism? In our opinion, neither is probable in the short run, given how much what characterizes quietist Salafism is distinct from any kind of impatient waiting when it comes to changing French society, as is the idea of fusing the *tawhid* agenda with that of other currents. The type of recruiting that characterizes this movement for now really seems to be the principal reason why it is very difficult to imagine a move to an expressly militant state. The focus on an apolitical socialization is even one of the crucial factors behind its success, so much have we seen that the demand hinges on the offer of religious meaning. Nevertheless it does not mean that this religiosity will always shy away from entering the rest of the social space in a more consequential manner. The potential is there, as we have seen. Factors such as Islamophobia and the Israeli-Palestinian conflict may push practicants toward a change in posture for which the religious principles would be reinterpreted to structure a more activist ethic.

Thus it is more difficult than ever to set up an unequivocal picture of Salafism in France and in the world. The same goes for the Islamic faith landscape. If any element has to be put in perspective, it is the explanation of the religious by factors endogenous to French society. Our gaze henceforth must be directed toward the fraught sociological and political trends that characterize its development. In part, its future depends on the nature of relations between French Muslims and their country. The growing awareness of such an evolution, to which it is hoped that this work will have contributed in a modest way, will let our country envision its future in a more optimistic manner and, who knows, to become reconciled with itself.

Index

For the benefit of digital users, indexed terms that span two pages (e.g., 52–53) may, on occasion, appear on only one of those pages.

Tables are indicated by *t* following the page number

Abdel Aziz Al Sheikh, 59–61
Abdeljalil (interview subject), 74–75
Abdeljalil (scholar at Montreuil mosque), 159–63
Abdelkhaliq, Abderahman, xxvi
Abdelsamad (interview subject), 59–62, 76–78
Abdelwahid (interview subject)
   in Algeria, 115–16, 123–24
   Al-Mouslim bookstore and, 12–13, 115–16
   on Chavez, 116–17
   education of, 12
   Halaldom brand and, 116
   Islamophobia in France confronted by, 115–16
   Muslim Brotherhood and, 13
   Palestine and, 13
   on political quietism, 13
   The True Face of the Prophet Muhammad and, 114–15
Abdou, Muhammad, xxiv, 164–65
Abdullah (king of Saudi Arabia), 138, 140
Abou Hanifa, 164–65
Adnan (interview subject), 6–11, 128
Al-Afghani, Jamal-Dine, xxiv, 164–65
al-Afghani, Jami'ou Rahman, 57, 58
Afghanistan, 57–58, 152
Al-Albani, Sheikh Muhammad Nassirdine
   Abdeljalil's story about, 161
   electoral politics and, 52
   Palestine and, 110
   preeminent stature among Salafis of, 148–49
   quietism of, 40–41
   Salaf as source of all truth for, 28–29

   on Salafism and the "return to the ancients" of earliest Islam, xxi–xxii
   Syrian educational system and, 41
Algeria
   Battle of Algiers (1957) and, 123–24
   French diplomatic presence in, 123
   French Salafists' *hijra* (departure) to, 91, 121–23
   macheikh (religious scholars) in, 96–98
   Salafi Orientalist views of, 141
   war of liberation (1954-62) in, 123–24
Algeria: The Past Revisited (Chitour), 123–24
'alim (Islamic religious scholar)
   as anti-system player, 180, 181–84
   buttressing of secular power and, 181, 183–84
   as guarantor of Islamic legitimacy, 27
   Islamist conceptions of, 180
   political holders of authority *(wali al amr)* and, 37–39
   quietist conceptions of, 179
   Salafism's emphasis on practicants' personal closeness with, 33
Amara, Fadela, 145
Arab Spring (2010-2011), 154–56, 181, 185–86
Ardisson, Thierry, 72
Aulnay-sous-Bois mosque (Lille), 10
Al-Azhar University, 88–89, 180

al-Baïda website, 9
banlieues (working-class suburbs in France)
   alternative meaning-making in, 102–3
   electoral politics and, 52

banlieues (working-class suburbs in France) (*cont.*)
"leftist habitus" of, 106–7
Lyon metropolitan area and, 106–7
Paris metropolitan area and, xli–xlii, 106–7
poverty and racial segregation in, 103, 104
Salafism's appeal in, ix–x, xiv–xvii, 101–3, 105–8, 187
al-Banna, Hassan, 164–65, 167, 172–73
Becker, Howard, xxxvi–xxxviii
Belhadj, Ali, 114
Ben Ali, Zine El Abidine, 20, 154
Bennani-Chraïbi, Mounia, xli
The Bible according to Barnabas, 76
Bilal (interview subject), 51–55, 57–58
Bin Laden, Osama
in Afghanistan, 57, 58
conspiratorial views of the West and, 108–9, 112
jihadist interpretation of Salafism offered by, xxiv, 32–33
Saudi Arabia and, 151–52
September 11 terrorist attacks and, 10, 112
takfir declarations by, 112
Bourdieu, Pierre, 24
Bouteflika, Abdelaziz, 116
burqa (women's face-concealing garment), xv–xvii
"burqa ban" (France's law prohibiting concealment of the face in public spaces, 2010), xv–xvii, xli, 51, 96–97

Carré, Olivier, 103–4
Chafi'i (Salafi 'oulama), xxii–xxiiin25, 164–65
Chavez, Hugo, 116–17
Chechnya, 58
Chirac, Jacques, 52, 113
Chitour, Chems Eddine, 123–24
Christianity, 48
Copé, Jean-François, 72
Council of Senior Scholars (Saudi Arabia), 153–56

Dahabi, Sheikh Muhammad, 177
Day of Retribution (*youm ad-din*), 30

deviance, xxxvi–xxxix, xxxviii*t*
Donegani, Jean-Marie, 54–55
Durkheim, Émile, xxxiv–xxxv, 99–100

Egypt
Arab Spring uprising (2010) in, 154
Al-Azhar University in, 88–89, 180
British control during early twentieth century of, 165–66
French Salafists' *hijra* to, 57, 88, 109
Israel and, 182
Markaz Al-Ibana in, 88
Muslim Brotherhood in, 165–66, 167, 175–76, 182–83
Salfist parties since fall of Mubarak in, xxiv
Society of Muslims (Jamaʾat al-Mouslimin) in, 177
Takfir wal-Hijra organization in, 176–78
Ennahada Party (Tunisia), 20, 174–75
ethnomethodology, xl
Étienne, Bruno, 87

Faisal (king of Saudi Arabia), 138, 146, 151, 181
Faraj, Muhammad Abdessalam, 180
Fatah Party, 61
al-Fawzan, Sheikh Salih Ibn Fawzan, 41–42, 57, 80, 149–50
Ferkous, Skeikh Mohamed-Ali, 96–98, 115–16
fitna (sedition), xxv–xxvi, 32–33, 79–80
France
adan (Islamic call to prayer) in, 51
"burqa ban" (law prohibiting concealment of the face in public spaces, 2010), xv–xvii, xli, 51, 96–97
Council of the Muslim Faith in, 22
economic regulation in, 65
"exclusive Muslims" in, 26
headscarf ban in public schools (2004) in, 26, 51, 52–53
Islamophobia in, 85–86, 88, 94, 106–7, 112, 114, 115–16
Muslims and electoral politics in, 51–52, 66, 105–8, 114, 192
"private Muslims" in, 25

quietist nature of Salafism in, xiii–xvii, xxiv, 4–27, 32–33, 104, 105, 129–32
secularism in the political culture of, ix, 55
socialization to Salafism in, xxvi–xxvii, xxix–xxx, xxxi
traditionalist *versus* nontraditionalist Muslims in, 25
Turkish Muslims in, 118–19, 121, 124, 127
Freemasons, 108–9, 112

Gabriel (archangel), CP.P27
Gayant-Douai housing projects, 7
Gaza, xli, 59–61, 62, 110, 136–37. *See also* Palestine
genealogical socialization, 3
Gérin, André, 106–7
al-Ghannouchi, Rashid, 20, 21
ghettoes. *See* banlieues (working-class suburbs in France)
Giscard d'Estaing, Valéry, 144
Gülen, Fethullah, 125
Gulf War (1990-91), 39–40, 150, 153–54, 181

Hadith 4603, 3n2
hadith of sixty-three sects, 47–48
Hamas, 61, 110–11, 136–37, 146, 174–75
Hanafi school of jurisprudence, xxii–xxiiin25
Hanbalite school, xxii–xxiiin25, 152–53
Hassan (interview subject), 121–22
hassanat (good coming from action or speech), 81
Hassan II (king of Morocco), 129
Al-Hawali, Safar, xxvi
headscarf ban in public schools (France, 2004), 26, 51, 52–53
Hezbollah, 61
hijra (flight of Muhammad from Mecca to Medina)
economic independence compared to, 65, 76
Egyptian Islamists conception of, 177–79
Ferkous on, 96–97
"globalized hijra" and, 175
Salafi discussions of leaving France compared to, 54–55, 56–57, 192–93

Salafist socialization in France viewed through lens of, xxv–xxvi
withdrawal from ungodly society compared to, 79–82
Hirschmann, Albert Otto, 50n1, 59, 168–69
Hobsbawm, Eric J., 186

Ibn Abdelwahab, xxiii–xxiv, 36–37, 39–40, 153–54
Ibn Baz, Sheikh Abdelaziz
Abdeljalil's stories about, 160–61, 162–63
Fawzan and, 41–42
"global mufti" status of, 39–40
Ibn Abdelwahab and, 39–40
Ibn 'Otheimine and, 41
Madkhali and, 42
The Nation of Tawhid depiction of, 138
al-Saud family and, 39–40
Ibn Hanbal, xxiii–xxiv, 34–35, 145, 152–53, 164–65
Ibn Houmeyd, 138
Ibn Kathir, 145
Ibn Saud, Muhammad, 36–37
Ibn Taymiyya, xxiii–xxiv, 35–36, 69, 145
Ibn 'Otheimine, Sheikh Muhammad Ibn Salih, 41, 82–83, 138–39
Idriss (interview subject), 89–90
ikhwan. See Muslim Brotherhood
Ilyas (interview subject), 111
imaginary socialization, 133–48
Iraq, 57–58
al-Islah, 174–75
Islamic Tendency Movement, 174–75
Islamism. *See also* Muslim Brotherhood
'alim within, 180
anti-regime preaching and, 181–83
Arab Spring (2010-2011) and, 185–86
cooperation with state power as a possibility for, 168–70
decolonization and, 174
definition of, 163
democratizing elements of, 184
"Islamic socialism" and, 172–73
militant dimensions of, 167–69, 173–74
"post-Islamism" and, 163–86
rational action in finality and, 166–67, 168

Islamism (*cont.*)
   rehabilitation of the Islamic state and, 184
   religiously aligned state structure as goal of, 168–69
   Salafism compared to, 168–70, 173–75
Israel, 182. *See also* Palestine

Jamaat-e-Islami, 174–75
Jam'at at- Tabligh. *See* Tabligh
Jesus, 8, 13–14, 76
jihadism
   anathema on "deviant" political leaders proclaimed by, 38–39
   Bin Laden and, xxiv, 32–33
   Gulf War and, 39–40
   jihad al-talab (defensive jihad) and, 57, 58
   Merah and, ix
   September 11 terrorist attacks and, xxiv–xxv
   tawhid doctrine and, 36
jilbab (shapeless robe or coat designed to hide the feminine form), 69
Judaism, 48
Justice and Charity movement, 129

al-Kabtani, Abu Farid, 44
Kamal-dine (interview subject)
   birth name of, 17
   Catholic family of, 15, 17
   Salafist conversion of, 14–17
   Tablighis and, 18
keffiyeh (Palestinian headscarf), 146
Kepel, Gilles, 87, 182–83
Khalaf (generations of Muslims after Muhammad), xix
khourouj (exit from the path of God), 8, 9, 17, 73–74
Kishk, Sheikh Abdelhamid, 182–84
The Koran
   prayer and, 110
   Prophet Muhammad's inspiration recorded in, xix
   Salafism's emphasis on adhering to, 5, 30, 110
   sura 3 and, 3n1
al-Koweïti, Sheikh Fayçal, 82–84

kufr (those living in unbelief), 79–80, 93, 95, 111, 122
Kuwait, xxiv, 152n16, 177

Lapeyronnie, Didier, 101–2, 104
Larcher, Gérard, xiv–xv
Lille (France), xli–xlii, 34–35, 106–7
Londonistan (Thomas), 86–87
al-Luhaydan, Saleh, 59–60
Lyon (France), 106–7

al-Madkhali, Sheikh Rabi Ibn Al-Hadi, 42
Madrassat Muhammad (The lectures of Muhammad, Kishk), 182
Maffesoli, Michel, 157–58
Malaysia, 118–19
Mali, 57
Malik (Salafi *'oulama*), xxii–xxiiin25, 164–65
al-Maqdis, Sheikh Abu Muhammad, 32–33
March of the Beurs, 144
Markaz Al-Ibana (Cairo), 88
Massoud, Ahmad Shah, 58
The Matrix (film), 66
Mayer, Jean-François, xx
al-Ma'moun, 34–35
Meddeb, Abdelwahab, 136–37
Mekki (interview subject), 85–88
Merah, Mohammed, ix
Meyssan, Thierry, 136–37
Milli Görüs (National Vision), 125
Mitterrand, François, 144
Morocco, xli–xlii, 4, 129, 141
Mouline, Nabil, 153–54
Al-Mouslim bookstore (Paris), 12–13, 115–16
Mouvement de la tendance islamique (MTI, Tunisia), 20
Movement for the Islamic Society, 174–75
Mubarak, Hosni, xxiv, 90n13, 154
Muhammad. *See* Prophet Muhammad
Muhammad cartoon controversy (2006), xli, 114
Muqbil Ibn Hadi al-Wadi'i al Yamani (sheikh in Yemen), 10
Muslim Brotherhood

British control of Egypt in early
    twentieth century and, 165–66, 190
  educational and welfare activities
    by, 167
  founding of, 164n11
  Muslim critics of, 111, 144, 146
  Nasser's suppression of, 151,
    175–76, 182
  political engagement by, xxvi,
    144, 166–67
  Qutb and, 175–76
  rationalist clerics and, 164–65
  "return to basics" of earliest Islam
    approach and, xxiv, 164–67
  Sadat and, 176
  Salafism and, xxiv, 163–65
  Saudi Arabia and, 151
  Sheikh Mansour (interview subject)
    and, 20, 21–22
  takfir doctrine and, 111
  zakat emphasized in, 172–73
Mustafa, Shukri, 176–80
Mu'tazilism School, 34–35

Nasser, Gamal Abdel, 151, 167,
  175–76, 182–83
Nassim (interview subject), 92–96
The Nation of Tawhid, Like It or Not
  (video), 136–39
Nawawi, Imam, 159–60
niqab (women's garment that covers
  the full body except the eyes). *See
  also sitar*
  France's attempts to ban, 51, 53, 71, 109
  gender norms within Islam and, 53
  Gérin's campaign against, 106–7
Nordine (interview subject), 114–15
Nou'man (interview subject), 43–45

Omar (interview subject), 109–11, 112–13
Operation Cast Lead (Gaza, 2008-9), xli,
  59–61, 62
Orientalism
  Orientalism of the interior and, 140
  Orient as an object of reification in, 134
  reverse Orientalism and, 141
  Saïd and, 134
  Salafi Occidentalism compared to, 147

Salafism and, 134, 135, 140–41
Saudi Arabia viewed through the prism
  of, 139–40
Western views of the Orient and, 135
Othman (interview subject), 63–66
Oum Daoud (interview subject)
  biographical background of, 69
  on *niqab* bans, 71–72
  sitar worn by, 69–71

Pakistan, 58, 174–75
Palestine. *See also* Gaza
  Abdelwahid on, 13
  Albani on, 110
  Fatah Party and, 61
  Hamas and, 61, 110–11, 136–37,
    146, 174–75
  Hezbollah and, 61
  keffiyeh and, 146
  Operation Cast Lead (2008-9) and, xli,
    59–61, 62
  Salafism and, 59–61, 110, 195
Paris (France), xv–xvii, xli–xlii, 12–13,
  106–7, 115–16
"post-Islamism," 163–86
postmodern socialization, 157–59
Presence and Spirituality of Muslims
  organization (PSM), 129

Al-Qaeda, xiii–xiv, xxvn33, 86, 176n28
qamis (men's plain long garment), xv–xvii,
  64, 68n29, 89, 116
Al-Qarni, ʿAïd, xxvi
Qutb, Sayyid, 167, 172–73, 175–76, 182

Rajib, Sheikh, 42–43, 82–83
Ramadan, Tariq, xxxviiin61, 26, 54–55, 56,
  87, 136–37
Rida, Rashid, 164–65
Riyad as- Salihin (*Garden of Virtues,*
  Nawawi), 8, 159–60
Roubaix (France), 106–7
Royal, Ségolène, 145
Rushdie, Salman, 44

Sadat, Anwar, 167, 176
Sahwa (Awakening) Movement (Saudi
  Arabia), xxvi

Saïd, Edward, xiii, 134, 147–48
Salafism
   'alim relations with political authority figures in, 37–39, 169–70
   "anti-me" figure and, 130
   banlieues (working-class suburbs in France) and, ix–x, xiv–xvii, 101–3, 105–8, 187
   burqa in, xv–xvii
   conspiracy theory and, 108
   dalil (proof) and, 31
   deviance concept and, xxxvi–xxxix, xxxviii*t*, 4–5, 28
   economic independence encouraged in, 63–67, 107–8, 117, 179
   election phase of, 130–31
   electoral politics and, 66, 96–98, 105–8, 114, 144, 145, 167, 169–70, 174, 192
   elitist orientation of proselytization and worship practices in, 73–75
   "emancipated neotraditionalist Salafis" and, 11
   "epistocracy" and, 37–38
   family socialization and, 117–21
   fitna doctrine in, 32–33
   as fundamentalism, xvii–xx, 54–55, 174–75
   genealogical socialization and, 3
   generational effects among, 129–32
   guardianship of dogma and, 46–49
   Gulf War (1990-91), 150
   hadith of sixty- three sects and, 47–48
   heterogeneity within, 148
   Islamism compared to, 168–70, 173–75
   Islamophobia confronted by, 114, 195
   legitimist Salafism and, 171
   long beards among adherents of, xv–xvii, 64, 94, 143
   Maghrebian background among converts to, 4, 14
   media discourse about Islam and, 84
   Muslim Brotherhood and, xxiv, 163–65
   neo-communitarianism and, 55
   neotrialism and, 157–59, 173
   "Noah Syndrome" and, 48
   non-Muslim background among some converts to, 4, 13
   orthopraxy and, 47
   Palestine and, 59–61, 110, 195
   positive retrogression phase of, 131–32
   post-Christian Salafis and, 13, 117–18
   post-Islamism and, 163–86
   postmilitant Salafis and, 19
   postmodern socialization and, 157–59, 191
   predominant Sunni schools of jurisprudence and, xxii–xxiii, 34
   proselytization and, 73
   qamis in, xv–xvii, 64, 68n29, 89, 116
   quietism and, xiii–xvii, xxiv, 4–27, 32–33, 54–55, 56, 104, 105, 129–32, 168, 171, 180, 188–89
   rational-legal legitimacy and, 29
   "redection upward" among converts to, 5
   reform of corrupted morals of Muslim coreligionists as goal of, xviii–xx, 11–12, 23, 46–47, 73–74, 81–82, 142–43, 165–66
   relationship to time in, 81
   resistance and persistence as principles in, 49
   "return to basics" of the Prophet Muhammad's era of Islam as primary goal of, xiii–xiv, xv–xix, xx–xxiv, 3, 4–5, 24, 29, 30–31, 33, 46–47, 157, 158–59
   "Salafi Occidentalism" and, 147
   Salaf Salih (Muslims living at time of Revelation) and, xiii–xiv, xv–xvii, xix, 3, 35
   Saudi Arabia and, 152, 181
   separation from impious society emphasized in, xxvi–xxvii, xxviii–xxix, xxxii–xxxiii
   September 11 terrorist attacks (2001), xiii–xiv, xxxii–xxxiii
   sitar and, 52, 68
   soteriological moralism and, 59
   stranger axiom and, 49
   takfir doctrine and, 62
   terrorism and, 87
   Turkish Muslims in France's eschewing of, 118–19, 121, 124, 127
   views of the West and, 108–9, 147
Samir (interview subject), 142–48

Sarkozy, Nicolas
  banlieue electorate and, 52
  economic regulation and, 65
  election of 2007 and, 145
  The Koran and, 113
  Maghrebian cabinet members serving under, 145
  Saudi Arabia visit (2008) by, 136–37
  sitar ban and, 52, 96–97
Sassanid Empire, 143
Al-Saud family, 39–40
Saudi Arabia
  Arab Spring uprisings and suppression of demonstrations in, 154–56, 181
  economic liberalism in, 103–4, 118–19
  French Salafists talk of *hijra* (departure) to, 146
  Gulf War (1990-91) and, 39–40, 150, 153–54, 181
  Hamas and, 136–37
  Ibn Saud's pact with Ibn Abdelwahab (1744) and, 36–37
  Islamic scholarly community in, 145, 146, 148–49, 151–56, 171–72
  Muslim Brotherhood and, 151
  oil industry in, 39, 104, 150–51
  Palestine and, 61
  politically legitimist Salafism in, 32–33
  Sahwa (Awakening) Movement in, xxvi
  "Salafism of the state" in Saudi Arabia and, 152, 181
  Salafis' Orientalist conceptualization of, 134, 136–37, 141–43, 146, 147, 178–79
  Sarkozy's visit (2008) to, 136–37
  shari'a law in, 52
  talk of French Salafists' *hijra* (departure) to, 57
  tawhid associated with, 136–40
  United States and, 39–40
Senegal, 57
September 11 terrorist attacks (2001)
  Bin Laden and, 10, 112
  conspiracy theories regarding, 112
  Islamophobia following, 84–85
  jihadism and, xxiv–xxv
  Salafism and, xiii–xiv, xxxii–xxxiii
Sharjah (United Arab Emirates), 65

Sheikh Mansour (interview subject)
  emigration to France by, 21
  Ennahada Party and, 20
  Ghannouchi and, 20, 21
  Muslim Brotherhood and, 20, 21–22
  Tunisian background of, 20
el-Sherbini, Marwa, 115–16
Shiite Muslims, xix, 35, 44, 136–37, 143
Sifaoui, Mohamed, 87, 136–37
The Signs of the End Times (Wabil), 113
Simmel, Georg, xxviii–xxix
sitar (*niqab* that covers the eyes behind a veil)
  France's attempts to ban, 52, 71
  harassment of women who war, 69–71
  Oum Doud on her decision to wear, 69–71
socialization. *See also* genealogical socialization
  identity construction as definitional quality of, xxviii–xxix, xxxi
  progressive nature of, xxx–xxxi
  socio-structural conditions and, xxx
Society of Muslims (Jama'at al-Mouslimin), 177
Süleymanci (Sunni brotherhood founded by Sheikh Süleyman Hilmi Tunahan), 125

Tabligh (Jam'at at- Tabligh)
  Adnan on, 8–9
  founding of, 6n6
  Maghrebian Muslims and, 124
  mass preaching style in, 73–74
  "redection upward" emphasized by, 5–6
takfir (excommunication) doctrine, 62, 111
Takfir wal-Hijra organization, 176–78
The Taliban, 58
tasfiyya wa-tarbiyya ("it makes for good politics these days to leave politics behind"), 57–58
tawhid (divine uniqueness)
  Ibn Taymiyya on, 35–36
  jihadist *versus* legitimist interpretations of, 36
  al-Koweiti on, 83

tawhid (divine uniqueness) (*cont.*)
  Salafism's effort to preserve worship of, xxii–xxiii, 5
  Saudi Arabia conceptualized as the epitome of, 136–40
  unification of the *umma* (community of believers) and, xv–xvii, 58
Thomas, Dominique, 86–87
Tocqueville, Alexis de, xiii
Tourcoing (France), 106–7
The True Face of the Prophet Muhammad: Beyond the Caricatures, 114–15
Tunisia
  Arab Spring uprising (2010-11) in, 154
  Ennahada Party in, 20, 174–75
  Mouvement de la tendance islamique in, 20
  Salafi Orientalist views of, 141
  Salafists in France with family ties to, 4, 143
Turkish Muslims in France, 118–19, 121, 124, 127
Türk-Islam Birliği de Diyanet İşleri (Turko-Islamic Union for Religious Affairs, DITIB), 125

umma (community of believers), xv–xvii, 55, 58, 79–80
Union des organisations islamiques de France (UOIF), 53, 54–55, 56, 144
United Arab Emirates, xli–xlii, 65, 118–19
United Kingdom, 71, 165–66
United States, xxiv–xxv, 39–40

Venel, Nancy, 54–55
Vénissieux (France), 106–7

Wahabism, 9
Walid (convert to Salafism at Montreuil mosque), 74–75
Weber, Max, xxxiii–xxxiv, 29–30, 67, 166–67, 174
The Women (sura), 138

Yade, Rama, 145
Yassine, Abdessalam, 129
Yemen, 10–11, 57, 174–75

zakat (alms), 172–73

www.ingramcontent.com/pod-product-compliance
Ingram Content Group UK Ltd.
Pitfield, Milton Keynes, MK11 3LW, UK
UKHW022153230426
12049UKWH00003BA/74